Inform,
Advise and Support

i

Inform, Advise and Support

The Story of Fifty Years of
the Citizens Advice Bureau

JEAN RICHARDS

Lutterworth Press
Cambridge

Lutterworth Press
P.O. Box 60
Cambridge CB1 2NT

British Library Cataloguing in Publication Data

Richards, Jean (Jean M)
  Inform, advise & support: 50 years of the Citizens'
  Advice Bureau.
  1. Great Britain.   Citizens advice bureau, to 1987
  I. Title
  361′.06

ISBN 0-7188-2753-8

Printed and bound in Great Britain by
The Guernsey Press Co. Ltd, Guernsey, Channel Islands.

Contents

Foreword

Fifty years ago, in 1939, the CAB service was born. It was the outbreak of war that brought it into existence and with the coming of peace there were those who thought its job was done. Others saw things differently, but at times it was touch and go whether the Service would survive. It did, and today it is inconceivable that it should not exist. Through over 700 bureaux and 400 other outlets, the Service now handles more than 7 million enquiries a year. Government and other official publicity leaflets point their readers to the nearest Citizens Advice Bureau for further information and advice, and in some cases the inclusion of such an indication is required by law. The Service is politically impartial and has the support of all the political parties.

The Service is, indeed, a typically British institution; and it is no accident that the few countries listed by Jean Richards as having at some time had similar services in being are almost all ones where the British influence has been strong. It is not merely that the Service, like Topsy, 'has just growed' but more importantly because it has relied on a large number of volunteers, or small paid staff, and support from public funds.

The foundation of the Service is the volunteers whose role is not to raise funds to employ professionals to do the work, but to do the work themselves. The demands made of our volunteers have been increasing all the time in terms of commitment, knowledge, and performance to professional standards. The ambassador of one of our neighbours in Europe, himself a great admirer of the CAB service, once told me it was impossible to conceive of such a service in his own country because individuals could see no reason why they should devote time and effort to the solution of other people's problems. In this country they can and they do, and that is the essence of the Service – not to take over other people's problems but to help them to find their own solutions to them.

If voluntary effort has been one of the foundations of the CAB service, the other has been support from central and local government. As Jean Richards' account shows, there have been a few but significant turning points in the Service's history when the government of the day substantially increased its financial support. The increased professionalism to be found in the Service today is largely a product of the centrally produced information service that is a model of its kind; the much more intensive and purposefully directed training of bureau volunteers; and the employment of more paid staff in bureaux in a managerial and specialist role in support of the volunteers. None of these would have been possible without the willingness of the volunteers to seize the opportunities and assume additional obligations, but equally, none would have happened without the substantial injection of public funds.

A fiftieth anniversary is a proper occasion for looking back. The service has been fortunate in having Jean Richards as its chronicler with her personal experience of working on the inside, combined with a capacity to stand back and take an overall view. Her account shows how diverse are the various strands that have been woven to form the present CAB service. Yet the principles that govern the service today were clearly identified right from the start. The volunteers and paid workers in 1939. were fired by the same dedication and enthusiasm that are the hallmarks of the service today – and, judging by the quotations in Jean Richards' book, shared the same sense of humour that is from time to time essential to remain sane. Both in the field and at the centre, they included some truly remarkable people who serve as an inspiration to those of us who have the responsibility and the privilege of taking the service into its next fifty years.

Sir Kenneth Clucas
Chairman, National Association of
Citizens Advice Bureaux
December 1988

Introduction

In writing this book my intention has been to show how the Citizens Advice Bureaux have flourished, declined and flourished again and to explain some of the difficulties which the CAB service has faced in the fifty years of its history. The story is complicated and if it were to be followed in detail it would require a much longer study than the present one but I hope that for all past and future friends of the bureaux it will fulfil the task of explaining to some degree how the CAB service came to be where it is today.

Terminology and Usages

In order to explain the terminology used it should first be made clear that every Citizens Advice Bureau is independent, in the sense that it has its own Management Committee which is responsible in every respect for the running of the bureau. Several bureaux may be run by the same Management Committee but that group, in its turn, is an independent unit within the CAB service. In order to become a member of the National Association of Citizens Advice Bureaux each bureau undertakes to run its affairs according to the rules and policies which are laid down by the membership of the Association, acting in Council, or, in some matters, by Resolution of the Annual General Meeting.

The National Association is a Company Limited by Guarantee, of which the members of Council are the Directors. Council appoints the Director of the Association, who is the Executive responsible for the employment and conduct of the staff of the Association. Staff working in the Central Office and in the Area Offices, together with some Project staff, are employed by the National Association. The bureaux in Northern Ireland have a slightly different relationship from those in England and Wales, while the Scottish bureaux belong to their own Association. It has not been possible to cover the story of Scotland in this book; it merits a study of its own.

CAB or CABx	A single bureau or a collection of bureaux. The word 'Citizens' is given here without the apostrophe, in accordance with current CAB usage.

The CAB service	All the bureaux taken as a collective group, plus the support staff.
NACAB	The support services in a situation of interaction with the bureaux.
The Association	The CAB service in its role as a national body, with the bureaux and the support staff acting co-operatively, often in relation to external bodies.
Headquarters	This usage has been retained in quotations taken from early documents but has been replaced elsewhere by the terms 'Central Office' or 'the centre'.
Organiser	Since this title was used for 47 of the 50 years, it has been retained save where the term 'Manager' appears in a quotation from a current document.

Acknowledgements

Thanks are due to all those who helped with the preparation of this book. To Sir Kenneth Clucas for his Foreword; to Elizabeth Filkin (Director) for granting access to the archives; to all those in bureaux who sent material which I have been unable to use although it contributed to the preparation of the text; to those who agreed to an interview and whom I had no time to fit into my programme; and, in particular to John Battersby, Gillian Borrie, Ron Bruce, Meg Bryant, Bob Chaundler, Ann Cumberbatch, Nesta Davies, Frank Fordham, Robin Forrest, Eileen Grommell, Ann Hawkins, Hazel Humphreys, Maria Kessler, Margot Kettle, Jeremy Leighton, Rhea Martin, Jean Pooley, Theresa Ricketts, Mimi Sanderson, Barbara Stow, Margaret Torbett, John Wallis, Veronica Weeks and Diana Whitworth, who kindly gave their time and allowed themselves to be interviewed, together with Jean Adams, Kathleen Ashcroft, Maureen Barker, Barbara Brandes, Ann Bright, Marjorie Brown, Ann M Calder, Paul Childs, Shirley Collins, Joyce Cooper, M Coote, S David Cotterill, Hilda Crossley, Barbara Dempster, Gary Dore, Mary Fillmore, Ray Forbes, Hilary Forrest, Eileen Glen-Davison, Grace Griffiths, Rena Haines, Angela Harding, Sona Higginbottom, Violet Highton, Joan Inglis, Chris Jago, Liz Johnson, Hilda Jones, Audrey Kelly, Marion Knight, Rosemary Landreth, P M Lloyd, Irene Macey, Stella Martin, M McQuarrie, G Myers, Mary North, Dorothy O'Connell, Pat Osborne, Diana S Payne, Anne Pearce, M A Pierce, Gladys Radcliffe, Alec Rae, Margaret Richards, Elizabeth Robertshaw, Julian Ruddock, Elizabeth Sanderson, Elizabeth M Simpson, Evelyn Soper, Phyllis Stainton, Elsie Strong, Betty H Taylor, Susie Tremlett, Rita Trevennen, Beryl Walkden, A C Watkins, Caroline Webb and Eva Wray, all of whom supplied me with material from which extracts have been taken and incorporated in the text.

I wish also to acknowledge the following for permission to use their photographs: Sorin Masca for photographs on pages 116 and 148; the NACAB for photographs on pages 45, 72, 77, 104, 144 (lower photograph) and 159; the *Essex Chronicle* for the upper photograph on page 144.

Sources

Where no specific source is given the information is taken from the minutes or other papers of the National Association.

Jean M Richards
Haddenham
Cambs
1988

CHAPTER ONE

Beginnings and Ends

The War Years: Prelude to Aftermath

War or the threat of war has a tendency to concentrate the mind. The evidence from the Spanish Civil War – and the Munich crisis – turned many people's thoughts towards the possible effects of a war with Germany on the civilian population.

Among the bodies which felt that preparations should be made was the National Council of Social Service which, in 1938, made the first moves towards setting up a national advice service for the country. The National Council of Social Service was the central body under whose umbrella many of the big voluntary casework agencies came together to discuss matters of mutual concern. It was a prestigious body, raising and distributing substantial voluntary funds and functioning in many ways as a clearing house for the voluntary social services. It was therefore appropriate that the NCSS should call together all the major voluntary social work agencies in the country, including the Liverpool Personal Service Society, the Birmingham Citizens Society, the London Council of Social Service, the City of Glasgow Society of Social Service and the Charity Organisation Society, for consultation.

The result was a Statement, issued in July 1939, which set out their conclusions and proposals in the light of the probable outbreak of hostilities. In view of the way in which the CAB service developed over the years it is interesting to note that many of the essential elements for a Citizens Advice Bureau were identified from the very beginning. The first initiators were clear in their minds that there would be need for sources of help and advice for the civil population. They believed that these would be crucial in the areas where disruption and disturbance were likely and they set about providing a blueprint for a network of advice and assistance through the means of a new service, to be called Citizens Advice Bureaux.

The original Statement sets the stage for the development of bureaux and makes a number of assertions. These include the basic require-

1

ments that the support of the local authority would be essential in setting up a CAB; that the bureau must be centrally placed and easily accessible; that there should be adequate accommodation, including a room or rooms for private interviews; that the bureau should be in the charge of a full-time, experienced caseworker, supported by part-timers, and that there should be proper recruitment and training procedures. *(For the July 1939 Statement see Appendix 1.)*

The preparations made led to the opening of approximately 200 bureaux throughout the country on 4 September 1939. In her autobiography, the first Secretary of the CAB service, Miss Dorothy Keeling, tells how 18 bureaux opened their doors to the public of Liverpool on that day.

> As always, the situation in London was more complicated than elsewhere and arrangements were made for the Family Welfare Association to be responsible for the Centres in London boroughs and the London Council of Social Service in the Greater London area. On the outbreak of war in September 1939 it was possible to open a Citizens' Advice Bureau in every London borough and in a large number of boroughs in the greater London area. It was also possible to establish two Legal Advice Centres, at the Mary Ward Centre and Cambridge House, Camberwell. When the intensive bombing began a Poor Man's Valuer Service was established to assist in dealing with war damage claims. *(Citizens Advice Bureaux – How they began. Report of the Citizens Advice Bureaux in Central London 1963/64)*

The arrangements for setting up a bureau were wildly different according to the circumstances. While the major voluntary casework agencies were frequently the active agents, in many cases the initiative came from people like Town Clerks – almost anyone could be involved. One lady described how her husband, a solicitor who was ineligible for military service because he had lost an eye, came home from his office in central London and announced that they were going to open a Citizens Advice Bureau in their front room the next day. She was given a copy of the Citizens Advice Notes (CANS), some government leaflets and circulars, and told to get on with it! When confronted with a problem which she could not disentangle her only recourse was to tell the enquirer to come back again at the week-end when her husband would give it his attention.

Another lady relates how 'My father looked after/was the CAB unit in Crediton, Devon. When I came home on leave from the ATS he told me he had been "shanghaied" into the job. He was the local benevolent secretary of the British Legion so he simply put up a hand-written notice to the effect that the office was now a CAB and would help anyone with any problem.'

These are two examples of what could, and evidently often did, happen and, looking back, it is quite clear that the seeds of some of the later mistrusts were sown at this time. The conflicting attitudes of the full-time, paid, professional bureau workers and the part-time, purely voluntary, workers took root and it was to be many years before the service managed to work its way through to a consensus about what the CAB service was and should be. The complications of multiple loyalties were also present, indeed were inherent in the way in which the CAB service was conceived and born and these were finally disentangled only after the Association (as it had by then become) became a separate charitable company with responsibility for its own affairs.

Not many months into the war it became clear that there was need for a central administration, working within the NCSS, to take responsibility for the Citizens Advice Bureaux and in February 1940 Miss Dorothy Keeling was seconded by the Liverpool Personal Service Society to be Secretary to the CAB Policy Sub-Committee of the NCSS, a post which she held until her release and return to the Liverpool society at Christmas 1945.

If the large voluntary casework agencies were responsible for the blueprint for the service it was Miss Keeling who was the architect who saw that the edifice, when built, was a sound construction. Variously described as 'a most dynamic personality' and 'a tartar but a very good brain', she was an experienced social worker, who had first-hand knowledge of pre-war conditions in some of the worst parts of Liverpool at a time when unemployment reached 31.5% at its peak.

She brought with her a keen appreciation of the importance of being able to influence the legislators and administrators in respect of conditions which came to light as a result of work with the most vulnerable members of the public. With her staff, she saw herself as the voice of the people, speaking up for them out of the knowledge of problems and hardships revealed by the day to day work of the bureaux. She established very early on a dialogue between the CAB service and the civil servants and others responsible for making and applying all the multitude of Orders and Regulations by which the lives of the civilian population came to be governed. So great an atmosphere of trust was built up that it was sometimes possible to tell bureaux what was about to happen while it was still confidential to the Ministry concerned. An example of this was clothes rationing, about which information was supplied in advance to bureaux in order to enable them to answer the anticipated deluge of enquiries which would come as a result of its introduction.

The funding for the central administrative services came from the Ministry of Health and from the NCSS, which housed and serviced the central staff and employed the administrative staff throughout the country. The NCSS had a structure of Regional Offices and the CAB Travelling Officers (as they were called) were attached to the various Regional Offices. In 1940, Travelling Officers were working from York-shire, the Midlands, Greater London, Wales, the South West and the

North West. A seventh Travelling Officer joined the staff in 1941 and the final total staff in this category was eight. They were paid a salary of £300 a year, which was quite a respectable sum by the standards of the time.

The network of bureaux expanded rapidly from the outbreak of war and by 1 January 1940 there were 169 bureaux in London and 875 elsewhere, a total of 1044. The records show that the number fluctuated sharply because the whole system had to be extremely flexible if it was to meet the needs of the time. For example, the first 18 bureaux which Miss Keeling quotes as having been opened in Liverpool were soon reduced to six, it having been found that many of those originally opened were in the wrong places and were not attracting sufficient enquiries to justify their retention.

In November 1940, the CAB Committee of the NCSS, which was made up of representatives from the Regional Advisory Committees, under which the bureaux had been grouped, made the first moves towards some form of quality control. The Committee granted official recognition to 433 of the bureaux. A year later, the Owl sign was produced and put on sale by the NCSS and all bureaux officially listed as authorised were permitted to use it. Plans were also made to issue certificates of recognition.

The peak of bureau expansion was reached in 1942, when there were 1074 bureaux in operation, of which 603 were recognised. By 1943 there were slightly fewer, i.e. 1060, but 621 of these were recognised.

The budgets for bureaux were, in the main, very small and those which were not part of one of the personal services societies depended on support from the local authorities, plus, in some cases, an allocation from the funds provided centrally by the Ministry of Health. The allocation of these funds evidently caused some dissension, so that a policy had to be adopted for dealing with them. This required that all applications from a Region were considered together, that those who received the money should be accountable for the way in which it was spent, that resources should not be wasted by giving sums of money to bureaux which were too small to be worth supporting and that all bureaux should endeavour to raise some voluntary money.

An example of the kinds of grant which were made shows how small most of them were, even having regard to the changed value of money.

DECISIONS MADE REGARDING APPLICATIONS FOR GRANT-AID
from Regions 4 & 5 – 1942/43

Region	Purpose	Amount Granted
REGION 4		
St Albans CAB	Towards salary of secretary and general expenses	£50.00.0

Region	Purpose	Amount Granted
REGION 4 – *continued*		
South Benfleet CAB	Towards general expenses	£12.00.0
Southend Civic Guild of Help *(Guild to be asked to refund £48 on 1941/42 Grant)*	Towards CAB expenses	£48.00.0
Cambridgeshire RCC	Towards expenses of CAB work	£5.00.0
Bedford CAB	Towards office equipment and general expenses	£20.00.0
Hornchurch CAB *(Bureau to be asked to refund £17.10.0 on 1941/42 Grant)*	Towards general expenses	£17.10.0
REGION 5		
Barking CAB	Towards general expenses	£25.00.0
Mansfield House Settlement CAB (West Ham)	Towards general expenses for period 1.7.42 to 31.3.43	£150.00.0

The central funding from the Ministry of Health reached its apogee in 1943/44, when a total of £35,525 was given – £25,000 for the individual bureaux and the Regional Offices, £4,125 for the Travelling Officers and £6,400 to cover the Central Office costs.

The first anxieties about future funding were recorded in November 1943, when the Chairman and Secretary were asked to 'raise with the Government the question of future policy, both short and long term, regarding the CAB Service', and in April 1944 a deputation attended on the Minister of Health to discuss both current problems and the possibility of post-war funding.

The Minister responded that the government valued the work done by bureaux and agreed that it would continue to be needed in the immediate post-war period but that was as far as he was prepared to go. He promised to give reasonable notice of any alteration in the grant-aid policy but was unhelpful in all other respects. His view was that the job of explaining legislation etc to the public lay with the government and while he did not rule out the future help of voluntary organisations he felt that the government was likely to undertake the duty of explanation itself in the future.

Those who took part in the consultation must have heard the Minister's response to their approaches with some apprehension and their fears became more specific when the grant-aid for the service for 1944/45 was set at the same level as the previous year but with the stipulation that 'grants should not be applied to any bureaux not established before 31st March 1944'. By July 1945 the writing was on the wall – 'the Ministry had allocated £16,750 towards the expenditure of individual Bureaux for the year 1945/46 ... and had stated that *no further grant* would be made in respect of bureaux'. The situation had deteriorated further by January 1946 when it was recorded that 'there was no question of a change of policy in regard to grant-aid for individual Bureaux nor for Area Bodies ... nor for Travelling Officers. The Ministry was prepared to consider an application in respect of headquarters and regional services on the ground that these would not be grant-aidable by any local authorities.'

At this point the NCSS stepped in and agreed to fund the Travelling Officers for a further year after March 1946 'in view of the extreme importance of the Travelling Officers' work'.

The earlier fears proved justified when the grant from the Ministry of Health, which had been £10,000 in 1949, was halved in 1950 and notice was given that this was the last payment which would be made.

The effect of the withdrawal was disastrous.

The provisional budget for 1951/52 showed expenditure of £5,035 for the Central Office and £1,059 for the Regions, sums which were described as 'the very minimum on which a national service could be maintained at all'. Even with the help of the NCSS there was an anticipated shortfall of £2,000–2,500 which, in the absence of other funders, could only be found from the bureaux.

This meant an average contribution of £5 from each bureau, but since the bureaux were themselves operating on minimal budgets it was clear that some would find it difficult, if not impossible, to find even this sum.

A last-ditch effort was made to change the decision by means of a debate in the House of Commons on the Motion for the Adjournment on 23 February 1951 but, in spite of widespread support and many speeches which paid tribute to the work of the bureaux, the grant was not restored.

The figures for numbers of bureaux plot the effect of the withdrawal of support from the service. The 1948 total was 572; by 1953 there were only 477 – a decline of 20% in five years. The trend downward continued, so that by 1960 there were only 416 bureaux operating.

The staff situation at the centre was even worse. Miss Keeling had resigned as Secretary on the declaration of peace and had been succeeded by Miss Kay M Oswald, who now faced enormous problems in attempting to keep the service in being with a totally inadequate staff and finances. Where there had been eight Travelling Officers there was now one part-time Advisory Officer to cover the whole of the North, while development in the rest of the country (outside London) had to depend upon three members of staff at the centre who dealt with things as best they could by means of correspondence and the occasional visit.

At no time did the bureaux' contributions ever reach the sum which had been estimated as necessary for the maintenance of even a basic service. As a result of constant efforts some small improvements took place over the years; the Nuffield Foundation made a grant of £1,200 a year for three years from 1956, in 1957 the Carnegie Trust granted £5,000 over five years for experimental rural schemes and in 1959 the Joseph Rowntree Memorial Trust offered a grant of £1,000 for three years. These sums were quite substantial when looked at from one point of view but, measured against the need, they were pitifully inadequate.

Renewal and Rebirth

Although the contributions from the various trusts had helped, if only as a stimulus to morale and a chance for the staff to do more than just hang on by their fingernails, the crucial break came with the restitution of government funding in 1960, when the Ministry of Housing and Local Government made a grant of £2,500 for three years 'in appreciation of the service rendered by the citizens advice bureaux to the community'. This grant was doubled in the following and subsequent years.

Housing queries had always figured high on the list of enquiries coming in to bureaux but the 1957 Rent Act lifted them even higher than before, until they reached 25% of all enquiries. By 1958 – the year before the Molony Committee started work – an increasing number of consumer problems were also coming into bureaux and by 1962 approximately 80,000 out of a total of one million enquiries were classed as relating to *Trade and Manufacture*, of which the majority dealt with some aspect of consumer protection.

The Report of the (Molony) Committee to the President of the Board of Trade in 1962 was the starting point of the modern consumer movement. The Report had a number of complimentary things to say about the CAB service. It cited CABx as the most suitable points to which consumers could be directed for advice and commented on the particular value of the impartial and disinterested advice which the bureaux were already providing. In its evidence to the Molony Committee the National CAB Committee had pointed out that the bureaux 'would be averse to become closely identified with any particular class of complainant, such as the consumer'.

The National Committee's point is a vital one. From the days of Dorothy Keeling the service as a whole had resisted all pressures to make it an arm of a particular funder. This was an essential element which went to maintain both the principle of independence and the generalist nature of the bureau service. Just as the local bureaux were not to be dictated to by their local authorities, so the central organisation resisted becoming the handmaiden of a particular government department.

The major recommendation of the Report was for the setting up of the National Consumer Council as an independent body, funded by government, charged with the task of overseeing all aspects of consumer protection.

In March 1963, Kay Oswald wrote a circular letter to the bureaux in which she said:

> We should like bureaux to bear in mind that we shall be in immediate and direct contact with the Consumer Council and shall want to be in a position to tell them what are the particular types of difficulty that arise ... and shall hope to receive indication of these from bureaux from time to time.

There was a good case for strengthening the central services in order to enable bureaux to respond to the expectations placed upon them and, in the light of the recommendations made in the Report, the Board of Trade gave its first grant in 1963, when the budget for the year included a contribution from that source of £24,000 for England and £5,000 for Scotland and Wales.

The grant was widely publicised, with the result that the public came to believe that individual bureaux had been given money to 'deal with consumer problems'. The level of expectation on bureaux rose and the public was misled into thinking that bureaux could do more than they were equipped to do. Although the grant had been given to enable the service to strengthen the central administration and regional structure, dealing with consumer queries was no easier. There was no infrastructure in place to which the CAB service could relate, no civil servants and other officials who could provide the backing required to enable the bureaux to help the public effectively.

The chance of obtaining recompense for an individual consumer was remote, the legislation being inadequate and the various voluntary schemes run by trading associations chaotic and ineffective in many respects. Referring matters to the Trading Standards Officers might result in the prosecution of offenders but was not much help to the consumer who had been tricked or swindled. Much remained to be done before the bureaux could do more than rely on their powers of negotiation between the disputants and the use of threats of publicity as a way of bringing local traders to heel.

In the next few years support for the centre from the Board of Trade rose steadily and there was a crucial difference between this funding and that from other government sources. The exchequer grant for the general work of the service was made on the basis of 40% from government and 60% from NCSS voluntary funds while the Board of Trade grant for development was given at the rate of 100%. In spite of the increased funding from the Board of Trade the CAB department at the NCSS was still under pressure. More bureaux were opening, generating more work at the centre, but the general budget was held down because of the incapacity of the NCSS to find additional money – every £4 from government meant that the NCSS had to find £6, and the money was not there. Frustration set in; the CAB service badly needed to increase its level of staffing but was unable to do so.

This principle of proportionality now began to emerge as an increasingly bitter source of irritation between the officers and staff of the CAB service and those of the rest of the NCSS. The CAB Secretary was head of the CAB department of the NCSS, on a par with other heads of departments, employed by and subject to the control of, the Executive Committee and the Director of the NCSS. As the 'Molony money' poured in, the balance between the CAB service and the other departments of the NCSS became increasingly distorted. One department of the NCSS was receiving more money than the others. The commitment of the NCSS to providing a matching proportion of voluntary funds before additional funding could be attracted to the CAB service meant that the feelings of frustration in the face of a legitimate desire to build up the service became steadily more marked.

Early in 1969 things became even more difficult. The NCSS resisted a move to change the level of proportionality to 50/50, on the twin grounds that such a move would endanger the independent status of the NCSS and that it would put more staff at risk should there be a national financial crisis and a consequent drop in the level of funding. One aspect of the conflict between the NCSS and the CAB was the refusal of the members of the Finance and General Purposes Committee of the NCSS to allow the representatives of the CAB service to participate in the negotiations with government for funding. This was on the grounds that there was a great deal of information in the application which referred to the rest of the NCSS, to Scotland and to Wales, and that the Committee did not believe that the CAB Council was capable of handling all the information.

In the face of the stonewalling tactics of the management of the NCSS, the tensions continued to grow and the CAB Council became convinced that the only way forward was to seek independence from its overlord. Discussions were undertaken and attempts were made to negotiate terms for an amicable divorce. These all failed and, in the event, the only outcome was the disappearance from the scene of the then Chairman and the Secretary. This caused a good deal of bad feeling and for a time there was considerable uncertainty about how to move forward. The Secretary was replaced by a new Chief Executive, Mr A J Leighton, whose first task was to work with the new Chairman to negotiate fresh working arrangements with the NCSS.

It was not until 1972 that an Agreement was finally signed by 'Mr J K Owens, Director, acting on behalf of the NCSS, and Mr A J Leighton, Chief Executive of the CAB service, on behalf of the CAB Council'. This

Agreement set out the conditions on which the CAB service would continue to be financed by the NCSS and it tied the hands of the CAB service in many ways. The NCSS retained total control over the finances of the CAB service and although it was stated that the representatives of the CAB service would 'accompany' the NCSS in negotiating with the government, they were clearly to have walk-on parts only. They were also not permitted to try and raise extra money from other sources without the prior permission of the NCSS. Once a budget had been allocated to the CAB service by the NCSS it was to be their responsibility to contain expenditure within that budget. The situation was one of responsibility without power.

In spite of the difficulties, the level of funding continued to rise and this defused the situation to some extent. By 1972/73 the total grant-aid for the support services had gone up to approximately £141,000, made up as follows:

Department of Trade & Industry	£80,000
Department of the Environment	£30,000
Voluntary funds, NCSS	£23,000
Other income	£8,000

In the following year the DTI grant was increased from £80,000 to £132,000, as a result of which the CAB Council was able to identify a number of priorities for expenditure which would reinforce and improve the work of the support staff at the centre and in the field. Two crucial needs identified at this time were those for a national Training Officer and for an advisor on local authority finance who could assist bureaux with their applications for funding. For the first time, it was possible to think in terms of a unified training service for bureaux and to take the necessary action to begin to bring this to fruition.

After all the lean years, NACAB could at last begin to build a proper framework of support for bureaux throughout the country, help to raise the standards of those which were struggling and improve the geographical coverage of the service. Government, however, continued to resist all suggestions that direct funding of bureaux from the centre should be reinstated. This was raised repeatedly with governments of all political shadings but the response remained the same – national bodies could be funded nationally; local bodies must be funded locally. In spite of the failure to progress on this front, in the face of the greatly improved central funding the atmosphere was one of modest optimism.

Lift-off

There was a lot of movement in the field of consumer protection in 1973. In particular, the recent legislation was seen to be putting enormous strains upon the Trading Standards Departments of the local authorities, and Trading Standards Officers, meeting with the Minister for Trade & Consumer Affairs, clamoured for more support in the discharge of their duties under the Consumer Protection legislation. An additional embarrassment for the government was the fact that it had become the custom for the direction 'consult your local Citizens Advice Bureau' to be printed on many government leaflets. This was all right in many cases and places but not where there was, in fact, no CAB – in such circumstances irate citizens tended to write to their MP or to the Minister himself. Late in 1973, Jeremy Leighton, Director of the Association, met Sir Geoffrey Howe, Minister for Trade and Consumer Affairs, who told him that the government was considering giving a separate Development Grant to the Association to enable it to improve the coverage of the country and to strengthen the ability of existing bureaux to act in support of consumers. This was finally confirmed in a letter which was reported to the meeting of Council in December 1973. The government proposed to provide £200,000 in 1974/75; £450,000 in 1975/76 and £500,000 in 1976/77, the money to be used for the promotion of new bureaux and the upgrading of existing ones.

To the local bureaux the announcement came as a total surprise – even the central administration had had only faint hopes that it would actually be made. At one stroke the landscape changed shape.

The grant was, in fact, part of a total package produced by the Department of Trade and Industry with the intention of bringing about 'a substantial improvement in consumer advice and complaint services over the next few years, both in the number of centres (whether CABx with local authority support or centres directly operated by local authorities) and in the quality of advice they give'. Some local authorities took advantage of the central funding to set up their own Consumer Advice Centres – which came to be known as the Shoppers' Shops – but others continued to be lukewarm about consumer protection and remained content only to carry out their statutory duties.

Understandably, the immediate reaction of many bureaux which were struggling along on totally inadequate resources was that all the money should be spent directly upon bureaux.

Equally understandably, the reaction of Council and the staff of NACAB in the first days was rather that of someone who has unexpectedly won the Pools. Here was all this lovely money – how on earth should it be spent?

As usual, the field staff immediately came to the forefront. In discussing the way forward, Council at once identified that promotion of new bureaux would place further burdens on the advisory staff in the field and went on to consider the spin-off effect upon the central support services as a result of any increase in numbers and the up-grading of existing bureaux. In order to obtain some insight into how to approach the problem of apportioning the new money most constructively, the advisory staff were asked to produce detailed assessments of the needs of their Areas.

The task of the Association in handling the additional money could only be heavy and in order to relieve pressure on the Executive Committee and to ensure that sufficient time could be given to working out criteria for the application of the grant, it was decided early in 1974 to set up a special Development Group. This Group passed its proposals to the Executive Committee and to Council for ratification in order to ensure that they were in line with the wishes of the federation as a whole.

As the financial affairs of NACAB grew in size and complexity it became more difficult for the members of bureau Management Committees relatively remote from the centre to understand just what was going on and, undoubtedly, there was some resultant alienation among them. For some Management Committees the rationale which called for additional spending on support staff rather than directly on bureaux was hard to accept.

Money, of itself, was clearly not going to solve all the Association's problems. None the less, just as one should 'never marry for money, but marry where money is' this golden shower liberated the Association and gave it freedom to develop in ways which, only 15 years earlier, would have been beyond its wildest dreams.

Summarising the results of the use of the first tranche of the Development Grant money, the Annual Report of the Association for 1974/75 said:

> Last year was the first of the five years that central government would be providing money for the development of the service – and NACAB made the most of it. The go-ahead was given for 23 new bureaux to be promoted using the national development grant and there are proposals to use grant money to open about 50 more in 1975/76. The grant also meant that 90 bureaux could be upgraded and 25 were helped in emergency situations – in most cases, money being made available to cover shortfalls in local authority grant aid and immediate contingencies, such as having to move.
>
> In the spending of the £200,000 available for 1974/75, new promotions were considered before bureau improvements, and in turn large urban and difficult rural areas which were plainly underserved had priority over medium town and suburban areas where the service was already more complete. Decisions on where the money should go were also influenced, of course, by the special needs of a community, such as lack of accessible lawyers and other advice and information giving agencies.

After years of frustration and lack of ability to act, NACAB had been able to begin to fill some of the gaping holes in the network. Some large cities, such as Sheffield, had consistently resisted all approaches and endeavours to provide a CAB service for their inhabitants. Now it was possible to go to such authorities cash in hand and to open up possibilities for development.

The most easily quantifiable result of the Development Grant was the extension of the national network. The number of bureaux and extensions in the United Kingdom went up from 615 in 1973/74 to 818 by 1978/79. Parallel with this increase was the increase in the number of enquiries, which climbed from 1.9 million to 3.3 million in the same period.

Over the years. NACAB had received funding from a number of different departments of state under a variety of headings and this made for a complicated situation from both NACAB's and the government's point of view. In 1975 it was agreed that the grant should be consolidated within one departmental budget. Clearly, as the largest funder, the (then) Department of Prices and Consumer Protection was the logical one to take the responsibility and from that time it, and its successors, have sponsored NACAB and monitored the financial management of the service to bureaux. Although this meant that the source of funding was related to consumer protection, the Association stood firm on the fact that what the bureaux were offering was a generalist service *not* one which was focussed upon consumer affairs in the narrowest sense, i.e. the purchase of goods and services.

In fact, as the consumer movement developed over the years, there was a tendency to enlarge the concept of the 'consumer' to cover almost all aspects of life, so that those who were ill could be seen as 'consumers' of the Health Services, while those on Social Security became 'consumers' of social welfare services. Given this extension of definition even a generalist service could be classified as consumer-centred. The CAB service never adopted any such definition but it currently defines itself as 'client-centred', which possibly comes close to being the same thing.

One of the ways in which the Development Grant money was used was to set up a much improved Area structure. There were 10 Area Advisory Officers in 1971/72 – by 1976/77 the number had risen to 16 in England and Wales plus four in Greater London (funded by NACAB but employed by the Greater London CAB Service). Each of these Officers had a minimum support staff of an administrative assistant and a clerical worker. For the first time, the work of the Area staff began to be put on a more realistic basis. Staff now had a manageable number of bureaux with which to work, although it was still true that areas such as Greater Manchester contained an enormous concentration of bureaux which were somehow expected to relate to a single Area Officer. Arrangements were different in Scotland, which had its own Chief Executive Officer and staff, and in Northern Ireland. Scotland had three Area Advisory Officers and Northern Ireland one.

All this progress and expansion was exciting and rewarding but it was not long before anxieties began to be expressed about what would happen when the Development Grant money came to an end. Would the process go into reverse, the structure contract again, the staff be declared redundant? There was very genuine concern for all those whose future might prove to be at risk. This was the beginning of a long dialogue between NACAB and its funders about the uses to which the funding could be put.

The Development Grant given by Sir Geoffrey Howe had been linked with funding made available to local authorities for their Consumer Advice Centres. The development of these was uneven; they were mainly confined to the metropolitan counties and inner city areas in particular. The West Midlands Metropolitan County Council established a widespread network of Shoppers' Shops but, as a result of a change in political control, these were suddenly closed. The effect on the bureaux in their catchment areas was immediate.

Queues formed in waiting-rooms, the telephones ran red hot and the bureaux found that their workloads were being distorted to such a degree that they could no longer serve their normal clients adequately. The Birmingham bureau and its fellows reported their plight to the Association and struggled to take measures which would enable them to cope.

Because of this experience, when the Minister of Consumer Affairs, Mrs Sally Oppenheim, announced in 1979 that the Consumer Advice Grants scheme for local authorities would be ended from 1980, the Association was able to present her with a reasoned case warning of the effects on bureaux which could be expected when the local CACs closed.

The Association had become more accustomed to quite large-scale financial planning; consequently its application to government contained development proposals to cover the local effects of the CAC closures, plus the more diffuse effects on the service as a whole. When Mrs Oppenheim announced that the grant to NACAB would be raised from £1.85m in 1979/80 to £4m in 1980/81 the situation was thus quite different from what it had been when Sir Geoffrey Howe made his announcement in 1973. The application had contained proposals in excess of the total granted by Mrs Oppenheim, so the problem facing the Association was that of cutting back the proposals rather than producing plans for the use of unexpected resources.

One complication in the use of this additional funding was that 68% of the grants made to bureaux went to those in a comparatively small number of Areas. Bureaux in Areas where there had been no Consumer Advice Centres were not entitled to help and there was considerable resentment on the part of some bureaux' Management Committees, which found it difficult to accept the selective nature of the criteria on which grants were made. The balance of the money not used for direct help to those bureaux affected by the closures was used to strengthen and enlarge the training staff nationally and to develop extra resources of both information and training for the benefit of all the bureaux, but the gain to individual bureaux was not immediately apparent or easily measured in a local situation. Once again the technicalities of government grant-in-aid caused some friction between the member bureaux and their central administration.

During the period following the end of the original Development Grant, an extension was negotiated; staff employed on what had, in the first place, been time-limited engagements, were transferred to permanent posts; and the various grants were consolidated to enable them to be used as constructively as possible under the Conditions of Grant-in-Aid. Increasingly sophisticated financial management was required as the Association's finances grew. Relations with the civil servants of the sponsoring authority were close and amicable although there was always the consciousness of the Treasury lurking in the background with the power to veto requests to add more members of staff to the establishment or additional funding. None the less, NACAB was able to make further modest progress, so that by 1982/83 the grant from the Department of Trade had risen to £5,626,465. It seemed that the wind stood fair.

The Vaughan Affair

24 March 1983 marked the opening of the storm. On that day, the Chairman, Lady Ricketts, opened the meeting of Council by announcing that she had, the previous day, received a letter from Dr Gerard Vaughan, Minister of State for Consumer Affairs, the Minister responsible for the government grant to NACAB.

Members heard with consternation that Dr Vaughan proposed to authorise only 'a six month grant to the Association for 1983/84, with a review thereafter'.

The Minister had met the Chairman twice during the previous month and had discussed various issues with her, after which she was under the impression that he was satisfied with the information given to him. It appeared that this was not so.

Dr Vaughan claimed to be worried about

– the quality of advice provided by some bureaux
– the organisational efficiency of the Association
  and
– alleged activities by bureaux workers and NACAB employees which could be construed as party political.

The Chairman provided details of the work being undertaken at the time to improve the quality of the Association's work, and its efficiency, but the Minister remained adamant that he was not satisfied. He insisted that the Association had strayed into the area of party politics and cited three complaints which had been received by the Ministry. Assurances that these, on investigation, had proved to be founded upon misunderstandings, were not accepted by him.

What was particularly difficult about this sudden announcement was the fact that it was made within days of the start of a new financial year. The Council faced an impossible situation should the second half of the annual grant be withheld. Expenditure had already been planned and contracts entered into with staff – a sudden withdrawal of resources could in no way be seen to contribute (as Dr Vaughan claimed he wished) to the organisational efficiency of the Association. Far from this, it inevitably must lead to the distortion of the workload and interruption of planned programmes while the threat to the life of the Association was fought off. Staff time and energy which would normally have been devoted to the support of the bureaux must, in the face of the emergency, be withdrawn and re-directed to the prime aim of saving the services which enabled the bureaux to function.

With all this in mind, after it had recovered from the first moments of shock, the Association's Council formulated and passed a Resolution which acknowledged its responsibility to be accountable for the expenditure of public funds, restated its adherence to political impartiality in its work and expressed its concern at the impossibility of maintaining normal financial management in the face of the Minister's decision, which it asked him to reconsider. The Resolution, together with a letter explaining the Association's position, was sent to Dr Vaughan on 29th March and copies were sent to eight senior Ministers, all of whose Ministries liaised with the Association and made use of the bureaux to interpret the work of their ministries to the public. Up to this point only members of the Association were aware of what was happening but eventually the journalist, Martin Kettle, broke the silence in an article in *The Observer* and the whole affair became public property.

An immediate effect was that many bureaux were galvanised into action. They had been accustomed to work with and through their local MPs and they at once sought support from them for the reinstatement of the grant to NACAB. Letters flew in their hundreds to backbenchers of every political colour, to Ministers and to local and national newspapers. The normally calm bureau workers, both paid and voluntary, were roused and were particularly incensed because Dr Vaughan had implied that one of their number, namely Mrs Joan Ruddock, Organiser of the Reading CAB, was guilty of making use of the CAB service for her own political ends. Mrs Ruddock was Chairman of the Campaign for Nuclear Disarmament but before taking office as Chairman had agreed with her Management Committee that she would work for restricted hours in her bureau while she held the Chairmanship; there was absolutely no question of the two functions overlapping in any way. Bureau workers felt that the Minister had failed to understand the disciplines of the CAB service and the extreme care with which bureau

Organisers guarded the good name of the service and maintained the Principles of Independence, Impartiality and Objectivity.

On 12 April, Dr Vaughan made a Parliamentary Statement in the course of which he modified to some extent the tone of his earlier remarks and expressed the Government's 'full confidence in the Citizens Advice Bureaux movement'. To the bystander it appeared that he had become aware of the danger of being seen to attack the bureaux as such and had decided instead to concentrate his forces upon the central administration. He promised Parliament that a Review would be set up to examine the affairs of the Association.

The Terms of Reference for the Review which Dr Vaughan reported to the House of Commons on 27 April tended to reinforce the view that he had decided to modify his approach. The Terms of Reference were:

> to review the functioning of the National Association of Citizens Advice Bureaux and to make recommendations, with a view to ensuring that the Association offers the best possible service and support to local citizens advice bureaux; and that the monies available to the Association are spent in the most effective way.

One of the most baffling aspects of Dr Vaughan's earlier statements had been his claim that he had been trying for a year without success to discover just what the Association was doing. This brought a reply from the Director, Mrs Elizabeth Filkin, that 'The Department of Trade has a representative sitting as an observer at every Council meeting and on the Executive Committee of the Association, and we are in weekly contact with Department officials . . . Our accounts are, of course, public and are given detailed scrutiny by the Department of Trade.'

When he set up the Review, Dr Vaughan announced that management consultants would be appointed to assist in the examination of the staffing and management structure of NACAB. He also stated that NACAB was anxious that the Review should start as quickly as possible in order that the Association could quickly be free to get on with its normal work. Once his proposal had been agreed, the Minister confirmed that grant aid for the year 1983/84 would be restored and continued on the customary basis.

In the wider field of voluntary work many people saw the Minister's actions as an attack upon the integrity of a well-known and, largely, respected voluntary body. Such an attack could not be viewed with equanimity because of its wider implications. His attitude was all the more surprising in the light of the government's oft-stated dedication to the idea of the value of co-operative effort, using voluntary resources. Concern existed within other voluntary bodies at the degree of control being posited by Dr Vaughan; previously NACAB had always been treated as an 'arm's length' body. The whole problem of 'charitable action' had become more difficult in the light of the views expressed earlier by the Charity Commission in relation to the work of some crusading charities, such as 'War on Want'.

The Chairman of the National Council for Voluntary Organisations (formerly the National Council of Social Service), Mr Peter Jay, wrote a letter which appeared in *The Times* on 15 April, setting out many of the anxieties which the Minister's actions raised. He said

Sir, The Dr Vaughan 'affair' has potentially raised a number of crucial questions about the relations between Government and independent bodies in receipt of Exchequer financial support and about the proper balance between independence and accountability.

For many years voluntary organisations have received grants from public funds. Such funding has increased very considerably over the past decade and today many of our social and other welfare services depend on the contributions of voluntary organisations working in partnership with local authorities and central government.

While those who work with the elderly or handicapped, with children in trouble or ex-offenders, with the mentally ill or chronically sick and those assisting the poor or unemployed or seeking to improve our environment have a primary interest in providing services, they may also seek to improve conditions or address the causes of problems. This may well lead voluntary organisations and others to advocate change in the policies and practices of a local authority or of a government department in the interest of those they seek to serve.

Successive ministers and civil servants have benefited from the advice given by voluntary organisations. It would be a sad loss to the evolution of social policy and to the processes of government if voluntary organisations in receipt of public funds were forbidden from expressing their views on policy and administration as it affects their proper aims.

Political suasion by government paymasters would be as dangerous and improper in this context as in the other areas of our free society where the principle of the 'arm's length grant' (support without control of policy, though subject to scrutiny of propriety and efficiency) has also long been recognised, e.g. the arts, university teaching and research, the BBC, the judiciary, royalty and certain international bodies and causes. There is already adequate protection in the existing charities law against 'political' abuse by the recipients, but it is for the Charity Commissioners by due process to enforce, not for ministers by administrative whimsy.

There remains lamentable confusion about what is and what is not 'political' activity. Case law suggests that some aims are classified as political whereas others are not, even though both seek to influence public policy, legislation, etc; and this breeds suspicion that the judgment between them is itself 'political' with a bias against those who would change rather than conserve the status quo.

It would be more in accordance with the principle that law should be clear, ascertainable and predictable if a simpler, more objective test were adopted, namely – that politics is essentially about the retention and transference of government power and that, in a democratic society and in the present context 'political' activity consisted only of activity whose aims include, overtly or covertly, the influencing of the electoral process in favour of (or against) any person or party.

Contributing to debate on public policy and administration would not, as such, constitute 'political' activity in this context. If it did, every body that ever sought to influence government and Parliament, including many highly respected and worthy charities would be caught.

If they are excluded, then the line can only be drawn either 'subjectively' according to how controversial the influence is or 'objectively' in relation to the electoral process itself. Objectivity is better.

I believe that the recognition of these principles would both uphold the proper freedom and independence of voluntary bodies (and others receiving 'arm's length' government support), satisfy Parliament as to the proper and efficient use of the taxpayers' money, reinforce desirable partnership between central and local government and voluntary bodies and correct the present unsatisfactory confusion – and resulting suspicion – over the definition of 'political' activity.

Our free and plural society would be healthier for thus dissipating the shadow of 'Big Brother', while leaving the electoral process as the proper domain of the parties and the politicians.'

With hindsight, and in the face of the later behaviour of the Conservative government, there is some irony in the list of organisations cited by Peter Jay. The arts, university teaching and research, and the BBC, were all later to be subject to the same kind of assaults upon their independence of action as NACAB suffered at this time. Mr Jay's letter epitomised views widely held by workers in the voluntary field, pointing up the position of peaceful cooperation and coexistence between the official and unofficial arms of social welfare which had developed over the years. This could be seen as complacency but there is little doubt that in a climate of trust it enabled many voluntary organisations to go about their business with the minimum of fuss and, in many cases, the maximum of effective action within the financial constraints to which they were subject.

Further discussion took place in Parliament on 28 May, when Mr Alf Dubbs initiated an Adjournment debate, to which the Minister for Consumer Affairs replied. In the course of his reply Dr Vaughan paid tribute to the CAB service

Our citizens advice bureaux are a major national asset – the envy, indeed of many other countries without a comparable system ... we have nearly 1,000 serviced by over 10,000 voluntary workers ... run by a relatively small professional staff ... citizens advice bureaux are an excellent example of how a small number of professional people, properly trained and deployed, can run a large number of volunteers, who, of course, bring a rather different approach to their work ... They bring a fresh and valuable approach. I see the citizens advice bureaux as a most desirable example of how the volunteer can work effectively with the professional ... a large proportion of the money that we provide centrally is spent on seeing that the professionals train the volunteers properly.

He went on

> The dedication, competence and impartiality of the service are known to all who are in contact with it. All hon. Members know ... how helpful the citizens advice bureaux can be ... The bureaux offer free ... and confidential advice to some 4 million enquirers a year. That is a tremendous contribution to the welfare of our community. (*Hansard, 28 May 1984*)

Later in his speech Dr Vaughan referred to his concern over the 'atmosphere of privacy' required for dealing with enquirers in bureaux. His consciousness of this was doubtless coloured by his medical background but he appeared unaware that there were clear stipulations about both aural and visual confidentiality in the Requirements for Membership (*see Appendix 6*) and that the Association had been working for years to find satisfactory solutions to problems which existed in some bureaux, due to inadequate or, in some cases, substandard premises which were all that they were able to obtain owing to the under-funding from which they were suffering.

Another of the Minister's worries related to the proliferation of advice agencies. According to him: 'There is too much overlap between the albeit limited number of advice centres in one area. People are still confused about where they should go for particular types of help.' (*Ibid.*) Following Dr Vaughan's announcement of the Terms of Reference of the Review on 27 April, the next few weeks were spent in trying to come to agreement as to the people who would make up the Review Team. Heading the Review as its Chairman was Sir Douglas Lovelock, First Church Estates Commissioner, formerly Deputy Secretary, Departments of Trade, Industry, Prices and Consumer Protection. It was agreed that he would be joined by a representative of the field of voluntary work, together with a senior member of whatever firm of management consultants was appointed to undertake the management inspection. After some discussion, Lady Limerick, a founder member and Executive Vice-Chairman of the Foundation for the Study of Infant Death, agreed to be the second member of the team, and on the appointment of Inbucon Management Consultants Ltd as the management consultants, one of their directors, Mr Charles Waghorn, became the third. Inbucon were appointed in July 1983 and their appointment enabled the work of the Review Team to begin. The task assigned to Inbucon was to undertake an examination of the work of the staff of NACAB, its organisational structure, the numbers and grading of staff. It was agreed that the work done by Inbucon would replace a proposed staff inspection which had been requested by NACAB and which the DTI had put into its programme for 1983/84.

In the next six months not only were 100 members of the staff of NACAB interviewed, discussions held with members of the Council and seven bureaux visited by the management consultants, but the Review

Team (who themselves paid a number of visits to bureaux and to Area Offices) also invited 70 organisations to comment (57 responded to the invitation) and advertised widely for comments from the public on the CAB service. 75 letters were received as a result of this invitation, some of which were inevitably from those with a grudge or an axe to grind. Similarly, when bureaux were asked to comment the principal response came from a bureau which was already in dispute with the Membership Committee (which had judged its work as not of a high enough standard) and which endeavoured to whip up support for its own view of the matter.

In the final 'Review of the National Association of Citizens Advice Bureaux' which was 'Presented to Parliament by the Secretary of State for Trade and Industry by Command of Her Majesty February 1984' the Team said:

> We would like to thank those individuals, organisations and bureaux who wrote to us, in particular those who responded to our requests for evidence. We would also like to pay a warm tribute to the courtesy and co-operation we have received from the staff of NACAB. Despite the unsettling circumstances in which the Review was set up and the uncertainty which our investigations must have induced in their minds, they were consistently helpful and responsible in meeting our requests.

In fact, the whole episode had a devastating effect on all members of the staff of NACAB who were employed at the centre and an only slightly less acute one on those working in the Area Offices. For months their work schedules had been interrupted, some had volunteered to work for excessively long hours – early on in the emergency staff worked round the clock and through weekends in order to maintain a continuous presence and to produce the necessary publicity and other material in defence of the Association – and both the Chairman, Lady Ricketts and the Director, Mrs Elizabeth Filkin, held themselves almost continuously available for meetings, discussions and interviews with journalists, radio and television reporters. The bureaux, too, gave time to talking to MPs, writing letters, trying to interpret what was happening to the officers and members of their funding authorities, entertaining visiting members of the management consultants or the Review Team, and generally acting in loyal support of the work of the staff of NACAB. Life was made considerably more difficult for a great number of people and, for the staff, there was the added anxiety lest there should be a final recommendation or set of recommendations which would put their jobs at risk.

Throughout the period of the Review everyone was under stress and it was remarkable that so many bore that stress so philosophically.

One famous incident concerned the Director, who was offered a lift back to the Central Office from the House of Commons by Dr Vaughan, a journey of perhaps ten minutes. It so happened that the journey coincided with a bomb alert, with the result that they were closeted together in the car for approximately two hours, at the end of which Dr Vaughan remarked that 'I think you are going to come out of this better than I am!'

When the Report of the Review Team was presented to Parliament it came as something of an anticlimax – at least to those who were hoping to see NACAB put in the pillory of public denigration. The Team commented on some things which it saw as requiring attention but its conclusions and recommendations were couched in mild terms. More significantly, far from recommending financial restrictions, the recommendations included that of an increase of £900,000 in the grant for a full year.

The Review Team disposed of the Minister's anxiety about overlapping agencies quite succinctly, saying

> relatively few of the organisations that gave evidence to us suggested that there was overlap and those that did indicated that the overlap arose from the failure of CAB to refer. The great majority of the organisations commented on the good relations they had with either their local CAB or with NACAB and the co-operation they received from them.

The other major stumbling block and cause for dissension, both with the Minister and with some members of bureau Management Committees, was the working of the Association's Second Aim.

As finally formulated and set out in the 1974 Requirements for Membership, the second of the Obligations of Membership is:

> – to exercise a responsible influence on the development of social policies and services, both locally and nationally.

This part of the work of the bureaux was developed right from the start, Dorothy Keeling having been quite clear in her own mind that part of her function was to act as a channel of information back to government, and the need for work in this field to be developed had been reiterated many times over the years. The constraints upon implementing the Second Aim lay rather with lack of resources than with lack of will. None the less, it remained an area of work which was misunderstood by many and one which was subject to criticism from those who confused the Principle of Impartiality with passivity or neutralism.

The Review took the view that

> This aim is proper and useful, but it should be ancillary to the First Aim and should be treated as such by the National Association of Citizens Advice Bureaux (NACAB) and the bureaux. In pursuing the Second Aim NACAB and the bureaux should ensure that any representations they may make are based clearly on bureaux' experience, that they take the form of reasoned argument and that they avoid a campaigning style, particularly on issues that might fall within the party political domain.

When we consider the case put forward by Peter Jay for a re-definition of 'political' activity as that which relates to 'influencing of the electoral process in favour (or against) any person or party' it can be seen how helpful such a move would be in reducing the area for dissension over the working of the Second Aim.

In looking at the operation of the Principles of Impartiality, Confidentiality and Independence, the Review found no cause for anxiety, but commented that

> It is desirable that the Service should be seen to be independent in order to maintain its impartiality and the confidence of its clients. *However, the Service should recognise that it is dependent on public funds and accountable for them* (My italics.).

The management consultants had some detailed recommendations to make in the light of their conclusion that 'NACAB's overall performance was affected by shortcomings in its management structure and management practice.' After making specific recommendations for the correction of these shortcomings, their only other pertinent comment was that the Greater London Citizens Advice Bureaux Service (GLCABS) should be 'made clearly subordinate to the Council of NACAB'.

Having made its report to Parliament, the Team disbanded and went about its business.

NACAB took a deep breath and prepared to begin discussions on the changes to be made in the light of the recommendations of the management consultants.

Dr Gerard Vaughan ceased to be Minister of Consumer Affairs a few months later and was given a Knighthood in 1984.

Consolidation

The level of funding was increased as a result of the Lovelock Report; by 1987/88 the grant reached the level of £8,028,000. On the face of it, this was a considerable improvement, but in reality, once the funding for the additional management posts recommended by Lovelock had been granted, the level of grant aid was tightly tied to the official rate of inflation, which meant that after 1985/86 the Association's finances lagged behind the rise in costs (such as postage) which were beyond its control; each year saw an actual reduction in available resources. As part of the effort to meet the situation, the Association moved into marketing in order to raise additional money. The Information Service, films, videos and all kinds of teaching materials etc. were sold to outside bodies and individuals. The additional revenue from these sources came to £48,344 in 1987/88.

The finances of the central support systems of the Association are, of course, only one element in the financing of the CAB service as a whole. From the days when a bureau, in order to be recognised, had to have an income of 'at least £7.10s.-d. a year' to the present time, when a single bureau can have expenditure which runs into six figures, the contribution of the local authorities has been essential. Some of this – particularly in the years between 1945 and the 1970s – has taken the form of 'help in kind', which is difficult to tot up in any realistic way. Over the years the commitment of the local authorities has risen steadily and is now estimated at £15m a year.

The greatest increase in costs for the local authorities has resulted from the payment of salaries for Organisers (and other members of staff) at the proper grades. It is hard to compare non-comparable figures, i.e. to do so adequately would require calculations in respect of inflation and the value of money, but a bureau like Cambridge, serving both a city and its surrounding rural area gives some indication of the changes which have occurred over twenty years. The bureau was re-founded in 1969, at which time it was established with a part-time salaried Organiser. The total income for the bureau in its first year was £2,620 of which £1,070 was the salary element. By 1988 the income was £68,675 and the salaries totalled £39,250. A small bureau – Potters Bar – ran for years on a shoestring. Its income (not untypical of the time) was £70 in 1966; by 1976 the income was £1,305 and the Organiser was being paid an 'Honorarium' of about £600; ten years later the income was £11,320 and the salary paid amounted to £7,630. Most bureaux would show similar changes, particularly in relation to the salary element.

Although direct government funding for bureaux has still not been accepted in principle, central government money has gone into the bureaux by many routes over the last years. The earliest of these was by means of the successive Urban Aid programmes and bureaux have subsequently made use of the many different schemes run by the Manpower Services Commission to employ staff to strengthen the service they offer. The problem about such initiatives is that they are often temporary in nature and unless the bureau is able to find an alternative source of funding the benefits may be only short-term.

A more fruitful use of central government funds has been that of the development by NACAB of the use of partnership agreements with local authorities. These work on the principle of changing percentages, i.e. in the first year of operation NACAB provides 75% of the cost, the local authority 25%. The balance shifts from year to year, according to the length of the partnership agreement, until the local authority is providing 100% of the funding. It has been possible to improve many existing bureaux and to promote new ones by means of this procedure. It is permitted under the Conditions of Grant-in-Aid because it enables a proportion of the grant to be moved round, never used as permanent funding, and its use as seed money has proved particularly valuable.

The comparatively vulnerable position of local authorities as we go from the 1980s to the 1990s must be a cause for unease but the position of the bureaux in the fabric of national life is probably their greatest guarantee of survival.

CHAPTER TWO
Relationships

Parent Bodies

From the inception of the CAB service, the Councils of Social Service of Scotland and Wales, with the National Council of Social Service, were central to the existence of the bureaux. The National Council of Social Service had drawn up the preliminary plans through the medium of a meeting of the Standing Conference of Councils of Social Service, convened by Sir Wyndham Deedes, and both the Scottish and the Welsh Councils took responsibility for the service in their own countries. Many of the bureaux were constituent parts of a local Council of Social Service, Guild of Help or similar personal service casework agency.

The relationship of these various bodies was a loose one. Though the National Council was, in title, the chief body, and was responsible for the Standing Conference of Councils of Social Service, it had no powers over the members nor could it insist upon a Council of Social Service becoming a member. Affiliation to the Standing Conference was a matter of choice and many Councils of Social Service (and their equivalents under other names) did not choose to join. The size and scope of these bodies varied widely, ranging from modest collections of local voluntary organisations which combined together to run a small Council of Social Service on a pittance to large and well-endowed agencies which had attracted donations and bequests from charitably minded philanthropists at the end of the nineteenth and beginning of the twentieth centuries.

There was nothing tidy about any of this.

When the service was inaugurated the CAB department was established within the NCSS on a basis of equality with other departments of the Council. Its members were part of the staff structure and shared the support services, such as printing and despatch, with the rest of the NCSS. Its management and staff grading was integrated within the NCSS and final powers of decision on policy and finance rested with the NCSS Executive Committee. CAB staff were thus directly responsible to the

NCSS for their actions and directly dependent upon the NCSS for all finance, whether from government or voluntary sources.

The first body set up for the guidance of the CAB central staff was the CABx Policy Sub-Committee of the NCSS, which met for the first time in November 1940. This was found to be inadequate for the needs of the service and in December 1941 the CABx Committee of the NCSS was instituted under the Chairmanship of Sir Wyndham Deedes. The members of the Committee were drawn in the main from the Regional Advisory Committees; a constitution was adopted, and the Committee worked under this until July 1947, when it became the Central CABx Committee of the NCSS, under which title it functioned until January 1951, when it became the National CAB Committee of the NCSS.

These changes are not to be seen as purely cosmetic. Rather they chart the way in which the CAB service was attempting to establish its identity within the framework of the NCSS and to bring decisions on matters of policy under its own control. The fact that all decisions relating to expenditure lay with the Finance and General Purposes Committee of the NCSS meant that the only significant decisions which the National Committee could take were those which carried no direct financial implications, such as the way in which bureaux should be organised and how they should deal with the public. Resolutions on matters which required expenditure could only be forwarded to the NCSS in the hope that they would be accepted and implemented.

Most of the time the system worked smoothly enough but naturally the perspective of the CAB service was different from that of the NCSS and there were times when the CAB staff found themselves with instructions from their National Committee which could not be carried through owing to lack of support from the NCSS Executive Committee. The NCSS often acted with great generosity; for instance, it was a great help that it continued to fund the Travelling Officers for a further year when government funding for them was withdrawn. None the less, it was faced with competing claims for its voluntary funds among its various departments and dissatisfactions were bound to arise.

This situation was commonly mirrored within local Councils of Social Service, where there was a further complication in that the Secretary of the CSS often operated as Organiser of the CAB as well. The Management Committees of Councils of Social Service were not always willing to give the importance to the work of the bureaux for which they were responsible that the service felt was their due, nor were they always sensitive to the need for the integration of their bureaux within the national CAB service.

An indication of the problems is given in the minutes for July 1958 where reference is made to the difficulties arising from ill-advised promotions undertaken by local CsSS and similar bodies, which sometimes resulted in the establishment of bureaux which did not meet the standard required.

It is probable that a Council of Social Service would have seen things rather differently. It would have identified the need for a bureau, have felt able to meet that need and have seen no reason why it should not promote one as an integral part of its organisation. There was an in-built tension between the entirely independent CSS, which was answerable only to its own Management Committee, and the CAB, which – if it was to be a registered member of the CAB service – was also answerable to the National CABx Committee. The NCSS could impose no rules on a Council of Social Service and, unlike the CAB service, could impose no sanctions. Therefore a CSS which acted in a way which struck at the relationship with the CAB service could not be hauled back by the NCSS. In some cases, this compounded difficulties already being experienced.

A former CSS Secretary/CAB Organiser who was appointed in 1960 described the job as 'fraught with difficulties'. One aspect of this was that the CSS was endeavouring – in her view – to get two workers for the price of one, which meant that she could do neither job to her full satisfaction.

The CAB service was at that time pressing CsSS to set up separate CAB Committees in order that there should be proper supervision and also adequate support for the work of their bureaux. Most CsSS already had an Executive Committee, an Old People's Welfare Committee, a Care Committee and possibly others. The last thing their Secretaries wanted was yet another committee and they resisted the idea, with the result that some bureaux existed in a vacuum.

Confusion about their relationships and loyalties to internal and external bodies of various kinds could make life exceedingly uncomfortable for conscientious Secretary/Organisers. Some had no doubts as to how to handle the situation, for others it led to considerable stress. In places where the Secretary and the Organiser were different people problems also existed and the relationship was not always an easy one.

Over the years the field staff worked to persuade CsSS that it was in their best interest to divest themselves of the responsibility for running a CAB. It became the policy of the service to encourage separation whenever it was a practical possibility and the process finally culminated in November 1980 when Council passed a Resolution which required separation from all parent bodies to be carried through if a bureaux was to retain its membership of the Association and continue to enjoy all the privileges which that involved. By the end of 1983 all bureaux had established their own identities as self-governing units within the federation of Citizens Advice Bureaux. The process of separation was often difficult and sometimes painful but worth the effort in the end.

Independence, as any major change, was not achieved without a struggle, but the result was exhilarating, especially when a brand new typewriter could be purchased to replace an ancient hand-me-down. There was even satisfaction in being able to make one's own economies. (*Organiser*)

Another bureau found that

as a result of its steady expansion and high profile it had become a cuckoo in the nest of its over-stretched parent organisation and tension was apparent in the need to defer to the CVS on all financial questions, or indeed on any important issue.

The inevitable severance came and the Management Committee was rudely jolted out of its leisurely ways. Suddenly it found itself the employer of a growing number of salaried professionals, and co-ordinator of the activities of many more volunteers. Suddenly there was a large budget to handle, and the need to develop political skills in competing for scarce resources.

The most immediate problem was the increase in the workload of the Management Committee. Meetings were protracted, debates complex, and there was always a long list of outstanding business. In voluntary agencies where management committee members are themselves volunteers the need not to overburden them has to be balanced against the demands of the organisation. Our solution to this problem was to create sub-committees which would meet frequently and make decisions, subject to ratification by the full Committee. Such devolution can of course enable a few individuals to shape the thinking of a whole committee at the expense of full involvement by the majority of members. This is an imbalance which poses a problem for management throughout the voluntary sector. The Chair must always be alive to it, and the role of the Organiser as facilitator and communicator is a crucial one. (*Ex-Chairman, Bureau Management Committee*)

Once the dust had settled, bureaux came to enjoy excellent relations with Councils of Social Service and to work actively with them in many parts of the country.

The fact that, in the end, it became necessary to insist that bureaux should have a separate life should not obscure the vital role played by the CsSS. When government funding was withdrawn and the number of local authorities which were willing to fund a local bureau was limited, it was often only the sponsorship of a Council of Social Service which ensured the survival of the local bureau. The contribution made over the years by Councils of Social Service cannot be measured; the CAB service gained from their support – so did the nation, in that they helped to keep the service alive in times of decline.

In order to get some understanding of the complexity of the relations between the various national Councils of Social Service, the Family Welfare Association, the London Council of Social Service, the CAB service as a whole and the NCSS, it is necessary to look in some detail at the way in which these developed over the years. Anyone endeavouring to disentangle the threads cannot help but be struck by the potential for conflict which was built into nearly all these relationships and can only marvel that they managed to work at all.

London

The story of the evolution of the CAB service in Greater London is even more difficult than most to disentangle. At the outbreak of war the Charity Organisation Society, which later changed its name to the Family Welfare Association, established bureaux in the Inner London boroughs. These were not the boroughs as we know them today but the old boroughs which existed before the reorganisation of London local government in the late sixties. The rest of the Greater London area came under the suzerainty of the London Council of Social Service, which did not run bureaux (as the FWA did) but oversaw those run by a wide variety of organisations in Outer London.

From the outbreak of war, the FWA bureaux were staffed by paid and experienced caseworkers, many of whom had already been employed by the FWA. These bureaux were different in kind from the great majority of CABx throughout the country but they were required to conduct their affairs within the policies and practices of the CAB service as a whole as it developed under the leadership of Dorothy Keeling, the secondee from the Liverpool Personal Service Society, and the various committees to which she worked. It was a rather bizarre chance that the Director of the COS (FWA) at that time was Ben Astbury. The comment has been made that he 'as head of the COS was very much in competition with the Liverpool set-up, which is possibly why there was so much antipathy between headquarters and the COS'. Relationships got off on a bad footing and remained decidedly bumpy for many years.

The London Council of Social Service depended upon the NCSS for much of its income and its staff were employed by the NCSS, though housed by and responsible to the LCSS. It employed staff to work with the Outer London bureaux – which were largely (though not entirely) run by volunteers – and these staff were also answerable to the CAB Central Committee and its successors.

Though the two components of the London situation were able to coexist, it cannot be said that they were always able to see each other's point of view. The FWA employed a member of staff as CAB Liaison Officer, with responsibility for its bureaux and as the link with the National Committee; another officer worked with the LCSS in an advisory capacity.

The time came when, faced with the reorganisation of local government in London, the Chairman of the LCSS, Sir Parker Morris, began to plan for a new independent body to cover the whole of the Greater London area, drawing in both the FWA bureaux and those in the LCSS area of influence. Early in 1967 a working party was set up to draw up proposed Terms of Reference for such a body. The tripartite negotiations came to nothing and the matter was 'referred to the NCSS Finance and General Purposes Committee', where it seems to have made no further progress.

The NCSS decided to go ahead with the appointment of an officer to be the CAB Officer of the London Council of Social Service, to act as the CAB Council's Advisory Officer for London. (It was normal practice for the NCSS to make appointments to the staff of the LCSS.) The appointment was made without any prior discussion with the FWA or its existing CAB Liaison Officer, who had been at work in the field for a number of years. This episode underlines the intricacies of the relationships involved and the administrative difficulties which stood in the way of achieving Sir Parker Morris's desired objective.

Although discussion and deliberations did not cease, no real progress on the unification of the London CAB service was possible until, as a result of an internal review, the Family Welfare Association, under the leadership of a new Director, Miss Janet Lacey, came to the conclusion that the bureaux could be hived off from the parent organisation. It then became urgently necessary to find a way of saving the FWA bureaux and providing an employer to take responsibility for all their staff.

Setting up the new body involved a great deal of work but, under the Chairmanship of Sir William Hart, who was supported by an excellent committee, it was finally possible in June 1972 to bring into being the Greater London Citizens Advice Bureaux Service Ltd, a charitable Company, Limited by Guarantee, which took on the employment roles formerly undertaken by the FWA and the NCSS. From that date the Greater London CAB Service was responsible for all bureaux pan-London, although those in the outer boroughs still retained their independent Management Committees and, in some cases, were the employers of staff.

Not everyone approves of the final solution. One long-serving voluntary worker comments that 'it was a mammoth undertaking to set up GLCABS to cover the extensive and densely populated area of Greater London. It might have been wiser if they had concentrated their activities on the inner London areas and the CAB in the outer London Boroughs had joined their respective neighbouring country areas with whom they had more in common.'

The Greater London CAB Service, as a Limited Company, is run by its Management Committee, which is its Board of Directors, but four other bodies also function within the London Area. These are the Area Committees, all of which send representatives to the National Council of the Association. The Management Committee can decide on policies in London but must do so within the same rules as other member bureaux throughout the country. Its Area Officers and bureaux are answerable to the Council of NACAB, as are those in other parts of the country. The fact that the GLCABS set-up is different from that obtaining anywhere else means that it is widely misunderstood within the CAB service and its concentration on retaining a salaried staff, rather than making use of volunteers, has created suspicion in the past.

Undoubtedly GLCABS is an anomaly; one which was subject to examination by the Review Team in 1984. At that time the management consultants decided that 'GLCABS is operating effectively and the removal of this anomaly is not a priority.'

At the time of writing its position remains unchanged.

Scotland

The original Scottish bureaux were opened in 1939/40 under the aegis of the Scottish Council of Social Service. It is not clear how many bureaux were established at this time but it was in the range of six to ten; no doubt numbers fluctuated, but there is no readily available record of the maximum number reached. The bureaux undertook the same work as those in the rest of the United Kingdom and were loosely affiliated to the Central CAB Committee.

After the war a number of local authorities in Scotland were running their own services; in 1964 the CAB Council took note of this and agreed that

> providing the Scottish CAB Committee are satisfied that the service of advice and information provided by the Town Clerk or other local authority officials is the best service that can be provided taking into consideration population and local circumstances, the central information service should be made available to the Local Authority.

There had been problems about local authority bureaux in other parts of the country – specifically problems relating to independence – and the position was peculiarly difficult in Scotland as there were so many of them, comparatively speaking. After further discussion in the CAB Council in 1965 it was decided to continue to supply the Information Service to the local authority bureaux in Scotland. At the same time, Council identified the need for more field staff who could promote independent bureaux and reduce the dependence on direct local authority services.

The local authority bureaux were not the only cause for friction. The CAB staff of the Scottish CSS did not 'wholly subscribe to the decisions of the CAB Council in regard to registration procedure'. Scotland felt that it should undertake the registration of its own bureaux; the Council was fearful that it would not be possible to maintain comparable standards if the process of registration was not carried out on a UK basis. Relations became strained, though both sides made every effort to try and reach agreement. The fact that the National CAB Council was, at the same time, in process of trying to negotiate its own position within the NCSS only made things more complicated, and by June 1969 there was still no formal agreement between Scotland and the National CAB Council though by that time the Scottish CAB Committee was registering Scottish bureaux. The National CAB Council, putting aside its fears, expressed a 'real wish to join in a common standard of service' when it accepted this position.

It was important that both systems should be kept in line and in 1970 there was agreement that staff from each side of the border should make registration visits together from time to time.

The Information Service was the next cause of dissension. Much of its contents did not apply to Scotland, since Scottish law was based on Roman law and operated in different ways. It was unhelpful to distribute information which was inapplicable to Scotland direct to bureaux. It was agreed to send the Information Service to the Scottish central office, rather than to bureaux, from January 1971. This procedure, in its turn, produced a typical niggle when SCSS asked London to continue to invoice the Scottish bureaux and London, rather huffily, replied that 'it would not be appropriate now that there was no direct contact with bureaux in Scotland for invoices to be sent by CAB headquarters to individual bureaux in that country'.

Tempers were kept, but only just.

As the National CAB Council found itself constrained by its position in the structure of the NCSS, so also the Scottish CABx were not satisfied with their position under the control of the SCSS. They sought separation from the SCSS and this proved easier to achieve than did that of the National Association. The Scottish Association of Citizens Advice Bureaux (SACAB) became independent of the SCSS in October 1975, adopted a new Constitution and moved to separate offices in Edinburgh. Technically, SACAB retained the status of an Area Committee of NACAB, a situation which continued until 1980, when complete independence was achieved. SACAB bureaux became Associate Members of NACAB and the General Council of SACAB became the ultimate authority for the CAB service in Scotland. SACAB's final step on the road to full independent status was taken when it became a charitable Company, Limited by Guarantee, in 1984. In 1988 the name 'Scottish Association of Citizens Advice Bureaux' was changed to 'Citizens Advice Scotland' and a new logo was adopted for the Scottish bureaux. The object of the changes was to heighten public awareness of the role of Citizens Advice. A Liaison Committee has responsibility for ensuring that NACAB and Scotland do not get out of step with each other.

Prior to 1974, Scotland was largely under-developed but it was able to make use of money from the Development Grant to such good purpose that whereas there were 44 bureaux in 1975/76, dealing with 180,838 enquiries, by 1987/88 the number of outlets (main bureaux and extensions) had risen to 83 and the enquiries to 508,319.

Like the National Association, Scotland is promoting the use of modern methods of extending the service, including computers and microfiche systems for outreach work. It has revised and refined its membership system for bureaux since it became independent of NACAB, leading the way in new approaches to the assessment of bureaux, and has developed its own training strategy and methods to meet the special needs of Scotland.

Northern Ireland

The story of the CAB service in Northern Ireland is that the first major initiative occurred after there had been two terrible air raids on Belfast in 1941, after which the Belfast Council of Social Welfare was asked to take charge of Information Centres in the city. In the event, these were not needed but general enquiries came in and, as a result, the Council of Social Welfare decided to appoint a worker to deal with them. A room in Bryson House, home of the Council for Social Welfare, was designated as the Citizens Advice Bureau and the worker, a woman barrister, was housed there. It is not clear how long this continued but there was no other CAB presence until, in 1964, a CAB Advisory Committee was formed. From this, and from discussions with BCSW, it became possible to establish the first bureau in Northern Ireland which was run in accordance with the requirements of the national CAB service. This, like its predecessor, was situated in Bryson House and its Organiser was a member of the BCSW staff. During the 1960s the Northern Ireland Council of Social Service was instrumental in promoting bureaux outside Belfast and a number were opened. Additional bureaux were opened in East and West Belfast in the early 1970s and these developments were drawn together when, in 1974, a Northern Ireland Association of CABx, serviced by the Northern Ireland Council of Social Service, was set up. This became the governing body of the Northern Ireland bureaux, linked to the National Association by means of its representative to Council, enjoying both the privileges and the duties of membership but separate from it.

The Northern Ireland situation is different from that in the rest of the United Kingdom. Its committee performs much the same function as an Area Committee in England but it is not serviced by NACAB staff, nor does it receive money from the government departments which fund NACAB and SACAB. Indeed the conditions of Grant in Aid make it impossible for NACAB to use its funds to help the Northern Ireland bureaux directly.

The administrative situation in Northern Ireland differs from that in the rest of the UK; it also has variations of law. It was therefore essential that there should be additional information for the bureaux in the province and an essential member of the staff was the Information Officer, who supplied supplementary material covering aspects of the

law or administrative arrangements which were different from those on
the mainland. The first Information Officer was a member of the staff of
the NICSS, appointed in 1968.

The constitutional position of the bureaux in Belfast and in Northern
Ireland generally was somewhat complicated and the impetus for
disentangling all the strands was given by the requirement of NACAB
Council that all bureaux must become independent of their parent
bodies. This led in 1984 to the formation of the independent Northern
Ireland Association of CAB, which, like NACAB and SACAB, is a charit-
able Company, Limited by Guarantee. This body employs the staff of
NIACAB and services its Council, which is the governing body of the
Northern Ireland bureaux.

Wales

The Wales Council of Social Service, like its brethren in England and
Scotland, made itself responsible for the establishment of the CAB
service at the outbreak of war. It is thought that there were initially
something in the region of fifty bureaux in the principality, though no
list has survived as far as is known. Numbers of bureaux have fluctuated
over the years, in Wales as elsewhere; the total number of outlets listed
for the year 1987/88 was 87, of which 29 were in North, and 58 in South,
Wales. The term 'outlets' is used because it includes such things as
specialised support units as well as conventional bureaux. The special
problems of Wales relate to the difficulties of communications and
access, one aspect of which is the language problem in Welsh-speaking
areas; there are also minor variations in the administrative services and
provisions which relate to the special position of the Welsh Office. The
differences are not as great as those in Scotland or Northern Ireland but
still need to be provided for.

Mention has been made of the conflicts between the Scottish Council
of Social Service and the national Registration Committee over the
registration of bureaux. This situation was to a large degree mirrored in
the case of Wales, the CSS there also holding out for the power to
register the bureaux in the Principality. These problems were at their
most acute between 1968 and 1972. It was during 1969 that the Welsh
Committee 'registered three CABx' for which they levied 'the usual 10/-
fee'; they also proposed to design a Welsh registration certificate. One
result of this was that for some time the Welsh bureaux were disenfran-
chised – a matter which was of some importance when the Standing
Conference of Citizens Advice Bureaux met in June 1971.

Not only was the Wales Council of Social Service in dispute with the
national Registration Committee but it also was increasingly at odds
with the bureaux in Wales as a whole. The field staff were employed by
the WCSS and carried out the same functions for it as did their
counterparts in England who were the employees of the NCSS. In 1972

the Secretary of the Wales Council of Social Service decided to organise a referendum in order to discover the wishes of the bureaux under its jurisdiction; he then called a general meeting of all the bureaux.

As a result, shortly after his appointment in 1972, Jeremy Leighton, the new Chief Executive of the CAB service, was faced with a potentially destructive situation. Fortunately, before attending the meeting, he had been able to agree with the Administrator of the NCSS, Col R. C. Chaundler, that if the situation ended badly, he would be in a position to offer employment to the existing field staff. It was a wise piece of forethought for, when the vote was taken and the bureaux opted to leave the Wales Council of Social Service, the Secretary of the WCSS washed his hands of all further responsibility and walked out of the meeting.

From that time the Welsh bureaux were integrated with those in England and the support staff was employed by the NCSS in the first instance and NACAB from the time of independence from the NCSS.

Going it Alone

There was an increasing feeling of dissatisfaction with the position of the CAB service within the structure and management of the NCSS during the 1960s.

It was realised that the constitutional position was complicated and in 1966 a Constitution Committee was set up, charged with the task of carrying out an examination of possible constitutional change. The bureaux had been accustomed to meet together as the Standing Conference of CABx, an 'associated group' of the NCSS. One issue raised was the 'extent to which the NCSS was answerable in law as trustee for an associated group'.

The CAB service felt that the most satisfactory relationship would be an equal partnership with the NCSS and it began to press for this. The NCSS had set up a Review Committee in 1967 to examine its internal structure and relationships and in 1969 a meeting was held between the Review Committee and Officers of the CAB service. This proved unproductive; the Committee was committed to the retention of 'associated groups' and to the view that only the NCSS should be concerned with the allocation of finance.

This was not to the liking of Council, which passed a Resolution in June 1969 reaffirming its view that 'the work of the CAB service should be carried out as a separate entity in equal partnership'. The NCSS responded by expressing its view that 'the Service should be governed by a committee appointed by the NCSS, that committee being the CAB Council'. The NCSS was quite unprepared to make any concessions on the lines sought by the CAB Council and limited the amount of control allowed to the Council to that of the 'day by day affairs of the CAB service'. Unsurprisingly, this response was not welcome. The Constitution Committee commented that 'It was not considered realistic that a developing national voluntary organisation should remain satisfied unless it had the management of its own affairs under its own control.'

One proposal from the NCSS was that staff employed in the CAB department should be treated as interchangeable with those in other NCSS departments. This was judged to be potentially very damaging to the service to bureaux. It was suspected that the underlying purpose of the proposal was the development of a commitment by staff to the NCSS rather than to the CAB service.

Within the framework of the NCSS, only the CAB service and the Charities Aid Fund gave direct services to the public. In the opinion of the CAB service this was 'material to the degree of control it should exercise in relation to finance and staffing'.

The grading of staff, coupled with job evaluation, was a further cause for conflict. Other sensitive areas related to dual loyalties and the needs of the administration of the CAB service.

In October Council voted by 16 to 1 (with five abstentions) that it was not prepared 'to accept dual control of staff or to surrender policy decisions although ready to discuss these with others on a partnership basis'. Council then went on, perhaps tactlessly, to claim that 'until CAB had an entity of its own it was incumbent upon the NCSS to continue to provide some voluntary money'.

The first suggestion that a charitable company might be the answer for the CAB service appears to have been made at this time.

Discussions were entered into with the Officers of the NCSS. Unfortunately, the Chairman of the NCSS, Dr Leslie Farrer Brown, and the Chairman of the National CAB Council, Sir Harold Banwell, did not find it easy to talk to each other and relations between the Director of the NCSS, J. K. Owens, and the CAB Secretary, Joan Pridham, were not much better, with the result that neither side succeeded in addressing the problems facing them in a way which would have enabled them to come to a mutually acceptable agreement. Their discussions resulted in the production of a draft agreement under 15 heads; by May 1970 agreement had been reached under 12 of these heads but no resolution was possible on the remaining three.

The Chairmen met again in February 1971 under the neutral Chairmanship of a civil servant from the Cabinet Office and, with the consent of their respective Councils, jointly prepared new heads of agreement.

These were presented to, and rejected by, the National CAB Council, which formulated a Motion to be put forward to a special meeting of the Standing Conference of Citizens Advice Bureaux which was called for 8 June at the Friends' House, Euston Road. The Motion called for the National CAB Council to adopt a constitutional position separate from the NCSS, giving the bureaux collectively the control of their affairs.

A large proportion of member bureaux sent representatives to the meeting. Among those present were representatives from the Welsh bureaux but because there was an unresolved conflict between the Wales Council of Social Service and the CAB service over the registration of bureaux, the Welsh bureaux had no vote.

The meeting was scheduled to open at 10.30 a.m. but, to the great puzzlement of those attending, the platform party withdrew and the representatives sat waiting for approximately ninety minutes before the proceedings began. It was then announced that a final attempt had been made to reach agreement with the NCSS and that it had failed. The ensuing debate was not very satisfactory and bureaux were left with the impression that although unofficial approaches had been made to the Home Office about funding for the future, these had borne no fruit. The sum of £26,000 was bandied about as the possible shortfall which would have to be met in the event of secession from the NCSS. This swayed the bureaux against the Motion – many of them could not look forward with any confidence to the possibility of this money being found. After the Motion had been put, an Amendment was proposed by Martin Grundy, General Secretary of the Exeter Council of Social Service. This Amendment turned the CAB Council back from its position and required it to negotiate new terms on which it would remain integrated within the NCSS.

The Amendment was put and passed by 163 votes to 132, with six abstentions. It is an irony that had the Welsh bureaux been allowed to vote the result might have been different. It was not much later that the Welsh bureaux voted unanimously to leave the Wales Council of Social Service.

What followed is recorded in the Annual Report of the NCSS for 1970/71:

> The NCSS Executive on 10th June welcomed the resolution. They considered very seriously what steps should be taken to ensure its implementation and authorised the honorary officers to take the necessary action. It was with great regret that the honorary officers came to the conclusion that agreement could only be reached if there were a new secretary of the National CAB Council. Although the representatives of the National CAB Council with whom the matter was then discussed did not agree to this view, it was decided that the previous secretary should be dismissed and a new secretary appointed. Miss Joan Pridham was retired on pension ... A special meeting of the National CAB Council took place on 6th July 1971, and after expressing their dismay at the action in dismissing the secretary, the Council decided that their first duty was to strengthen and unite the CAB service in the light of the decision at the meeting of the bureaux. It was agreed to seek informal meetings leading to formal negotiations in a more constructive atmosphere.

The Council members had been taken aback that the NCSS Executive Committee, only four days after the meeting of the Standing Conference, had decided to terminate Miss Joan Pridham's appointment and require her to take paid leave of absence. This decision had been taken without reference to the National CAB Council and against the advice of the Chairman and the two Council members who were called to a special meeting with the NCSS Honorary Officers on 28 June.

The ostensible reason for her dismissal was that Miss Pridham had 'advocated a policy in complete contradiction to that agreed by the National Standing Conference of CABx'. This, with hindsight, looks a little specious, since the Secretary had been instructed by her National Council to work towards freeing the CAB service from the overlordship of the NCSS. The argument was that, because of her previous commitment to the aim of independence, she would not be able to implement the decision of Conference that the CAB service should remain an integral part of the NCSS. It is likely that the public statements of the NCSS were somewhat disingenuous and that, underlying the whole fiasco, were clashes of personality among both the Honorary Officers and the employees of both bodies. The NCSS at the time was somewhat resistant to change, possibly because many of its most prominent members were elderly and set in their ways.

Naturally enough, the newspapers had a field day over the rumpus and it was written up in various ways, the headline in *The Observer* of 4 July, 'Power Battle in Bedford Square', being typical of the type of thing which appeared.

The NCSS brought in one of its Regional Officers to be Acting Secretary until a new appointment could be made. Three of the more senior members of the Central Office staff resigned in protest at the dismissal but the remainder of the staff continued with their work as usual.

The Chairman of the CAB Council, Sir Harold Banwell, had given notice of his intention to retire as soon as a successor could be found but Council members were surprised when he announced at the first meeting following the Standing Conference meeting that he was withdrawing immediately. Faced with this situation, Council prevailed upon one of the Vice-Chairmen, Mr John Wallis, to take over as Chairman. His first task was to pour oil on troubled waters. John Wallis had long experience in conciliation work, as he had been Training Officer with the Marriage Guidance Council for some years, and knew how to be emollient. His first letter to bureaux ended with the paragraph:

> The CAB Service is at present divided between those who still want independence, those who want to remain within the NCSS and those who did not attend or vote at the Standing Conference. It is therefore surely unlikely that your Council or anyone else will quickly produce a result to satisfy everyone, however tired we are getting of the dispute. Fortunately, there is one firm basis on which we are all united; the CAB Service fills an invaluable and unique place in present society and in the lives of the men and women who turn to us daily for information, guidance and help.

The bureaux which had, over the months, been deluged with papers of enormous length and complexity, found themselves bemused and bewildered about what exactly had happened and why. Their proper concern was to maintain their service to the public and once the fuss died down they shrugged their collective shoulders and got on with the job.

Mr E J Nichol, NCSS Midland Regional Officer, kept things going at the centre until the appointment in 1972 of Mr A J (Jeremy) Leighton as head of the CAB service, with the new designation of Chief Executive. He was at once faced with the need for a negotiated settlement with the NCSS, together with progress towards a more satisfactory constitutional position. Discussions and consultations went on throughout the next year and by May 1973 it was possible to present a new Constitution to the Standing Conference for adoption. The Constitution was accompanied by a new Agreement between the NCSS and the National CAB Council which set out the terms under which the two bodies would in future conduct their affairs.

As a result of the adoption of the new Constitution, the National Standing Conference of CABx was wound up, as was the National Citizens Advice Bureaux Council, and their assets were transferred to the new body – the National Association of Citizens Advice Bureaux. This was a real advance, though it did not take the Association as far as some would have liked.

The effect of the new Constitution was to turn the Association into a federation of independent members which, through the representative machinery, controlled the policies and practices of its members and of the staff who were employed to implement its decisions. Under the terms of the Agreement the staff continued to be engaged and employed by the NCSS. The Chief Executive was appointed a member of the NCSS Chief Executive Team, and the involvement of members of Council in the selection of senior members of staff was spelt out.

Quiet negotiations continued but it was not until there was a Management Review of the NCSS that further progress began to be a real possibility. The Civil Service Management Review Team, at an early stage in its work, recommended that NACAB should be separated from the NCSS. They recommended that work should be done to define the financial implications, ascertain the attitude of the Treasury, look at the problems of legal and charitable status – in short, to lay the foundations for a separate existence.

In the period between the unsuccessful bid to separate from the NCSS in 1971 and 1975 there had been two vital changes. One was the financial situation of the NCSS, which had become more difficult, and the other was the acquisition by NACAB of the Development Grant. Whereas at the earlier stage there had been a conflict of interest, it was now much clearer that separation would benefit both parties. The essential difference was that, in the light of the recommendations from its own Review team, the civil service was prepared to provide the financial support necessary to maintain the central CAB services. No longer would the NCSS be called upon to finance any deficit; apart from income derived from the sale of the Information Service, publications and bureaux subscriptions, all income would in future come from the funding departments, via the consolidated grant and the Development Grant.

While the position was straightforward in terms of the central organisation, some bureaux still had grave doubts about the desirability of NACAB being entirely dependent upon government funding. They felt that it made NACAB too vulnerable; just as the NCSS had argued, years before, against relying on too high a proportion of government money, so these bureaux were uneasy about NACAB's freedom of action in the future. However, at the Extraordinary General Meeting held in London in May 1976, a Resolution that the Association should move towards separation from its parent body gained overwhelming support.

In spite of any reservations still felt, the die was now cast and from November 1975 onwards it was a case of slow but steady progress towards disentangling NACAB from the NCSS and establishing it as an independent body. There were many technicalities to be gone through. It was not possible to go ahead with the incorporation of NACAB straight away and for the interim period Custodian Trustees were appointed to provide the legal identity necessary for such matters as the holding of leases etc. The three brave men who undertook this for the Association were Professor Roy Goode, Mr John Methven and Lord Selwyn-Lloyd. As a final gesture of goodwill, the NCSS gave an independence grant of £50,000 from its voluntary funds. When the staff finally moved from the old NCSS offices in Bedford Square and took up residence in Drury Lane it was the end of nearly forty years of close association.

The final step was taken in 1979 when, after some delay caused by industrial action at Companies House, the Association became a charitable Company, Limited by Guarantee and having No Share Capital. At last it was its own body, standing on its own feet and able to act as a legal entity. The Council members became the Directors of the company and began to come to grips with the nature of the change in role that this implied. The Association is a federation of independent members – each bureau (or group of bureaux) has its own Management Committee which is responsible for the acquisition of funding, premises, equipment etc. and and for the employment of the staff (whether paid or voluntary). To be a member a bureau must be a registered charity and must conduct its affairs in accordance with the principles and practices of the Association as laid down in Council. Every bureau sends a Representative to its Area Committee and, in its turn, the Area Committee elects one of its number to go forward to Council as its Representative. Since it is customary for the Organiser to represent the bureau on the Area Committee, the odds are that the Area Representative on Council will also be an Organiser. Some Management Committees are unhappy that the Area Committees, and Council and its committees, are made up in the main of members who are the employees of bureaux. Although Management Committees are consulted on all policy matters, in the last resort it is in Council that decisions on policy are taken. This has been an issue from time to time and remains one which is unresolved.

Because the bulk of the membership of Council is made up of the practitioners it is in close touch with the day to day situation of bureaux throughout the country. This is its strength, in that it prevents Council going off at a tangent down some inviting path which looks enticing but which would lead nowhere in terms of the development of advice services; it is also its weakness, in that many become Council members without experience of managing anything with a budget running into more than five figures or with employment responsibilities for more than a handful of paid staff. Coming from the point of delivery keeps your awareness of reality high – it also tends to make you keep your head down and tackle the work which flows in on a one-off basis, rather than lifting your head and looking at the wider perspective.

Looking back, it is possible to perceive missed opportunities over the years, opportunities which might have been grasped by a Council which did not get bogged down with detail and which was capable of taking a larger view. It is also true that due to the 'a-political' stance of the CAB service, a certain naivety has, in the past, marked the relations between the Association and the various government departments which have funded it. There was in the minds of many of the devoted and excellent Organisers of the 1960s and 1970s (and also their Management Committees) an idea that presenting a case for proper funding was in the nature of political action; therefore it could not be contemplated. What many people see as a perverse form of pride, pride which finds satisfaction in managing on almost nothing, held many a bureau back, so that it could not develop and improve the service it offered. It also led to the potential of the service being under-estimated by many officers and members of the local authorities.

As a result of the report from the management consultants who took part in the Review of NACAB set up by Dr Vaughan in 1983, the membership and the committee structure of Council has been revised, with the object of making its work more effective. With its enlarged responsibilities Council faces an ever more taxing duty to ensure that the decisions it takes are not only right for the service as a whole but are also seen as right by the individual member bureaux, their staffs and their management committees. The new structure was introduced in the autumn of 1985.

Prospects for the Future

It has been necessary to give some account of the complications of past relationships in order to show how the CAB service has arrived at its present situation. A great deal of energy has been absorbed over the years in the conflicts which arose as a result of unclear arrangements. To all those who feel that constitutional matters are boring and to be avoided if at all possible, the story of the development of the CAB service into what eventually became the National Association of CABx should act as a warning. The lack of clear lines of executive authority made the running of the service difficult; the inter-relation of various independent and semi-independent bodies hampered decision-making in ways which made for frustration. Similar mistakes should be avoided in the future and this can best be achieved by means of a sound constitutional framework.

One option to be considered in the future is that of devolution. This may or may not prove acceptable to the service but is one which may need to be considered as the Association continues to grow. It must be prepared to think carefully about how it is to face the years to come and make proper arrangements to ensure that it is neither top-heavy nor unable to sustain a sense of the unity of the whole. Keeping all parts of a dispersed organisation together is not easy but it is essential that it should be done.

The time when the Citizens Advice Bureau was the only source of information and advice has long passed. The underlying assumption that people need only be told as much as is good for them to know, which marked the first half of the century, has been blown apart by the increasing awareness that knowledge is power and, conversely, without knowledge we are all powerless in our situation. Making access to information a reality for the population as a whole is what faces the CAB service; it must make sure that its structural arrangements are effective and powerful in pursuit of this aim.

CHAPTER THREE
The Development of the Bureaux

Opening Up

We have seen that there were two quite distinct types of bureau – those which were instituted by the Personal Service Societies, Guilds of Help, Councils of Social Service and similar organisations and those which were sponsored by individuals or by other voluntary organisations. Two organisations which were prominent in this role were the Women's Voluntary Service and Rotary International, but the churches and other organisations were similarly involved.

Although the Statement of July 1939 had set out that 'as a minimum there would have to be one full-time person, experienced in family casework in charge of the bureau' there was a limited number of such people and by no means all bureaux were staffed in such a way.

The report 'Citizens Advice Bureaux: A Record of Five Years' Work', published in 1945 summarised the position.

> The first Citizens' Advice Bureaux were managed and staffed by people already engaged in social service work: many of them salaried and experienced workers. In central London, for instance, most of the Bureaux are part of a Charity Organisation Society Office; in Greater London they are organised by the London Council of Social Service; in Liverpool, Sheffield, Bristol and the other great cities they are run by the Personal Service Society, or other casework bodies.
>
> But these Bureaux soon needed many more workers: and towns which had no social service organisations needed Bureaux. An army of new people were [sic] recruited for the service, many of them newcomers to social welfare work; men and women from every walk of life – housewives, business men, teachers, workmen, retired civil servants, students – all kinds of people ready to share their varied knowledge and experience with fellow citizens who needed it.
>
> More than 10,000 men and women work in Citizens' Advice Bureaux, and 90% of them are voluntary workers.

In addition, many more staff the local committees which manage the affairs of the different Citizens' Advice Bureaux.

The only thing which many of the early bureaux had in common was the name – 'Citizens Advice Bureau' – and even that was not universal. Two variations which have come to light were 'Citizens Advice and Help Bureau' and 'Hazel Grove Advice' – doubtless there were others. The accounts of bureaux in the first months of the war reveal a great variation both in the way they came into existence and in the kind of facilities which they were able to offer. For example, the foundation of the Newport (Monmouthshire) CAB in September 1939 was brought about when:

the Secretary of the Rural Community Council approached the Borough Council, which kindly provided the use of premises and agreed to pay Rent, Heating, Lighting and Telephone charges. With laths and some linen the premises were divided into two parts, the outside for Enquirers and the inside for private interviews and general office. Furniture consisting of two trestle tables, a couple of chairs and an old writing desk, was begged or borrowed. The windows had to be boarded up because of the Black-out. All work had to be done in artificial light and the only ventilation was through the 'Open Door' ... By the middle of December there were 11 members of staff.

Having no experience on which to base the work, everything had to be done by 'trial and error' but by April 1940 we had succeeded in establishing a satisfactory and useful system of records.

... the bureau was open from 10.00 a.m.–1.00 p.m. and 2.30 p.m.–5.30 p.m. five days a week. During the first four years, when the need was urgent, the bureau remained open long past these hours and was open on Saturday afternoons and public holidays. All the staff were volunteers and paid their own expenses; the volunteers worked an average of two sessions each per week.

Another account – this time of a one-man bureau in Crediton – says that

information files were unknown. The service depended very much on the compassion and knowledge of the person in charge but, believe me, they did excellent work. There were no set hours. My father was available in the office and at home 24 hours a day, 7 days a week and I can remember my mother complaining bitterly that she couldn't listen to the radio (which was in our sitting-room) because someone was in there 'crying out their troubles to your father'. Dad never gave up. If something was beyond him he would refer the client to some other body but he always followed it through to make sure satisfaction was obtained. Postages he paid out of his own meagre pocket. Holidays he never had.

A contrast to these somewhat haphazard beginnings was that of the Holborn, Finsbury and City of London office of the Charity Organisation Society.

In preparation for air-raids, instructions were given to civilians to identify their nearest Citizens Advice Bureau.

Ours was a long established COS office and our case files went back many years, so one of the first things we did was to dust down those for August 1914 to find out what had happened then. The main problem then was delay in receipt of allowances by wives and families. In 1939 this proved to be a very minor problem but we thought it wise to alert our local SSAFA representatives, only to discover that these were mostly advanced in years and had had little work to do since the end of the Great War! I may say that this situation was quickly solved by SSAFA.

We realised that we would need extra staff. Luckily, our local COS Committee was very active. Most of the members were trained social workers who could offer varying amounts of time to help, some of them knowing that their own jobs would grind to at least a temporary halt in a war situation.

3 September, 1939 was a Sunday and I was at the Church of Scotland in Pont Street with my mother. Two events I remember. First, our Minister appeared in uniform (he was Chaplain to the London Scottish) and the Air Raid sirens went off in the middle of the service. Not a soul in the large congregation moved. We heard later that it was a false alarm. In the afternoon a few of us went to the office to prepare it for the following day and we opened early on Monday morning in our new role of COS/CAB.

I cannot, at this stage, remember our opening hours, except that they were much longer than our usual ones of 9 till 5, and for the first few weeks we were open on Sunday as well as weekdays.

We soon collected a willing band of volunteers, both professional and lay. Owing to evacuation this included hospital almoners and school staff who had remained behind. All of them knew our area well, which was a great help with home visiting, which carried on as before.

The regular supplies of CAB notes did not start at once and our caseworkers had to rely greatly on their own commonsense in dealing with problems. Our telephone bill for that quarter must have been a very high one!

Another bureau was situated in the Green Room of the Civic Hall and 'We all sat at a long table and answered clients as best we could publicly. We had one private interview room, mostly for matrimonial questions.' Other premises included empty shops, church vestries, church halls, a Quaker Meeting House, libraries, Labour Halls, a room in a café, the Organiser's house – in fact, almost any corner which became available could be made use of.

Whether they were trained caseworkers or the new breed of volunteers struggling to get to grips with a difficult task, the workers in the bureaux were very much in the dark about how to conduct the affairs of their new service. At the beginning it was a case of taking a deep breath and tackling the work as best they could.

In the opening months of the war the most common problems coming into bureaux were those of young wives left to cope on their own on drastically restricted budgets. As one person said, 'many of them were little more than girls and they were in great difficulties over the payment of their rent or mortgage out of a totally inadequate allotment. Debt became the great headache at that time.'

A report in the *Manchester Guardian* of 16 January 1940 reinforces that view. It outlines some of the 'Questions that Reveal a People's Difficulties', listing those most frequently turning to the bureaux for help as

> young wives who had never faced a difficult problem single-handed until their husbands were called up, parents whose sons, now in the Army, had been their chief support, men whose businesses are now frowned upon as a luxury trade, middle-class unemployed who do not know of the special register for them and young people who have begun to buy a house and cannot go on paying while the husband is away... By far the most important questions are to do with financial difficulties of which there are two principal sources. These are sudden and unexpected unemployment or loss of business caused by the war, and inadequate allowances for the families and dependents' allowances raises really serious difficulties.

THE SOLDIER'S WIFE

The allowance for a private's wife is usually 17s, with 7s from the man's pay and 5s for the first child, 4s for the second and 3s for each of the remaining children. This gives 33s for a man, wife and two children, and the hardships caused where the man has hitherto been in a good job earning from £3 a week upwards are easy to imagine. As there is no body except the Public Assistance Committee which will supplement Army allowances, one of the results of enlisting – either voluntarily or under the Military Service Act – is commonly to reduce one's wife or parents either to running into debts which there is no reasonable prospect of ever repaying or else applying to the Public Assistance Committee. Supplementary allowances up to an additional £2 are theoretically payable in cases of hardship but, up to the present relatively few people have received these allowances.

FINANCIAL HARDSHIPS

Rent is the main stumbling block, coupled with building society repayments and rates, and followed closely by hire-purchase agreements. The only protection in these cases is given by the Courts (Emergency Powers) Act, 1939, under which no action can be taken to recover a debt on a pre-war contract without leave from a court of law to do so. This is, however, small comfort to a respectable person who would never ordinarily dream of incurring debts, much less of appearing in court as a debtor.

The fact that the Act only applies to contracts made before the war began is important, particularly in the case of hire purchase contracts, because if the company can in some way induce a debtor to enter into a new contract – by offering, for example, a new agreement allowing reduced payments over a longer period – the protection of the Act is removed. If the hirer then falls into arrears the hire-purchase company is at liberty to exercise any remedy it can, subject only to the Hire Purchase Act, 1938. In addition to this hire purchase companies in particular try many ways to secure payments which they can only legally recover by applying to a court. Wives of soldiers are persuaded that they must pay on their husbands' or sons' contracts and all kinds of threats are made to remove the goods.

Chance (and the care of one individual) has preserved the Annual Reports of the Southwark Citizens Advice Bureau in spite of the fact that it was bombed out, and through them it is possible to trace the problems as they arose year by year.

September 1939/September 1940 gives us

> First the rush of evacuation for children, aged and invalid in the first weeks of the War then ... the problems connected with the abandonment of civil life, the altered income and change in family conditions. With the fall of Norway and Holland came a stream of Red Cross messages ... Finally, the tidal wave of consequences arising from the bombardment of London, with its forced change of habits of so many homes ... Requests to trace missing relatives in the bombed areas poured in. Each search often required five or six visits: to the address given, to hospitals, rest centres, police casualty lists, estate agents and employers.

In the year 1940/41

> The volume of work has followed closely the events of the war – a heavy wave of air raid problems and evacuation in October and November 1940, and again in April and May 1941, closing the period in September 1941, with a mass of clothes rationing problems. The office in the Causeway was demolished by enemy action in May with the loss of all records and all equipment ... new quarters were found on the floors above the Boro Air Raid Information Centre. In the destruction of the office the addresses of many Red Cross Message senders were burned.

In the year 1941/42

> Clothes rationing queries have accounted for 43% of the applications but many other problems arose ... not least ... the loneliness of old age pensioners. Though there is more money coming into many homes ... there is constant evidence that the expense of keeping two homes is a heavy burden where the wife and children are evacuated or the husband is transferred to another part of the country for essential war work ... The call-up of women, fire-watching, income tax assessment, price control, soap and fuel rationing have all had their influence on the questions brought into the Bureau. War Damage compensation problems continue ... but, with one severe exception of a local bomb explosion, air raid problems have decreased sharply.

In the year 1942/43

> Clothes rationing problems bulk as largely as before ... Emphasis this year has been on employment, call-up difficulties and the search for accommodation. Red Cross Messages, utility furniture, price regulation and supply problems arising directly from the war are frequent, but in addition, there seem to be an increasing number of queries ... less

directly concerned with the war, not least among them being those concerned with health and personal or family problems.

In the year 1943/44

London's long rest from bombing since the 'blitzes' of 1940-41 seemed to have made its inhabitants peculiarly sensitive to the attacks by the flying bombs ... Though V1 caused comparatively few deaths, the devastation of houses was indeed a severe ordeal ... The after-math of the flying bomb attacks is showing now in the number of questions about reduction of rent for uninhabitable rooms, complaints of leaking roofs and windows, furniture destroyed by damp while owners were evacuated, the total disappearance of furniture left behind, re-starting of small businesses in blitzed premises, and many utility furniture requests.

In the year 1944/45

The coming of peace seems to have stimulated the flow of citizens ... September 1945 showing an increase over any previous month since August 1944 in the flying-bomb period ... The year has seen the return from evacuation with its contingent needs of accommodation, bedding, fares, costs of removal, utility dockets, and belated war-damage claims. Parcels to SEAC [South East Asia Command], release from HM Forces, and re-settlement problems are recent developments.

These synopses of the work of one bureau throughout the war are given to indicate the changes and developments which occurred for a bureau which was in a metropolitan area, subject to attack. Elsewhere, the problems were different; some were 'mirror image' problems. Where Southwark was busy arranging for the evacuation of the homeless, elderly and ill, High Wycombe, for instance, was arranging to receive them. The then Organiser writes:

On December 1st 1939 I arrived in High Wycombe to take up the job of Organising Secretary of the Central Aid Society ... to find that I was committed to starting a new branch of our work – a Citizens Advice Bureau ... The population of the town – about 30,000 – had been swelled by evacuees; local families were divided by the call-up and official regulations proliferated, so there were plenty of problems ... a steady stream of people found their way to the Office, conveniently situated over W H Smith's and opposite the Red Lion. I did all the interviewing myself, as such volunteers as were available were occupied in visiting for the Central Aid ... When the London bombing started, refugees from the raids flooded in and contingency plans were made to continue the service in an emergency centre planned by the local borough. I acquired a full-time typist. The telephone rang continuously, often with heart-rending requests for emergency accommodation for someone bombed out ... Information was built up from newspaper cuttings, but very soon a loose-leaf book of notes – CANS – was started.'

Not all places were as quick off the mark. A diary of the events leading to the opening of the CAB in Camborne/Redruth indicates a rather more leisurely approach.

January 24th, 1941
Miss Shergold CAB called to discuss setting up of Bureau here.

March 30th, 1942
School for workers in CAB. Miss D Keeling, Ass. Sec. of the NCSS spoke, &
Miss Joyce Shergold, Regional Travelling Officer for CAB & Mr Cotton,
Regional Officer of the NCSS.

July 16th, 1942
CAB meeting in Redruth. Two committees formed. Voluntary workers
enrolled. Pretty poor show – great mistake in my opinion to open on only
one day per week.

August 14th, 1942
Local Defence Committee Emergency Committee to consider its pre-
paredness for Air Raids. I gave report . . . and complained that the CAB had
not been established.

October 21st, 1942
Believe it or not the CAB opened in Camborne.

December 1st, 1942
Mrs Woodbridge & Mr Cotton called to see how the CAB was going and
expressed themselves well pleased with the progress – much to my
surprise. I jumped at their suggestion that there should be a revision
training course. This was fixed for Jan 28th.

January 28th, 1943
CAB Camborne-Redruth Training Course Day. Great success.

July 16th, 1943
Annual Meeting of the CAB. We are now registered at Central Council and
thereby must have a representative committee. Camborne had in 10
months dealt with 136 enquiries and 87 letters, many more dealt with
unofficially and out of office. Redruth 58 enquiries and 30 letters.

Although most directly war-related problems can be seen to cease
from the date of the final declaration of peace, problems concerning the
difficulties of living in post-war days were still heavily influenced by the
effects of the years of war. In 1946 there is reference to bread rationing;
in 1947 'rationing and control problems fell'; 1948 saw a further fall in
such problems, while housing problems rose sharply, as did those
relating to Social Insurance; 1949 showed 'a heavy fall in rationing
queries, while Housing and Personal and Matrimonial problems rose';
bureaux were still tracing missing persons. The 1950s opened with the
passing of the Legal Aid & Advice Act, which 'brought a number of
citizens with legal and matrimonial problems'. Housing problems rose
steadily in 1951/52 and 1953, even overtaking family and personal
problems in 1954 and 1955. The effects of the passing of the Rent Act of
1957 were even more decisive and continued for some years, while the
Landlord and Tenant (Temporary Provisions) Act, 1958, and the Legal
Advice Regulations, 1959, also brought work to the bureaux.

Remembering those days, a worker from Newcastle upon Tyne writes:

> Our main problems were Family & Personal – matrimonial, problems with
> children etc. This was followed by the after-effects of the 1957 Rent Act and
> the virtual eviction of tenants with a rateable value of over £30. H/P also
> caused quite a few problems. The clientele was very much of a working
> class nature ... 1965 – Rent Officers and registered rent brought in many
> more. The Divorce Reform Act and the Leasehold Reform Act of 1967
> changed the clientele to much more middle class.

By 1965 it was estimated that the national total for enquiries had
reached 1¼ million. Accurate figures were not available, since 25% of
bureaux failed to make the necessary returns, but the estimate was an
extrapolation from those figures which were received. On this basis it was
possible to say that the highest category was *Family & Personal* (28%),
followed by *General Information* (23%) and *Housing, Property & Land*
(22%), with *Trade & Manufacture* fourth (8% of which were classified as
strictly consumer matters). What in reality happened to enquirers
coming in to seek help with their troubles is something to be considered
later, as we look at the daily work undertaken by bureaux.

Pulling the Threads Together

Dealing with the immediate situation was the priority for both the first
bureaux and the Central Office staff, but after a time it was felt that there
was need to formulate some guidelines for their work. The first of these
were issued as a small pamphlet, published by the National Council of
Social Service in May 1941. It is not possible to discover who was
responsible for this pamphlet but anyone who has knowledge of the CAB
service over the years will find it interesting that so much which is central
to the organisation was laid down as early in its existence as this.

The pamphlet is entitled 'Principles of the Citizens Advice Bureaux
Service' and it sets out the Objects and the Guiding Principles (*for the full
text see Appendix 2*). This paper was the first in a long, and continuing,
series which seeks to define both the principles and the practices of the
service. The remarkable thing is the consistency which the service has
shown over the years; having defined itself in the first place, it has never
found it necessary to repudiate that definition. This was also the first step
which was taken in the continuing process of trying to control the quality
of the service offered to trusting members of the public who brought their
problems to bureaux.

Use was made of the grants system to impose some discipline upon
bureaux. Writing to Miss Keeling in May 1943 one of the Regional Officers
says:

> I have recommended that in this case a rider should be added, in the event
> of the grant being approved, stating that the Bureau Committee must be

called together at least once a year ... it seems to me very unsatisfactory that the Bureau committee has not met since 1941 ... the position is not as simple as it might be as the Bureau was set up by the Hitchin Council of Social Service which body is now dead. The present is, therefore, the right time for getting a real and effective Bureau Committee.

In July of the same year it is recorded that the CABx Committee

considered the case of the unsatisfactory Bureau at East Molesey where the Chairman of the Bureau had objected to the suggestion made by the NCSS Regional and Travelling Officers, supported by the Local Authority, that the Bureau should be closed and the work transferred for the time being to the neighbouring Bureau at Esher.

It can be seen that the work of the Regional and Travelling Officers contained an element of basic quality control and that they were made use of in this way.

Although many bureaux continued to draw enquirers even after the end of hostilities, it is recorded that 'the reasons for the closing of 224 bureaux during the period May 1945–May 1946' were:

Lack of enquiries, coupled with staff difficulties	70%
Staff difficulties	7%
Financial difficulties	7%
Premises	3%
Miscellaneous	13%

How the bureaux came to see themselves is important. One Annual Report, published in 1949, defines the function of CABx as

that of the Casualty Clearing Station; some emergencies; some first-aid dressing; some direction to the specialists such as the Free Legal Bureau and the Marriage Guidance agencies. In one respect however the analogy ceases: CAB is the whipping boy of the citizen with a grievance and a patient ear to listen is essential and often remedial.

Agreeing with this view, another person, writing of the late 1940s, adds that enquirers

often returned to the bureau after visits to such places as the Housing Department or the Ministry of Labour for us to explain to them what they had been told at the various offices.

It is clear, however, from the surviving records of the Southwark bureau that the practice there (and probably in the other bureaux run under similar auspices) was much more active.

It will be remembered that the money to employ the Travelling Officers ran out in March 1946 and all possibility of keeping any continuous check on quality became unrealistic after that date. Those bureaux which stayed open did so as a constituent part of some other organisation, e.g. the Family Welfare Association in central London, Councils of Social Service and others of that ilk elsewhere, on minimal Local Authority funding, or by existing on a shoestring at an extremely low level of function.

In small places round the country, individuals who had been working in CABx during the war kept them open, often as a purely personal endeavour. For many of these people the bureau had become their life and for them to give up the work was unthinkable. Often they were well known and trusted figures in their own communities but as the years went by they became more isolated and divorced from the mainstream of the CAB service. Some of them were still operating at the end of the 1960s and into the early 1970s. An Area Officer (the ultimate inheritor of the work done by the earlier Travelling Officer) who had twelve such bureaux in her Area when she started in 1963 remembers visiting one.

> I went to this town and asked for the Citizens Advice Bureau but no one had ever heard of it. I asked for the house by name and found myself at a fine house, standing in a lovely garden. I knocked at the door and this dear little lady in black taffeta came to the door, expecting me of course, and we sat in her front parlour, sipping coffee, and there were the information envelopes stacked in a corner, unopened. We talked about her cases, she drawing on her diary and saying 'Oh yesterday Mrs So-and-So met me in the High Street' and she told me this and that story – no sort of organisation at all. I asked her if they asked her these questions and came to her with these problems because she was a Citizens Advice Bureau or because she was a figure locally who was known to be helpful and very knowledgeable, and it was on that sort of argument that we were able to strike her off the list.

Things were not managed so amicably everywhere and it could be a cause for grief and grievance with some people, who felt that they had been devalued and denigrated when they had intended only to be of service to their fellows. It was similarly difficult to gain the acceptance of isolated and often dedicated Management Committees that the time had come when they would have either to reorganise the bureau or accept the fact that they must close down because the service they offered was no longer meeting the standards of the day.

In such cases it was not necessarily the staff members who were the prime movers. Nothing embarrassed a good bureau more than having one with unacceptable standards nearby. Bureaux in such a situation felt sensitive about the impression of the CAB Service as a whole which might be given by these lame dogs.

A view of what it was like to work within a Council of Social Service in the late 1950s is given by an account written by a worker from Exeter CAB.

> There were five full time paid employees, two of us trained social workers and all having received in-service training. We each spent one day a week manning the CAB which was open every day. The most serious problems received by the bureau included the problems of the elderly, problems

resulting from insufficient income, consumer, matrimonial and landlord & tenant problems.

There was no information system, just a series of pamphlets and a few information sheets sent to us by central office, and a constantly used, dog-eared copy of CANS was our only reference book. Every enquiry had to be researched by us, often in the local library, and clients frequently had to be asked to return for the answers.

At this time there was very little legislation giving people 'rights' especially in the consumer and housing fields and in the vast majority of cases all we could do was plead on behalf of clients on the grounds of reasonableness. We frequently paid personal visits to the managers of shops, or asked landlords to call and see us and we were often surprisingly effective. The offenders were probably afraid of adverse publicity.

Welfare benefits were at a very low level and covered far fewer groups of people than now. Women who left their husbands suffered considerable hardship and benefits for the sick and disabled were totally inadequate. We spent many hours therefore making out cases for financial assistance to the many local and national charities. Exeter CAB was an agent for the Law Society and we helped those women brave – or desperate – enough to sue for divorce using legal aid. This included making out the case for the divorce which, if it was to have any hope of success, needed to include evidence of misdemeanour on the part of the husband which would stand up in Court. We soon learnt the meaning of legal proof. Unless clients could pay for the service it was almost impossible to receive legal advice and we used our Honorary Solicitor to such an extent that he had to restrict our calls to before 10.30 a.m!

The fact that the Council of Social Service ran the CAB and the two were very closely integrated gave us a great deal of flexibility. When we began to receive dozens of enquiries from old people who could not find accommodation where they could be looked after, the CSS started a 'boarding out' scheme with private families which received considerable publicity in the national press and on radio. Similarly, when the bureau was inundated with enquiries from families who were in debt – usually because the bread-winner had become sick – a family budgetting scheme was started.

We worked very hard on behalf of our clients. Numbers were much smaller. The Annual Reports for those years showed that we dealt with approximately 3,250 enquiries per annum.

The Secretary who was in charge of Exeter CSS during those years would not countenance the use of volunteers in the bureau, as was happening elsewhere. She was convinced that only trained full time staff could help clients properly and it did not seem to occur to her that volunteers could be trained. As there were not even guidelines for training CAB workers, let alone training courses, she would certainly not have had the resources to introduce any effective training.

We returned monthly statistics to London and received our annual updates for CANS and a monthly envelope containing a few pamphlets and information sheets, few of which extended to more than one page. Most of our information was collected on an ad hoc basis locally. Otherwise, we had no contact with the centre.

As an integral part of the CSS, Exeter CAB did not have separate funding, although it did have its own sub-Committee. There was no annual grant from the local authority and funding came from annual donations from individuals, societies and industry.

The Framework for Information and Advice

Building on the original 'Principles' pamphlet the NCSS, in 1947, issued 'CAB Pamphlet Number One "Aims and Methods"'. In the context of these two pamphlets the service was redefined.

First, the service must be accessible to all.
(This was formulated into what came to be known as the policy of the 'Open Door', the idea being that there must be nothing to prevent any member of the public from walking into their local bureau and seeking help of one kind or another without the need for an appointment or any form of introduction.)

Second, in order to be accessible to all, the service must be free.

Third, in order to retain the trust of the public the service must be confidential.

Fourth, in order to deal with all problems and all people the service must be impartial.

Fifth, in order to have freedom of action the service must be independent.

These principles have been defined and redefined formally over the years. The current statement of the aims of the CAB service is as follows:

The aims of the Citizens Advice Bureaux Service are:
– to ensure that individuals do not suffer through ignorance of their rights and responsibilities or of the services available; or through an inability to express their needs effectively.
– to exercise a responsible influence on the development of social policies and services, both locally and nationally. The Service therefore provides free to all individuals an impartial service of information, guidance and support, and makes responsible use of the experience so gained.

The Principle of Confidentiality is defined as follows:

Citizens Advice Bureaux offer confidentiality to enquirers. Nothing learned by a bureau from enquirers, including the fact of their visits, will be passed on to anyone outside the Service without their express permission.

The Principle of Impartiality and Objectivity is defined as follows:

The service provided by Citizens Advice Bureaux is impartial. It is open to everybody, regardless of race, creed or politics, and advice and help will be given on any subject without any preconceived attitude on the part of the organisation.

The Principle of Independence is defined as follows:

> The service provided by Citizens Advice Bureaux is completely independent. Bureaux are therefore able to offer impartial advice to all enquirers and to take up any issue with the appropriate authority on behalf of individuals or groups.

It is within this framework of principles and practices that the CAB service has developed its unique situation as the only national advice agency. Underlying all of them is respect for the individual, his freedom of choice and his ability to help himself, or to accept the help of others, as may be appropriate.

How, though, do bureaux apply these principles and to what extent have they developed in practice over the history of the service? Can bureaux adhere to them as closely today as they have done in the past? Have there been times when one or other of the principles has been misinterpreted either by the workers in the bureaux or by their Management Committees?

Although for many years it was the easiest of principles to understand, the policy of the 'Open Door' was not always possible to implement to the full because of the limitations placed upon bureaux by their financial circumstances which obliged them to take what premises they could get. The doors of the bureau might be open for many hours of the day, there might be no queue in the waiting room, but if the bureau premises were reached by a steep flight of stairs, they were not accessible to the handicapped or the infirm; if the premises were tucked away in a part of the town to which there was no public transport, they were not accessible. Theoretically the door was 'Open'; in practice, it was partially closed. This remains true in many cases, though encouragement and grants have been given to bureaux to enable them either to move or to adapt their premises to give access for the disabled.

A different factor that has influenced the last ten years or so has been the sheer pressure of work. An Annual Report from one of the London areas in 1975/76 referred to the dilemma facing the bureaux.

> It has been with great reluctance that various bureaux have eventually had to decide that they must, at least to some extent, control the 'open door' system. At the same time the quality of the service must not be diluted. In order to help more people, we must not take less action on our cases, or hurry our interviews, when the client needs time to talk through his problems. It would be wrong to give up trying to help in such a way that clients learn through it how to help themselves, or to help less those who we deem to have less important problems, or to be 'undeserving'. Yet we are only tackling half the problem if we do not involve ourselves in trying to prevent some of our clients' problems from continuing to occur. Workers have been feeling either guilty at not being able to see everyone requiring our help, or guilty because they were not able to do all the various other things which needed to be done, or guilty about both these

things. The only way, without further resources, to maintain the standards of our service, and to contain our workers' schizophrenia, has been to make cut-backs in the hours which we are open to the public.

It has proved necessary in an increasing number of cases to institute some form of appointments system, though this is often combined with open access. Nobody regards appointments systems as ideal but they are often the only means by which an acceptable service can be offered to the public. The 'Open Door' may be the ideal to which the CAB service would like to cling but it does not seem ideal to the person who sits for three hours, waiting to be seen. To an extent the CAB service, and its clients, are the victims of its success.

CONFIDENTIALITY is a principle which is central to the work of the CAB service. It is also one which has, in the past, been widely misconstrued. All bureaux workers, before being accepted on the staff of a bureaux, are required to sign an undertaking that they will at all times maintain the confidentiality of the bureau. There has never been any doubt about the fact that this means that there is no question of discussing with a third party the situation of a client without the prior knowledge and permission of that client, but there has, from time to time, been confusion about the right of the client him/herself to permit the bureau to disclose information on his or her behalf. Instances have occurred when Organisers so misunderstood this that they refused to pass information to the client's solicitor when requested to do so! The confusion springs from a failure to understand that confidentiality attaches to the client, not to the bureau, and if the client should take upon himself to stand in the street and tell the next person everything which he has just disclosed to the bureau, that is his responsibility and his right.

Where the principle of confidentiality can become most difficult, particularly for the part-time voluntary worker, is when the worker becomes party to knowledge which he or she feels should lead him or her to take the action of a 'responsible citizen' but is constrained against informing the authorities of that knowledge. Cases where the bureau worker may feel that confidentiality should be breached include such things as danger to children, threats of violence or suicide, a belief that a wanted man (such as the Yorkshire Ripper) has been in the bureau, or knowledge of a criminal offence, such as benefit fraud. All kinds of problems are thrown up from time to time and the Association takes a responsible view of the conflicting duties of its workers. Anyone faced with such a dilemma must first discuss the issue with the Organiser of the bureau, who will then (unless already satisfied that there is no case for breaching confidentiality) consult one or more senior members of NACAB staff about the situation being faced in the bureau. The Organiser will not disclose the information to the relevant authority unless those consulted agree that this should be done. In such a case, the

Association undertakes to support the Organiser in every way if any repercussions result from the disclosure. Over the years it has been shown that breaching confidentiality is very seldom necessary; usually other courses of action are possible.

IMPARTIALITY and OBJECTIVITY comprise two inter-related and complementary principles. Impartiality contains within itself both the need for the bureau to be able to deal even-handedly with the tenant and the landlord; the consumer and the merchant; the employer and the employee; and the ability to approach each problem from an uncommitted stance. It requires of the worker that he or she is able to explain the possibilities in every situation, whether or not the worker concerned approves of the options available. For example, a worker must be able to give information about the availability of an abortion even if he or she is unable to approve of abortion because of religious or other convictions.

Another aspect of impartiality is that of political neutrality – bureau staff may not be seen to take part in a personal capacity in political activities which can be seen to imply the commitment of the bureau to a particular political stance. This does not mean that the bureau cannot take part in any form of political activity: it does mean that such activity must be non-party in character. To produce a report on local conditions which is drawn from the experience of the bureau and to publicise such a report can be seen to be an a-political operation – provided that the report is both impartial and objective, based on the evidence revealed by the work of the bureau. Individual bureau workers are not debarred from political activity, provided always that this is clearly separate from their work in the CAB service.

Objectivity may be impossible to maintain in the rare circumstance of a bureau being approached by both parties to a dispute. This may mean that the bureau has to advise one of the parties to consult another agency in order to ensure that the advice which it gives is uncoloured by prior knowledge of the situation of the other party.

The discipline of the principles of impartiality and objectivity is one which is applied in the most rigorous manner to work which comes within the expressed Aim 'to exercise a responsible influence on the development of social policies and services, both locally and nationally'. Back in 1941 this had been expressed as 'To collect information on the kind of problems which are at any specific time causing difficulties or distress and to bring such problems to the notice of those who have power to prevent or solve them.' (*Principles of the Citizens Advice Bureaux Service – see Appendix 2*). Both these statements validate the work which has been done both locally and nationally by the CAB service to highlight the hardships and injustices suffered by ordinary people as a result of faulty legislation or administrative practices.

INDEPENDENCE is a principle which is assailed from time to time. All bodies which receive grant aid from public authorities are now and again subject to pressure to take a particular line of action. The CAB service firmly declares that 'No other individual or agency, even one giving financial support or other aid to bureaux, has any right to determine or influence these policies or practices.' The service recognises its accountability for the spending of public money but denies any claim on the part of funders to dictate to the service on the use of its resources, once granted. For example, a right-wing council might feel that a bureau which it was funding should not give advice to strikers and their families. In such a case, the Management Committee would have the weight of the Association behind it in resisting any pressure to prevent the provision of such a service.

The more general aspect of independence is that of ensuring that the public understands that the CAB service acts alone, in accordance with its agreed policies, though it may combine with other agencies and develop close working relationships with them. One of the ways in which the separateness of the CAB service can be maintained is through the use of the corporate image (as adopted in 1975) and the distinctive presentation of all material produced by NACAB, SACAB, GLCABS or by bureaux.

Setting the Standards

Over the years the CAB service has tried to achieve uniformity of standards among its members. Given the disparate nature and circumstances of the bureaux, this has never been easy. During the war the basic standards were set out as 'Signs of Recognition'. These were issued in April 1940 and were simple and straightforward (*see Appendix 3*). The earliest post-war form of control, introduced in 1947, was drawn up by the Standing Conference of Citizens Advice Bureaux and designed as a 'registration' scheme. The Standing Conference decided to make some changes in the earlier arrangements. Bureaux ceased to apply for 'approval'; those which qualified became 'Registered' instead and 'non-approved' bureaux became 'Associated' bureaux. Registered bureaux had voting rights; Associated bureaux did not. A more crucial provision was that

> Certificates of Registration shall be awarded by the Central Committee on the recommendation of the Regional Advisory Committee; Associated Bureaux shall be expected to reach Registration standard within a limited time, unless in the opinion of the Regional Advisory Committee some particular local condition renders this impracticable; the Central Committee shall have the right to withdraw their services from such Bureaux and to delete them from the national list in cases where a reasonable standard of efficiency is not maintained. (*For the full 'Conditions of Registration' see Appendix 4.*)

It will be noticed that the 'policing' agent in this case is the Regional Advisory Committee. The Travelling Officers had left the scene and there was nobody else to take their place. The scheme was therefore intended to be self-regulatory, i.e. bureaux overseeing other bureaux of the Region. Without the backing of field staff it was almost inevitable that the pursuit of standards proved ineffective and that it was not until much later, when the first effects of the renewal of funding from 1960 onwards began to be felt, that progress became possible.

The Report of the CAB Service for 1959–61 strikes an optimistic note:

> The emphasis today is in fact on quality rather than numbers and some bureaux have been encouraged to close down where, for one reason or another, they were found to be unable to measure up to the more exacting standards of today. Some, on the other hand, having accepted the need for reorganisation, are now making a valuable contribution to the service. As a help towards the achievement of these higher standards the National Committee has revived the system of registration the conditions for which, worked out in the early days of CABx, have been amended and brought up to date; and renewed efforts have been made in recent years to help and encourage more bureaux to reach the registration standard. It is a source of encouragement that so many bureaux have applied for registration and that all newly promoted ones look to this as their goal when they have completed the initial period of work.

By 1965 it was 'agreed that it would be well to consider some revision of the present conditions of registration to bring them up-to-date with present day demands on the bureaux'. One decision was that all bureaux, except existing local authority bureaux, should have to comply with the new Conditions of Registration; all of them were invited to apply for registration under the new scheme.

In order to oversee the standards of bureaux a Registration Committee to which reports were brought and by which decisions could be made was established. The Committee worked to define the requirements to be included in the Conditions of Registration; their revised scheme was introduced in 1967 (*for full details see Appendix 5*). The bureaux evidently found the work of the Committee not entirely to their liking and it came as 'something of a shock' because 'certain matters concerning the operation of bureaux which had been accepted for years – or, more accurately, to which a blind eye had been turned – were now being questioned'.

As reports on the bureaux came in, the Committee identified areas which caused it concern and tried to eliminate what it saw as bad practices. As a result of the many detailed reports laid in front of it, the Committee was able to identify issues which needed to be resolved. Some of the points which the members raised can be charted over the next few years.

The custom had grown up in some places of the local authority taking over the management of the finances of a bureau to the extent that bills were forwarded direct to it for payment. This was different from the more common practice of 'Help in Kind' and certainly made it difficult to claim any real independence for the bureau concerned. It also meant that there was no true financial management. The Registration Committee told bureaux that 'bureau committees should produce annual estimates of expenditure' in the future.

Another bad practice which needed to be eliminated was that of the Organiser being the Chairman of the Management Committee. The constitutional position was that the Management Committee was the 'employer' of the staff of bureaux, even if they were unpaid. A system of checks and balances cannot work when one person holds both the key positions. The Registration Committee, hearing evidence from all parts of the country, judged that the time had come to phase the practice out.

An even hotter cause for dissension was the question of age limits for bureau Organisers. This was first raised in June 1968 because 'it had been found that sometimes an elderly organiser was not able to cope with the necessary reorganisation if a bureau was to reach registration standard'. By November of the same year the matter had gone the round of the Regional Advisory Committees and the consensus was that there should be 'a recommended retirement age of 70'. It was also suggested that new Organisers should not be appointed after the age of 67.

This question became a much argued-over bone of contention. Management Committees, on the whole, resisted all idea of asking their Organisers to retire. In many cases the attitude was one of curiously artificial chivalry, whereby they protested that there was no way in which they could ask a 'lady' her age. This enabled some to hide from the need to take action to replace an Organiser who was no longer up to the job. There was even an extreme case when the Management Committee claimed that the Organiser would die if asked to leave the bureau! Council disagreed and in February 1969 'endorsed the recommendation of the Registration Committee that there should be a recommended retirement age of 70 for CAB organisers'. The trouble was that it was a recommendation which could not be enforced and it was possible for Management Committees to ignore it altogether.

It was at this time that Council formulated a policy on the payment of salaries to Organisers and 'in communicating this to CAB committees the recommendation was made that when a committee decides its situation justifies the payment of a salary, provision should be made for it in the annual estimates. It was further recommended that this should be done even if for the time being the bureau has the services of an honorary organiser, so that funds would be available if and when needed.'

In spite of increasing support for the policy over time, the resistance of many bureau Management Committees to what they saw as the 'erosion of the voluntary principle' meant that it was more than fifteen years before it was possible to make it a mandatory requirement on bureaux. Bureaux continued to enjoy the hidden subsidies which depended upon their Organisers either having private means or being the wives of sufficiently prosperous husbands not to need payment for the hours which they devoted to managing their bureaux.

During 1968 conflict arose between the Registration Committee and both the Welsh and the Scottish CAB Committees over the question of the registration of their bureaux. The claim was made by both bodies that they should be responsible for registering their bureaux. The national Registration Committee was gravely concerned that if this was done if would make the achievement of a national standard even more difficult, if not impossible.

Having discussed the problem, the Scottish CAB Committee 'agreed to inform the National CAB Council that a procedure was to be adopted whereby "applications for registration" from Scottish CABx and reports on them should be considered by the Scottish Committee and the final decision on registration taken and the certificate issued by the Scottish Committee'.

By June 1969 'the Welsh Committee had registered three CABx for which they had levied the usual 10/- fee and it was understood that they were designing a Welsh registration certificate'. This could be seen as a mark of defiance and the relations between Wales and Scotland and the national Registration Committee became decidedly difficult. It took some years for the situation to be resolved. Eventually Scotland became independent, registering its own member bureaux, while Wales remained an integral part of the Association.

The work of the Registration Committee involved receiving reports on the bureaux for which they had responsibility from the Area Advisory Officers, acting as the agents of Council. The Committee therefore came to have an overall view of the condition of the service in all parts of the country. The members listened to Advisory Officers describing the difficulties they had in submitting reports and recommendations to the Committee in the knowledge that they, as officers of the CAB service, had no sanctions which could be imposed to bring deviant bureaux into line. It was clear that something needed to be done; it was equally clear that, without the agreement of the bureaux, it would be quite impossible to impose a formulation of rules on them. The Committee therefore began a period of consultation, during which draft proposals were issued to all member bureaux, discussed in bureaux Management Committees and workers' meetings, in Regional Advisory Committees and in the national Council. As a result of this process a new scheme was approved by Council in October 1973, to take effect from July 1974. (*For full details of 'Registration of Bureaux' see Appendix 6.*)

One problem which was thrown up by the new scheme was the position of the local authority bureaux. In England and Wales a relatively small number of bureaux run directly by the local authority had been contained within the previous scheme but the new one required each bureau to have an independent Management Committee. This meant that the local authority bureaux could no longer be included and negotiations were opened to re-establish as many as possible on a different, independent basis.

Additional complications arose from the reorganisation of local government. Following the consolidation of small local government units into larger ones, it became quite common for two or more bureaux to find themselves applying to the same authority for funding. Because of the haphazard way in which the CAB service had developed, it was quite possible for those bureaux to be extremely different in character and level of function. If one was existing on a budget running into a few hundred pounds, the Organiser being given an honorarium, and the other was funded at a more realistic level and paying a salary, there was a great danger that the argument would be raised that if one could run on 'so little' so could the other. Area Advisory Officers made every effort to persuade bureaux to group together within their district authority or, if they were not willing to do so, at least to submit applications for funds which were compatible in scope.

Although there had been a long period of consultation, during which bureaux had been given every opportunity to comment on and to propose amendments to the revised registration scheme, the spectre of 'Big Brother' was raised again as some bureaux began to realise that if they were to remain members of the Association they would have to take action to put their house in order. The groundswell of discontent was sufficient to make it necessary for the Registration Committee to go to Council in October 1974 to ask for 'special support in assuring bureaux throughout the country that the decisions it reached were arrived at democratically and that the Committee itself was largely composed of working organisers representing large/small; urban/rural and voluntary/paid bureaux'. The Committee, in spite of itself, had become Big Brother to some. Despite these teething troubles it was reported that by 1975, out of a total of 619 bureaux, 273 had been registered under the new scheme.

The consciousness of the importance to the CAB service of a degree of uniformity in the status of Organisers led to the passing by the 1975 Annual General Meeting of a Resolution

> that central government should be approached to provide uniform financial aid directly to all bureaux to cover the cost of employing an organiser, in recognition of the work bureaux undertake for government in communicating people's rights and responsibilities.

The model to which the CAB service looked was that of the Rural Community Councils, whose Secretaries were directly funded by the Development Commission, while their support staff were funded by the local authorities. Though the case was argued with vigour, government again resisted any form of direct funding, ruling that local funders must take responsibility for the local bureaux.

It was not until June 1975 that the rule on the retirement age for Organisers was finally passed. The first proposal was put forward in June 1968 – Council approved the idea in 1975, the whole discussion having taken seven years to go the rounds. Just over a year later, in October 1976, a retirement age for bureau workers was also ratified by Council.

A few bureaux objected to being made to register as a charity but the lawyers ruled that the 'registration of a CAB as a Charity is a legal requirement, as all Bureaux hold some form of tenure for their premises and this falls within the "minimum of property" as laid down by the Charities Act 1960'.

The Registration Committee was aware that a bureau could conform to each and every one of the rules and yet not be giving a good service to its community. This led the members to express the hope that the "quality of advice" element previously not included in the scheme' would be introduced at some future date.

The task facing the field advisory staff of bringing the bureaux into line, so that they at least reached the minimum standards of conformity to the rules, was enormous. It was hoped that each bureau could be visited biennially but the load on the field staff and the amount of work which was revealed by the new scheme made this an impossible aim to fulfil. It was to be nearly ten years before the backlog of bureaux which were not conforming to the rules was finally cleared up. The staff had in their minds the aim that anyone should be able to go into a bureau anywhere in the country and receive the same level of service. There was a vast, solid block of competent bureaux throughout the country; there were many outstandingly good bureaux; and there were some which were below standard. Identifying the latter and working with them to raise their sights became a difficult and stressful area of work for the field staff. Often even the mildest criticism was seen as an attack, and complacency, in the form of 'Ours is the best bureau in the country', was the tone of many of their Management Committees. These resented the attempts of the field staff to persuade them that changes must be made.

Perhaps the most potent of the weapons which the field staff had was that of peer pressure, that is of other Organisers who made their views of what some of their colleagues were doing (or not doing!) clear. The Regional (now Area) Advisory Committee was a key factor. The new scheme contained a requirement that each bureau **must** send a representative to the Area Advisory Committee so there was no longer any possibility of a bureau going along happily in its own way without knowing what was happening in other bureaux in the Area. With the Development Grant, the evolution of a proper training structure reinforced the awareness among bureau workers of the standards expected by the service. By 1978 624 of the bureaux were registered under the new scheme.

A promise had been made from the beginning of the consultation process which produced the 1974 registration scheme that no changes would be made without the full consultation process having been followed and this process was set in motion in 1983 and finally, in 1984, Council laid a responsibility upon all Management Committees to include provision for a salary for the Organiser (and, where appropriate, the Deputy Organiser) in their application for funding, whether or not the salary was needed by the present occupier of the post.

Even after the consultation period there were some bureaux which objected to this ruling, one even approaching the media and launching a public protest at being required to conform to it. For such Management Committees the democratic process by which every aspect of the registration scheme was discussed at bureaux level, in the Area Committees and, finally, in Council – often following this route more than once before any decision was taken – meant nothing. If they did not like the decision, it had clearly been made by Big Brother and had nothing to do with them! The fact that there had been an examination of the work of bureau Organisers by LAMSAC (the Local Authorities Management Services and Computer Committee), which issued a report which evaluated the work of Organisers at a higher level than had previously been claimed by NACAB, meant that the local authorities found it harder than before to resist the claim for the proper payment of those who held these responsible and skilled jobs. The climate was changing and local authorities in many parts of the country came to understand much better the true nature and value of the work of the Organisers and their bureau workers.

As standards rose steadily, the Registration Committee (now renamed the Membership Committee) turned its thoughts back to the earlier statement about the introduction of some form of evaluation of the quality of advice given by bureaux. As it had with the earlier scheme, the Membership Committee began a long period of consultation in bureaux and finally presented proposals to Council for a new scheme, one which departed from the process of counting 'nuts and bolts' and moved into the field of self-assessment. This was adopted in July 1987, comes into operation in 1989 and is the framework within which the work of bureaux is now evaluated. The onus of making a judgement has been lifted from the shoulders of the Area and Advisory Officers and the process has become a joint one. When ten years have passed it will be possible to see whether, like the 1974 scheme, it needs replacing with yet another, but for the time being the system is the one under which both the effectiveness of a bureau and its relevance to the community it serves can be judged.

Taking the Responsibility

The first reference to a Management Committee is in the paper 'Signs of Recognition', issued in April 1940, where it is stated that the bureau must have a 'representative committee responsible for the Bureau, on which the Statutory Authority and voluntary societies of the neighbourhood have been invited to appoint representatives'. The 1941 'Principles' pamphlet adds that the Committee should include representatives of local interests, statutory, voluntary, religious and political.

By 1967 it had become a requirement that the Committee should include representatives not only from these but also from the bureau workers. It was required to have a charitable constitution and to meet at least four times a year. For those bureaux operating under the umbrella of another organisation the requirement was for it to have its own Committee within that organisation.

The requirements in the 1974 scheme were much more specific (*see Appendix 6*). The Management Committee comes more and more into the centre of things and responsibilities begin to develop as both the nature and the scope of bureau operation changes and enlarges.

While a bureau worked on a minimal budget, paying a small honorarium to its Organiser, the principal activities of the Management Committee were usually limited to 'chatting up' the local Borough Treasurer so that he would be persuaded to pass the customary allocation over to the bureau 'on the nod', scrounging second-hand furniture and equipment from firms in the town, and (sometimes) doing a bit of painting and decorating or fund-raising in support of the bureau. This is perhaps an unfair caricature but there is enough truth in it for it to be an uncomfortable memory. Bureaux which had this kind of Management Committee frequently had dominant Organisers, whose feeling was that the last thing they sought was a Management Committee breathing down their necks and asking questions about the work of the bureau. If patriotism, in the words of Dr Johnson, is 'the last refuge of a scoundrel', confidentiality could be made a refuge for the Organiser who wished to keep everything in his or her own hands.

As advisory staff were appointed in increasing numbers, they began to tackle the problem of improving the work of Management Committees and making their responsibilities clear to them. The first step was often to involve the Chairman and other members of the Committee in the selection of workers for the bureau. When this began to be done it was often difficult to persuade the selection panel that, because an individual had volunteered, it was not necessary to accept him or her on to the staff automatically. As understanding improved, committees began to appoint panels which included those with training or experience in selection. These operated in cooperation with the Organiser and the

Area Advisory Officer to ensure that volunteers were properly vetted before being enrolled on to the staff.

Every change brings problems as well as gains in its wake and this one brought the beginning of correspondence between the Central Office, in particular the Director, and disgruntled individuals who had been rejected as volunteers by bureaux. While the public appears to accept that the Marriage Guidance Council and the Samaritans must be careful about whom they accept for training in their organisations, it seems more difficult to gain that acceptance for the CAB service.

As more and more bureaux began to make a reasoned case for realistic funding by their local authorities and as more and more authorities accepted the need for proper support for their bureaux, so the scale of financial responsibility of Management Committees became greater. As salaries began to be paid, so the responsibilities of Management Committees enlarged – soon they were dealing with all aspects of employment, including (in the case of some large bureaux or groups of bureaux) the unionisation of staff and such matters as Health & Safety and other legislation relating to workplaces. The work of Honorary Treasurers became more demanding and the ultimate responsibility of the members of the Committee more alarming.

All Management Committees operate under a charitable constitution laid down by NACAB in agreement with the Charity Commission and the income tax authorities. One clause of this makes it clear that the members of the Committee are the charitable trustees of the bureau and would thus be personally liable, in theory at least, for any debts which might have been incurred by a bureau forced to close through withdrawal of funding. This became a cause for alarm among many Committees as the scale of their operations rose, so that some of the larger bureaux decided that, for them, the answer was to become incorporated bodies. This proved a difficult operation because it was necessary to ensure that an incorporated bureau did not act under a different set of rules from those governing unincorporated bureaux. The Association could not countenance the development of two classes of bureaux within its ranks. Harmonising the requirements of company law and of the membership of the Association proved a highly technical problem but, with expert advice, this was finally achieved and a number of the biggest bureaux have now become charitable companies in their own right. In such cases the Management Committee, like the Council of NACAB, has become the Board of Directors and the whole is run in accordance with company law.

These developments have not been accepted totally uncritically by all members of Management Committees. One such describes the situation in the bureau with which she was involved until recently. The bureau had started life as an integral part of a Council of Social Service (later renamed the Council for Voluntary Service). After outlining the steps taken to deal with the organisation of Committee business, the Chair goes on:

> A further problem lay in conflicting attitudes towards the role and function of the service itself. Within the Bureau there is no doubt that the new breed of CAB professional – young, radical, committed and some-times intolerant – were threatening to many of the older voluntary workers, who had yet to come to terms with the increasing demand for expertise in advice work. The tensions which developed at this level were reflected in the Management Committee in the feeling of some members that the needs of the clients were taking a back seat to the internal politics of the organisation. For some of them the protracted discussion over recognition of the union was the sticking point, and resignations followed the institution of a joint negotiating committee. These concerns afflict any growing organisation but the division between paid and unpaid staff which exists throughout the voluntary sector, and indeed in the judicial system, undoubtedly creates a special challenge for management. There is a delicate balance to be maintained and, in retrospect, I feel that we did not always get it right.
>
> Too far too fast maybe: in an ideal world the pace of change would have been moderated and the feelings of disillusionment experienced by some who had given many years to CAB might have been spared. But the queues in the waiting room were growing and the Bureau needed to establish itself quickly in a more assertive and professional role. This was achieved and the organisation has matured since independence. The past few years have seen a period of consolidation during which all involved in manage-ment have sought to establish a new equilibrium and harmony of purpose. The final goal is the incorporation of the Bureau as an independent charity. This change in legal status will mark the end of a turbulent but fascinating chapter in its history.

Just as the ability of the CAB service to cope depends on the recruitment of a body of volunteers prepared to put time, application and commitment into providing advice, information and support to the general public, so the future of the service depends on the dedication of members of Management Committees who are prepared to give their time to the exacting and difficult task of providing the infrastructure which makes everything possible. The service has in the main managed to carry the wealth of voluntary talent found among its bureau workers along with it; it is to be hoped that it will continue to attract a similar wealth of talent to serve on its Management Committees in the future, despite the increasingly exacting nature of the work of such Committees.

CHAPTER FOUR

The Work of the Bureaux

In the Beginning

It is possible to give some impression of the work of bureaux during the war years by drawing upon the reminiscences of those who can remember what it was like, accounts handed on from people who served in those days, and from such case records as are available and accessible.

The following extracts are taken from an account of what would appear to have been a fairly typical CAB in Newport (Monmouthshire), between 1939 and 1945, written by one of the volunteers out of her own experience. She wrote:

As a Distributing Centre the bureau proved invaluable to the public. It has directed enquirers to the proper organisations and authorities best suited to deal with their cases and by so doing has saved the time, labour and temper of the officials and the public. It has acted as mediator between Landlords and Tenants, Debtors and Creditors, Employers and Employed, and has in many cases succeeded in settling the difficulties between the parties amicably.

The completion of Application forms was a revelation and proved the need for a better system of Education. On one form where the Applicant was asked to state his nationality he had written 'Roman Catholic! . . . the volunteers found that much trouble was caused by the incorrect completion of application and other forms, by illegibility or by the omission of material facts. Many Pensions, Allowances, Grants, Priority Dockets for Utility Furniture and Bedclothes for returning Servicemen, etc, were delayed or refused because of this. Like the Scribes and Letterwriters of olden days, we have filled up many forms required by government departments, written letters for those unable to write and, since D Day, many letters written in French, Dutch, German and Italian have been translated by the bureau staff.

Many a sad story has been poured into the ears of the sympathetic staff – of griefs and anxieties, hardships and sacrifices, injustices and want – yet in spite of this the work has not been devoid of humour. A letter was received from Malta which ran as follows:

We the undersigned NCOs require your assistance in selecting two young ladies between the ages of 18 and 25 who are domesticated and don't use too much make-up. We are not handsome, full of sport, don't drink much, dark eyed dark complexion, 5'7" and 5'10" respectively and wish to meet with the approval of girls of Newport and District.

There was the lady who wrote asking if we could do anything for her. Her Landlord wanted to evict her. 'And I have' she wrote 'occupied the house for 10 years and lived in it 7 years.'

In May 1940 the government order that all persons must carry their identification cards brought in 89 enquiries in one week; everyone seemed to have either lost or mislaid them. In June 1940 enquiries re Missing Relatives rose to a great height after the evacuation of Dunkirk and much the same occurred after the fall of Singapore.

During 1940/41 Evacuee problems took up a considerable amount of time. There were two classes of evacuees – Official Evacuees, i.e. those who had been bombed out and whose fares and accommodation were paid for by the Billeting Authorities, and Unofficial Evacuees for whom no one was responsible. Some of the latter had known local people and arrived hoping that these would take them in, only to find that they were either full up or that they had left the town. Others just jumped the first train they saw in the station which would take them away from the bombing and arrived in Newport as the first stop. They had left all their possessions behind and had no clothes but those they stood up in; they had no place to go, little or no money and some had had nothing to eat for hours. Some had children with them and nearly all were suffering from frayed nerves. The first thing was to provide them with food, then find them accommodation and supply them with clothing. This we did and kept a Register of addresses of all Unofficial Evacuees.

Hundreds of enquirers have been thankful for the Missing Relative Service. Day by day enquiries have come in for relatives presumed killed, missing and wounded. Then there have been refugees and foreigners having relatives in enemy or enemy-occupied countries, making enquiries about their families. Last, but by no means least, were the enquiries for civilians, especially after the bombing of the towns. Through the bureaux, a 'link up' of all towns was provided and relatives were speedily traced.

The Red Cross Message Scheme by which people in this country could, on payment of 1/- (one shilling), send a 25 word message to relatives in enemy or enemy-occupied countries, proved a boon and a blessing to many, though it involved an immense amount of work.

It is worth noting that for the first four years, in case of Air Raids, all our records had to be kept in duplicate.

As time passed the enquiries changed – queries re Enlistment, Registration, Shelters etc., grew less but always some fresh legislation or some new Government restriction took their place and brought in shoals of new enquiries. War Damage Insurance and clothes rationing, each brought very large numbers of queries into the bureau.

Much time was also spent in preparation for Post-Blitz work. Bureau workers were primed with all the up-to-date information until they felt there was no question they could not answer. Great was the astonishment therefore of the recipient of a 'phone call one morning. 'A bomb was dropped at Rogerstone last night' said a voice 'It killed a number of cattle and sheep. What are we to do with the carcasses?' The first question put to us on Air Raid work was one which we could not answer!

In the light of experiences gained by other blitzed towns, provision was made to equip 10 centres and establish an Information and Administrative Centre at the Corn Exchange. This obviated the necessity of bombed out people travelling from office to office. On the night of June 30th 1941 came the Blitz. Bombs were dropped and damage occurred in several parts of the town but chiefly in the Maindee area. The CAB opened next morning at 7.30 and enquirers came in steadily throughout the week. An information centre was opened in the Corn Exchange at 9 a.m. and on Wednesday another one was opened at Maindee Library to serve the Maindee area. Both centres remained open from 9 a.m. to 9 p.m. for the remainder of the week including Saturday. The total number of enquiries recorded at the Corn Exchange and Maindee Library was 3,406 and in the week following 103 cases of War Damage alone were recorded at the Bureau. After this experience arrangements were again revised and many improvements suggested.

The involvement of bureaux with finding relatives was clearly widespread. The East Grinstead CAB records that:

> We were made responsible for the Casualty Recording for the town. This was a major undertaking. For some weeks we spent about 12 hours a day in the bureau, dealing with soldiers on compassionate leave and with bereaved relatives. Through the ARP Housewives' Service we were able to compile a next-of-kin Register for the town in preparation for just such an emergency.

Another aspect of bureau work which was apparently universal was the administration of the Red Cross Message Scheme. This is mentioned again and again in reports of the wartime work of bureaux, as at Havant:

> We helped people who were bombed out of their houses in Portsmouth to fill in their claims for war damage relief; we helped with evacuation problems and with family disruption caused by wartime requirements. PAYE came in and we helped people to understand the tables; we sent off and received the short messages sent to and from those who had relatives in the Channel Islands.

One person started as a voluntary worker in the Edinburgh CAB in January 1940 and shortly after joining the staff was put in charge of the International Red Cross Message Service for Edinburgh and South East Scotland. She remained in this work until the Message Service ceased at the end of the war. She describes the Service which she ran as follows:

> The messages could only be 25 words in length, in any European language. (We got up to ten by the end though people were asked to use French, German or Italian if possible, as these were the best known in general.) All messages had to be either typed or hand printed by us on the special Red

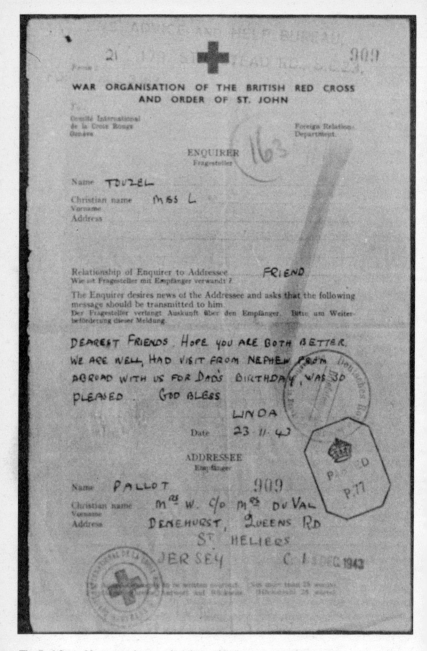

The Red Cross Message scheme, administered by bureaux, kept hope alive.

Cross form. The price of the message was one shilling, which pre-paid also the reply, if it was written by the recipient on the back of the form.

The messages were heavily censored both in Britain and by German censors in the occupied countries and had to be purely personal yet it was surprising how ingenious some people were at getting odd bits of information through, regarding their circumstances, especially our fellow Britons in the Channel Islands, who resorted to allusions to 'Mother Hubbard' and 'what Granny likes' – which was the caption of a well-known make of tea's advertisement – to let us know how short of food they were.

I had to post the messages in bulk once or twice a week to the International Red Cross in Geneva, who returned the replies to the British Red Cross HQ in London as only they knew our number, which was stamped on the form in lieu of an address. They then forwarded the replies to us and often sent us messages which had come from abroad with muddled addresses in the hope that we could guess what they might be and forward them. One example I recall was to 'Stuchison, Asylum 5, England' which I successfully translated into 'Hutchinson, Fife County Asylum, Scotland'.

It took about two months for a sender's first message to receive any reply but if the sender had gone on sending the permitted two messages a month he usually thereafter continued to receive two replies per month.

By the end of the war we were sending messages in nine languages and to British civilians interned in Singapore and Hong Kong by the Japanese. The final tally was roughly 500,000 and we also had a considerable number to forward from the enemy and occupied countries.

Another aspect of bureau work was the work of the Mobile CAB and of the Mobile Squads. The first was made possible by the presentation of a converted horsebox which was paid for by the British War Relief Society of America. The Mobile was staffed by members of the Friends Relief Service (after they had undertaken some CAB training). A report of the so-called Baedeker Raids gives some indication of the work of this unit. The report is dated August 1942.

Extracts from COMMENTARY ON THE RECENT BAEDEKER RAIDS ON BATH, EXETER, NORWICH, YORK AND CANTERBURY.

In the six Baedeker raids of April and May, 1,337 people were killed. To this total the Canterbury death roll must yet be added. When it is realized that only in the raids on Bath (50 planes and 30 planes) were more than twenty five planes used and that, in all the six nights, April 23rd to 29th, only 225 tons of bombs were dropped, it is clear that the devastation caused by this type of raid is very considerable. In the very heavy raids of April and May 1941 over the whole country, 6,065 and 5,394 people were killed respectively. These figures include the death roll of the London raids of April 16th and 19th and May 10th, when as many as 600 planes were used on one night. It is worth considering also some of the details revealed by an analysis of the figures – 400 killed in Bath alone, in Norwich 13,000 houses damaged of which 2,000 were completely destroyed, 3,000 homeless and an estimated 10,000 trekkers – this from a town with a population of

118,000 after two raids only, in Exeter the town cut in half and an average of 450 questions answered each day by a team with the Mobile Citizens' Advice Bureau.

Mobile rest centre and CAB workers proved of value in Norwich, Bath, and Exeter, and could be of even greater value if arrangements were made for calling them out to the town during or at any rate immediately after an attack.

The Mobile CAB proved its value without any doubt in both Bath and Exeter but not in quite the way for which it had been planned. Originally the Mobile CAB had been planned to serve the cushion belt around the target area to which homeless people and trekkers had moved out. In fact, outside both Bath and Exeter there were Information Officers, trained by courses held by the NCSS. These officers were able to cover this need and the Mobile Bureau was mainly used in areas which had been bombed out but which were some distance or cut off from the centre of the town and the central offices. It is uneconomic to keep open information bureaux in all parts of a town and there is therefore a great need for mobile CABx to be available for the towns likely to be attacked in each of the twelve [civil defence] regions.

Searcher Service

The information services were shown again to be the lifeline of civil defence and first among them the importance of the searcher service was emphasised by the nature of the raids, which resulted in a higher proportion of killed and injured for the number of planes used than in earlier raids. Much misery was caused by lack of knowledge of what had happened to friends and relatives which could be avoided by a well organised searcher service. In Bath, where there were as many as 400 deaths, the enquiries about lost friends and relatives at CABx and at the Mobile CAB formed a very large proportion of the total number of enquiries. Fortunately the searcher service in Bath was admirably organised but Rest Centre Registers should be completed and sent in more quickly to HQ. For a good searcher service it was shown to be vital for accurate and rapid registration to be made at all rest centres, for there to be a large number of CABx and information centres ... for there to be a central administrative centre to act as a clearing house and for there to be an adequate messenger service.

Records from the East Midlands show that a Mobile Squad was formed in 1942 'to provide the services of a Mobile CAB Squad to deal with personal and domestic needs in any area which may be subjected to heavy bombing and where the authorities request such help'. Doubtless other Regions took similar action but chance has preserved the record of the use which was made of this particular Squad. The following extracts are from a report which was made to the Regional Advisory Committee in July 1943.

REPORT OF THE MOBILE SQUAD AT WORK IN GRIMSBY

On the 14th July the Ministry of Health called for a Regional Mobile Team to go to Grimsby to assist at the Administrative Centre, as it was found that enquiries were too heavy for the local people to handle.

One interesting feature of this raid was that as the damage from blast was extremely widespread there was an impressive amount of slight damage, and the dwellers in these houses, contrary to our previous experience, were not suffering severely from shock and were therefore able to go to the Administrative Centre for help and advice.

The call was received in Nottingham about 10 o'clock and the first team of four arrived in Grimsby shortly after 2 p.m. – a further team from Gainsborough came in about 4 p.m. These were placed in the Administrative Centre, the greater number of them working at the initial enquiry table, directing enquirers to the various departments in the Centre, and a smaller number being at the table for assisting in the completion of forms and dealing with difficult problems.

When I arrived, shortly before 6 p.m., it was reported that, although over 1,500 had called at the Centre, there were still numbers on the damaged sites, attempting to salvage their furniture or guarding what had escaped damage. Many of these people were spending the nights in the shelters adjacent to their houses, and no contact had been made with them as they had not visited the Centre, and it was felt that the speediest way of dealing with these people would be to bring help to them. (There were three particularly bad areas in the town.)

At the Civic Intelligence Centre I also learned that many engaged in work during the day were returning to the damaged areas in the evening and spending their time there salvaging what they could before seeking assistance from the authorities. It was felt that the only means of getting to these people would be by making use of the CAB van, manned by personnel who would be able to remain working up to any hour, as sleeping and feeding facilities are provided on the van.

One of the weaknesses ... of our Regional Mobile Teams ... is that they wish to begin their return journeys about 5 o'clock and this is the time when workers are able to return to the damaged houses and help their families.

After consultation with the local authority it was decided to ask the Ministry of Health to call out the Mobile Van from London, and this they very kindly did.

On the 15th a team of six came from Nottingham, supported by a further team from Lincoln. It was rather unfortunate that the transport arrangements completely broke down in the latter instance and ... transport could not be obtained until the morning of the 15th.

It was estimated that on this day about 600 applicants called at the Centre. The CAB van arrived at noon, with a team of five, and was stationed at St Hilda's School, readily accessible to inhabitants in the damaged area.

Many applicants were interviewed and all kinds of enquiries answered. A hundredweight of soap had been supplied to the van, to be given to those who needed additional supplies for cleansing and before the evening was over this had been distributed and a further supply obtained.

After 7 p.m. that evening the van moved to Castle Street and Harold Street area, and again many questions were answered and details taken of particularly hard cases; for instance, elderly women the roofs of whose houses were damaged and who were incapable of moving their furniture downstairs for protection from exposure; houses where first-aid repairs were more urgently required on account of illness in the house.

On the 16th further teams were brought in – six members from Nottingham and three from Gainsborough. As it was found that the number of applicants at the Centre was falling off some of the helpers were divided into groups and allocated to various streets where they contacted the people at their houses and ascertained whether all the help required had been made available. In this way a very large area was covered and many complaints were received at an early stage and remedied.

A shortage of hot water was reported; the Local Authority ordered out mobile supplies and these were directed from street to street where the need was found to be greatest, the information being collected from those workers who were visiting the houses. On this day a further 3 cwt of soap was distributed and as this was again handed out in ½lb or 1lb lots, it gives some idea of the number of people contacted.

In all ... it would seem that nearly 3,000 visited the Centre and over 1,000 were contacted through the mobile teams in the badly damaged areas. Enquiries received through workers on the streets were passed on to ... the Centre with speed, through the messenger service, as messengers were attached to each group of workers who acted as shuttlecocks between them and the van; further messengers acted between the van and the Civic Intelligence Centre. In addition, the messengers acted as guides throughout the town. The enthusiasm, efficiency and dependability of these boys was a most valuable link in the smooth working of the service.

The staff at the Civic Intelligence Centre were of the utmost assistance in directing the mobile hot water supply and on any other points arising, such as shortage of food supplies to small grocery shops, etc. ... One of the problems which will cause not a little difficulty will be the means of cleaning carpets, etc. damaged by plaster and soot. Although the Assistance Board is willing to pay for this it is well-nigh impossible for the people to find any cleaners capable of undertaking this work at the moment.

... it was by our very close co-operation with the Civic Intelligence Centre ... that we were able to work in accord with the needs of Grimsby as they developed during the three days we were there.

Having brought in mobile teams it was extremely difficult to find the right moment to withdraw such help but at a conference on the evening of the 16th it seemed that the local volunteers would be in a position ... to carry on, as ... a great many of the cases requiring help had been contacted. It was decided therefore ... that the teams should be withdrawn.

Conditions varied, of course, according to both the geographical position of the CAB and the progress of the war; whether or not there was bombing, movement of troops, movement of population, conditions of life for the civilian population – all these factors influenced the work

Manned by the Friends Relief Service, the Mobile Bureau moved in to clear up problems arising from air-raids.

The friendly face of help in time of war.

of individual bureaux. For example, in November 1942 there is note of Worcester CAB setting up a special information bureau for American troops.

By 1944 weariness had evidently begun to take its toll. The Midlands identified its particular problem as

> being, on the whole a reception area for evacuation from Southern England, this has added greatly to the work of Bureaux. In many towns there has been considerable strain on the workers as not only has the weight of enquiries been very heavy but, in several instances, Bureaux have found it necessary to expand their hours and this without the assistance of additional experienced helpers. Prior to the official evacuation scheme being put into operation Bureaux were presented with many difficult problems and in areas where there is no official scheme these have continued to arise.

That bureaux varied enormously is quite clear but the account of one which was operating in Yorkshire stands alone:

EARLY DAYS OF A WEST RIDING CAB

I lived in a prosperous Yorkshire town. The main industries were engineering and woollen mills. Many of the women already worked in the mills and were able to take over mens' jobs as they were called up so families were not too badly hit by shortage of income. The wives did need help with form-filling and Income Tax matters however and I can imagine the shock they got on first visiting our CAB.

It was run by a lady with a double barrelled name. This was, to Yorkshire minds, far too high-faluting, and she became known as 'Mrs B at the Bureau'. She was completely unique – obviously wealthy, always well dressed, her hair was continually escaping from a huge bun in spite of being tethered by numerous Spanish combs; a statuesque person, wearing heavy horn-rimmed spectacles which did nothing to hide her piercing eyes.

As in most newly founded organisations the aims were not too clear. This was no problem to Mrs B. She had a war on her hands and not only was **she** going to win it – she was going to see that everyone else did their bit.

The office was over a High Street shop. No covering on the splintery floor but that was immaterial as the room was piled high with items that could 'come in useful'. While the rest of the population was still dithering she had realised that shortages were inevitable so she started her 'collection' while things were still available. There was a rack of suits and dresses. Most of her friends must have been bullied into parting with lovely evening gowns. Such was her foresight that she had also collected boxes of patterns which were handed out to mothers along with the clothes. The dresses were reserved to make party outfits for the girls – with the proviso that the patterns were returned **complete and well ironed!** Mrs B also had a collection of wedding dresses which were loaned out on a rota system – preference given to girls in the Forces coming home to get married.

Old blankets and curtains were handed out with a packet of black dye for curtains. Old tyres were cut into pieces to sole shoes with. She foraged for pieces of linoleum to keep the air raid shelter floor dry. Not only did she have a supply of very ancient sewing machines but she knew some ancient men who would repair them.

Before long, people realised that if she helped them, there was always something they could do in return, even if money was short and they couldn't make a contribution. If you could knit she would forage through her patterns and sort out knitting needles from a huge copper, hand you a garment to unravel and take your name so that she could keep tabs on you! Of course, if the article was for children of your own you were only asked to return unused wool. This was then given to some other unsuspecting client to make squares for blankets for babies' cots. Probably due to her connections with the weaving industry she always had large supplies of thick untreated knitting wool. It was no use saying your hands were too arthritic to knit. You were issued with a hank of this foul-smelling wool and told that the oil in it would do wonders for the pain – and just think how grateful the poor sailors would be for such warm socks!

Of course we all knew that steel domestic goods would be short as the engineering works had 'gone over' to making weapons but Mrs B went one step further. She put up a large notice advising everyone to lay in a small stock of needles, pins, safety pins and hair curlers and across the bottom of the notice:

DO NOT BE GREEDY. OTHER PEOPLE NEED THEM TOO

At one time she had quite a stock of perambulators. When this ran out even she was hard put to find any more so a young mother-to-be was advised to go and look in old barns and fields. 'If you find one, I know who can put it right for you.' In the meantime they had to make do with large laundry baskets.

I suppose, looking back, that this was a Citizens' Exchange and Mart. The town was not badly bombed, which meant that the CAB there was spared the harrowing experiences of homeless people. I know Mrs B would have been well able to help if that had happened but in the event she did what she could for 'her people'.

She must have known some solicitors although I can't recall people visiting them. Any difficult query was left with her and she would invariably have the answer when the client came back. I have heard of many bereaved families who found her a tower of strength and sympathy. She even arranged holidays for the really tired and needy.

Although life was hard and life was earnest, for the wartime workers in bureaux there were moments of light relief. The Newcastle upon Tyne Bureau has among its relics of the war a booklet which contains a number of parodies written by bureau members, in particular by Professor Arnold Duff, who apparently helped during his vacations from the University of Wales at Aberystwyth. One of his contributions sounds a familiar note.

A NOT SO VERY ORIGINAL POEM

When the chronic coupon-loser's not a-losing, not a-losing
  And the lodger treads not on his landlord's toe, landlord's toe
They find their war-time worries less confusing, less confusing,
  And darken not the doors of our bureau, our bureau.
But when clients come a-tumbling on each other, on each other,
  Then our weary heads appear to weigh a ton, weigh a ton,
O! take one consideration with another, with another,
  A worker's lot is not a happy one, happy one.
        Chorus: Repeat last two lines.

When the love-sick maiden's yearning for a letter, for a letter,
  From her boy who's been a twelvemonth on the sea, on the sea;
When the Tyneside Council can't do any better, any better,
  Than say 'Everybody's out excepting me, excepting me';
When the wife can never stick her husband's mother, husband's mother
  And the husband has his naughty bit of fun, bit of fun;
O! take one consideration with another, with another,
  A worker's lot is not a happy one, happy one.
        Chorus: As above.

When the Board of Trade says Ministry of Pensions, ... stry of Pensions,
  Which politely recommends the Board of Trade, Board of Trade;
We invoke the place that's paved with good intentions, good intentions;
  Can you wonder that at times our nerves are frayed, nerves are frayed,
So our staff keeping writing poems to each other, to each other,
  To illuminate the course that must be run, must be run?
O! take one consideration with another, with another,
  A worker's lot is not a happy one, happy one.
        Chorus: As above.

With apologies to W S Gilbert

(*On the feast of St CAB, in choirs and places where they sing, shall be
rendered the above Anthem.*)

How It Was for Some

To get a real flavour of the kinds of problem which faced bureaux in
these years it is useful to take a look at some of the cases recorded in
Annual Reports. In the 1940s we have:

> Soldier son called on behalf of his mother for help in filling up compensation form for furniture lost in raid; also for evacuation for his mother.
> She is British born but was married to an Italian. Her husband and
> daughter killed in raid. She is staying with son's friend for a week, but has
> nowhere to go afterwards. Referred to Lant Street Rest Centre and son
> invited to call again at office with his mother to arrange convalescence.
> Mother called. She lost everything in raid, including £12 in money and
> badly needs spectacles. Does not want to go away yet as daughter is still
> buried under debris. Referred to Mayor's Fund for help for spectacles, A

week later still very badly shaken. Referred to local representative of Women's Holiday Fund and also Personal Service League for clothes. Eventually arranged private billet and escort, Soldiers', Sailors' and Airmen's Family Association paying expenses. Unable to go on day arranged owing to Aliens Restriction Act regulations.

Visitor went to police with her, but they could do nothing until permit received from area to which she is going though she is British born and her husband is dead and her sons serving in the British Army. ARP still searching for daughter.

Arranged for visitor to call on local police and expedite permit.

The great British public was just as daft about its animals then as now, as witness:

Rooms damaged by blast and uninhabitable. Tenant wants to know whether she must continue to pay rent. Does not think landlord will undertake urgent repairs. The cat is still in the house and they come to feed it every day.

Unable to have it destroyed as the animal clinic it usually attends has been bombed. They are living at husband's firm in the City at the present.

Missing relatives caused many a headache:

Letter from a grandmother in the country to ask if CAB can trace her son, wife and children who lived in this district two years ago. She mentions that the children's names are 'John, Tom, Alec, James, Susan, Mary and two or three others'. Visited house – unoccupied and blasted out. Enquired from ICAA D/O and Infant Welfare Centre, who say family moved in July before bombing began.

Advised grandparent.

People were enmeshed in unyielding regulations:

Citizen employed in the ARP service received his calling-up papers and was admitted to hospital simultaneously. The Borough authorities cannot pay his wages as he is technically a soldier. The injuries for which he was admitted to hospital, though aggravated by effects of blast from enemy action while on duty, do not entitle him to Civil Injuries Act compensation.

Administrative tangles made life difficult:

How to cash a crossed cheque received from the War Damage Commission in payment of compensation claim? The cheque is made out to the husband, who is serving in the Middle East.

Young people were forced to take responsibility prematurely:

Boy of 17 came to ask how he could be granted authority to draw insurance money and see to his parents' possessions. His father, mother, sister and grandmother had all been killed by enemy action. He had crawled out of the home unhurt. Two of his brothers had been safely evacuated with their school and an aunt was going to make a home for all three, but she could not hear of a house large enough. She also wanted to know where she could apply for the children's pensions.

The 'Dear John' letter:

Her husband is serving in the Army abroad and has written to her that he
has heard things about her at home. Referred her to SSAFA and gave her a
note to employer to enable her to get time off to go and see them by
appointment.

Recollections from those who were there at the time include the
comment that 'We had, as I remember, an epidemic of babies taking 10 or
11 months to arrive!' Another person mentions that 'We had a big Dutch
camp here which made complications. We had one Sergeant who was
expecting 12 babies. As I recall, the Dutch authorities were very good
about maintenance etc. but it took a bit of sorting out.'

Another worker remembers visiting

one pregnant young wife who also had an 18 month old son. However, there
were *two* babies crawling round the room where her mother was immersed
in piles of washing. It transpired that whilst she was expecting her first
child, her father, a merchant seaman, was away at the war. Her mother,
having no financial support, took in a lodger and became pregnant by him.
Both babies were born about the same time and as my client was unable to
produce any milk, both were breast-fed by the mother, and now they did not
know which was which! They say it's a wise child that knows its own father.
These two didn't even know their own mothers!

The same person had

a client who was very ill with TB and very dependent on her husband, who
had recently been conscripted, but fortunately was with a unit stationed
locally. He had worked as a chef at the Adelphi Hotel before call-up. She
came in one day very distressed as he was being sent overseas. As luck
would have it, the same day a soldier from the same unit came in
complaining bitterly that he had been transferred to the cookhouse ashore
instead of going with his mates to fight the enemy. Luckily I knew the
Colonel of this outfit and rang him up. He was willing to switch the two men,
but No 1 was already on board ship waiting to sail. I rushed No 2 to the
barracks, collected the necessary papers, drove my fighting man to the
docks, and after some negotiations with the embarkation officer, secured
No 1 and delivered him to the cookhouse as a willing replacement. I
understood the company's meals were much improved!

Even after peace had been declared, there were lingering effects of
wartime traumas and wartime regulations.

Officialdom and red tape:

Bus conductress, a widow. Her home had been damaged in an air raid and
her claim had been turned down on the grounds that it was not presented
prior to 1st January 1947. She twice applied for, and was granted extensions
of time before putting in her claim as her furniture was stored where she
could not get at it to assess the damage. These earlier applications had been
overlooked – hence the Official refusal to entertain her claim.

Effects of new legislation:

Man came in with a bandaged arm, threw a pay packet for £1.19.0d on the table and complained that that was all his employer was giving him. He was in receipt of Industrial Injuries pay at the correct amount but was under the impression that his employer had to make it up to the full amount of his ordinary wage. Explained that under the new scheme, the employer was under no obligation to give him any money at all and that if his employer did so he was showing a generous spirit. If he was in need to supplementation he should make application to the National Assistance Board.

The legacy of great numbers of foreign troops in the country brought its own complications. A worker from that time writes:

In 1947 our main problem probably was the 'American Brides' i.e. young girls who had either married or become engaged to GIs and had gone to live in the USA. Unfortunately a great number had beeen taken in by the troops and things were very different from their expectations. This naturally caused great unhappiness to them and their parents who came to us for help, and advice. We did our best to try and sort out their distressing problems.

As we progress into the 50s the problems of war are left behind, though residual effects are still evident. The untidiness of life is demonstrated time and time again.

What is your name?

Young couple wish to change their name before the children go to school. They find their present name unpronounceable by many people and a source of derision by others. Advised about formal changing of name through the National Registration Office and Food Office with a statutory declaration before a Commissioner of Oaths. Also explained change of name by Deed Poll.

Lady lived for 25 years under the name of Mrs Q but was not legally married to Mr Q. He has left a Will in which her previous married name is given. She is frightened she will get into trouble for having lived under an assumed name. Explained that it is not an uncommon situation; her ration book and identity card are in the name of the testator and she can prove her right to her previous married name by getting a copy of her marriage certificate from Somerset House, linking the two names by an affidavit if necessary.

The mentally unstable:

Two sisters, very worried about their brother who lives with them. He was demobilised from the Army in 1946 after six years service. He shuts himself up in his room, refuses to go to work, sometimes refuses food, is sometimes very noisy, sometimes silent but often abuses his sisters and his father. He only goes out after dark and is very shabby and in need of care.

The confused mother:

She wants to join her husband, who is in the United States Army but says she has been told by the American Embassy that she cannot take the baby with her as her husband is under 21. They were married a month before he returned to the States and the baby has been born since. The Embassy explained that she must get a quota visa for the baby as he will not yet have acquired American citizenship. He has dual nationality.

Tax liability:

Middle-aged widow, very shy and worried. The Income Tax authorities have asked about the interest on her Post Office Savings account. She lost all the old Savings books in the blitz and wonders how far back she would be taxed. Her late husband had never declared the savings account and she has visions of being summonsed. The Income Tax office confirm that the check will only extend over past six years. She is much relieved.

Dental troubles:

She had her teeth extracted two years ago by a local dentist who is not now practising. Feels she would be in better health if she had a set of dentures but is now a widow on supplementation and cannot afford any payment towards the cost. Hospital dental department made appointment and said there would be no charge.

The curious accident:

His fishing tackle was removed by a passing speedboat while he was fishing from a South Coast Pier. The Insurance company informs him that it is the responsibility of the fisherman to keep tackle clear of shipping. Does this mean he cannot claim compensation?

Hire purchase:

He has legally committed himself to the purchase of educational books for his children costing over £20. He cannot afford the purchase and no longer wants the books. Will the firm cancel the agreement?

Housing difficulties:

Mr & Mrs E came about a notice to quit. The property had recently been sold to the lower floor tenant who said he had need of their rooms. They had received a solicitor's letter. Mr E had been ill and must change his occupation to something lighter. He is an ex-Regular Serviceman. They have been managing on his sickness benefit without applying to the national Assistance Board.

He is 80 and has received a notice of increase of rent under the 1957 Act. He has always paid the rent and does not understand why the rates have been included in the calculation for increased rent. Checked the form and pointed out two errors – the inclusion of the rates and a demand above the limit permissible under the Act. He returned later to say that the agents had apologised and amended the form.

Those bureaux which were operating as independent units, not being part of a larger social welfare organisation, went into the 1960s with very few resources. The principal information source available to them was CANS and this, together with Whitaker's *Almanack*, some basic information sheets from the Central Office, and such information as they had been able to compile through studying the national and local papers, was in most cases all they had to depend on.

CANS – the Citizens Advice Notes – was frequently believed to be produced by the CAB service but, in fact, it has an anomalous position in that, though it was started by Dorothy Keeling as a 'Bulletin of Information of Emergency Matters', it was produced by a separate unit within the NCSS and was widely marketed to subscribers who included members of the legal profession, local authorities, librarians, civil servants, social workers and many others. It was not designed principally as an information tool, though it became the 'bible' of many advice workers who managed to master its intricacies. It was the work of a typical NCSS mixture of professionals and volunteers who co-operated to produce a thoroughly reliable and authoritative publication.

CANS (which is still published but no longer used by bureaux) contains synopses of all social legislation, together with such criminal law as bears upon social law (for example, the Abortion Act), and is updated at regular intervals to take account of changes.

Given the paucity of tools that the interviewers had to hand, it is not surprising that the emphasis in the fifties and sixties was more on trying to ensure that the enquirers were 'pointed in the right direction' than on giving more positive assistance towards tackling the problems which came through the 'Open Door'. Probably one of the most valuable contributions made at this time was the availability to members of the public of a sympathetic and unhurried 'listening ear'. At a time when there were few places to which people could turn for positive help the bureaux at least filled the role of an uncensorious and patient partner in a discussion which was helpful in enabling the enquirer to clarify his or her mind about the problem which was the cause of worry and indecision.

Reports published in local papers at the time give a picture of a rather patronising attitude on the part of some bureau workers – one that grates today but was, presumably, acceptable according to the *mores* of the time. For instance, talking to a local group, an Organiser in the late sixties is reported as having said:

> The humbler sort of person usually comes to us – those scared of officialdom – wanting a bit of sympathy ... One case I always remember involved four young children all under 21. Their parents died almost one after the other and they were left to look after themselves. Apparently the father had owed money before he died and a moneylender came round to the house each week to collect £2. I was incensed by this, but unfortu-

nately I could find no evidence of money being collected. When I made enquiries I was told that the man went round 'to see if the kids were all right'.

He explained that:

The Citizens' Advice Bureau works closely with local authorities. The people who man the bureau are not technical or professional, but they do have well informed people to contact when in doubt or difficulty. We can consult the London office and we do have technical people who can advise us if we ask, but it really is appalling the terrible mess people can get into.

After outlining the troubles of one family, he went on to say:

Sometimes I feel that people are fools and I want to tell them so. It keeps you alive though, and you learn a lot of useful information too. Government sheets come through telling us about new Acts in very easy language, things you would have a job picking up from the national press. We do not have a great deal to do with criminals but one day a man came in who was awaiting trial for theft. He complained that a policeman had taken his torch. I had a quiet word with the local inspector who said it was just a figment of the chap's imagination. And even if it had been true, the torch would only have been stolen from someone else in the first place! But this man obviously felt a sense of injustice and wanted someone to listen sympathetically to him.

Another report, of the same vintage, has the Organiser saying

We never overstep our mark. If the problem cannot be solved by a phone-call or by simply talking and providing literature, we refer the person to someone qualified to help him.

A Chairman pointed out that the bureau was

not an agency to fight people's battles, but rather a signpost, directing distressed or baffled citizens to the organisation or body which could solve their particular problems. In the case of, say, a woman with several children being abandoned by her husband, the role of the CAB would be to co-ordinate the actions of statutory and voluntary bodies which would afford some assistance. We would suggest to her that she might have maintenance rights and assist her in applying for legal aid, so that she could have the services of a solicitor. We would also point out that the Ministry of Social Security might provide money for food for her family and that the local authority and housing association could help her with any housing difficulties. In short, our assistance is not material, but points to organisations which will provide such assistance...

It was often the case, that when people criticised the 'amateur' nature of advice bureaux they failed to appreciate that the CAB is not meant to be a technical body of experts. Our workers are not qualified to consult and act on behalf of clients... what they have to do is find out where there is a legal or social expert who will know and direct the citizen to him. Of course, there are some problems which can be dealt with on the spot but the technical queries will be directed elsewhere.

A present-day bureau worker who dates her service from the opening of the bureau in 1966 remembers:

> Once the premises were found and furnished with second hand tables, chairs, a filing cabinet and a typewriter, the workers who had been interviewed and accepted spent a couple of weeks getting a filing system together. The fourteen categories of information were contained in 14 manilla folders and all fitted easily into one drawer of the filing cabinet. Local information we found as we went along. It was all card indexed and for anyone who knew the alphabet quite easy to find again, chiefly because there was not much of it.
>
> We went on duty in twos so there was always someone to talk to during the long afternoons and for many years we interviewed in twos ... I don't think we were too forbidding – not to the clients – but my word, we frightened a lot of other people – recalcitrant shopkeepers, providers of second-class services and the local Rachman-type landlords. With local government officers we had to be much more circumspect. We knew them all and they knew us. It was a long time before they began to take us seriously. Just when we were being recognised as responsible people serving the public, local government reorganisation pushed us out into the big world and we had to start again.
>
> NACAB didn't exist for most of us ... Democracy reigned supreme. Decisions were made in the local bureau and our policies were our own. As long as we provided a free, impartial and fairly confidential service we could go our own way with no one to fault us. Even the Organiser was a shadowy figure who took the Saturday morning session on her own and wrote notes in the message book for the rest of the week. The main duties of the Organiser seemed to consist of making out the rota and buying stamps. Workers' meetings were held twice yearly and consisted of refresher training. Occasional special days of training were set up by the Area Office. I had been an Organiser for several years before anyone attempted to train me and there are people still in the bureau who never had a proper basic training course.

Bureaux in cities were, perforce, bound to move more positively into areas which the orating Chairman had categorised as 'technical'. One reminiscence tells that

> The problems we dealt with fell into the same categories as now but I would think the emphasis was on family/personal, consumer and housing matters rather than on employment and Social Security problems as at present. With employment matters one referred to the Law of Master and Servant which was far less complicated than present day legislation. On the other hand there were many landlord and tenant queries involving furnished/unfurnished and controlled lettings and the legislation of the Rent Acts was very complex.
>
> The general office was one small room, in the corner of which an interviewing room had been formed. This was little more than a large

cupboard. Our callers waited, sitting on a narrow bench, in the narrow hallway outside. (I was informed that these premises were a great improvement on those previously occupied. Apparently in earlier days one very able and knowledgeable woman dealt with most enquirers herself by calling each person to a hatch opening in the wall.) We then progressed to shop premises and interviewing there on a hot day was something which highlighted the determination and staying power of the workers. The interviewing rooms were in the shop windows and our callers also suffered.

An Organiser remembers how she took over in 1968 from the previous Organiser, who had been 94! This lady 'had taken all the information and burnt it. The bureau was therefore empty apart from mounds of paper, two desks, chairs and 2 filing cabinets.' Democracy in such cases had deteriorated into anarchy and individualism into eccentricity. The time had come for the CAB service to begin to assert a little discipline – if only for the sake of the people who came through its doors.

Alarums and Excursions

It could be argued that the conditions of war constitute a permanent state of emergency but, once the war was over, the emergencies to which the bureaux responded became more closely defined.

The first records we have of response by the CAB service to a peacetime emergency are those relating to the Lynmouth Floods in 1952, when the twin towns of Lynton and Lynmouth were devastated by flash floods.

Initially, when an approach was made by the Regional Officer of the NCSS, the offer of help was rejected, but a fortnight later the Town Clerk asked for a team of workers to be sent to Lynton to set up an emergency bureau. As a result, Kay Oswald, with the Regional Officer, a caseworker from Bristol and workers from Torquay and Birmingham, went to the town.

Homeless people were immediately circularised and visits paid to those living in the Red Cross caravans and in the outlying villages which had been affected. A bureau was set up in the foyer of the Town Hall and remained open for a week.

A report made by one of those involved describes the operation of the team:

> Our first task was to ascertain the names and number of people affected by the floods, which had caused devastation in a wide area around – apart from Lynmouth, Lynbridge and Barbrook, the most seriously affected areas.
>
> After exhaustive enquiries it was obvious that the only list available to us was one compiled by a Lynmouth resident affected by the flood, who had prepared his own list whilst helping to distribute sugar and bananas

to those affected. During the first three weeks we concentrated on assisting those who had been bereaved and who had lost their homes and all their personal possessions. This was a sad task and (involving as it did working through week-ends and most evenings) was depressing in the extreme. The last three weeks were spent completing the investigation of the remainder of the personal loss claims, including claims from visitors. At the time of our departure the majority of these claims had been settled.

As an example of the residual problems arising from the flood I quote the difficult problem of an aged mother in her eighties who had left her council house after the flood and inflicted herself on a married son. He was in despair about the effect of this on his family as his wife suffered from Angina and his two schoolboy sons and adolescent daughter were being greatly distressed by the selfish and cantankerous behaviour of the old mother.

The experience of dealing with the aftermath of the disaster stood the CAB service in good stead when the East Coast areas were struck by the devastating floods of 1953.

A full report of this was published by the NCSS in a pamphlet entitled 'Citizens Advice Bureaux in an Emergency', dated February 1954. Extracts from the report give an idea of the scale of the operation.

Emergency bureaux had been set up in Mablethorpe and Sutton, Lowestoft, Felixstowe, Whitstable, West Ham and Canvey Island ... advisory visits had been made ... to Sheerness and Harwich.

When the floods occurred all the units of the organisation co-operated and released relays of experienced workers, up to a dozen, at a time to man Advice Bureaux where they were needed. A combined team went at once to strengthen the existing bureaux at Louth and Alford, in Lincolnshire, where thousands of evacuees from the coast were sheltered.

After their experiences in the flood itself and the strain of evacuation and the bleak return, these communities were still shocked. They seemed robust and cheerful enough on the surface ... but even the younger people were shaken and tired and nearly all the older ones were too confused and upset to read and understand. There can be a world of difference between a public notice and a kindly answer from someone obviously anxious to help.

Each Bureau had to adapt itself to local needs and opportunities. Some entered more fully than others into liaison work with voluntary agencies, matching requests for help on the one hand with offers of help on the other. One adviser answered hundreds of questions seated at the end of a trestle table while tinned foods were being noisily dispensed at the other end.

The first strenuous period of helping people to get the basic necessities at last drew to a close but already a less spectacular and more difficult job was engaging the Bureaux.

Many thousands of [claim forms for grants for damaged furniture, clothes and property] were not only issued at the Bureaux but filled in there on behalf of the applicants. These seaside towns have a high proportion of elderly retired people, many of them of small means and living alone; many still dazed and nearly helpless for weeks – even months – after the floods. Sometimes they could think of nothing to claim for: 'Just a bed that's all right again and a few pans. That's all.' But when one of the advisers found time to visit the home, she would find broken furniture, rotted linoleum, ruined upholstery and clothes that the old people had forgotten all about.

The secretariat of the Lord Mayor's Fund relied very largely on the Citizens Advice Bureaux to investigate difficult or doubtful cases referred to them. All the time there was a constant flow of reports and recommendations from the Bureaux on the spot, through their headquarters, to the Mansion House Committee of the Fund, which was feeling its way towards a humane and just set of rules for discharging its complicated task.

The reports which appear from time to time over the next few years chart some of the international events which called for a response from the service. In 1957 it was the arrival in the United Kingdom of refugees from the Hungarian uprising. Services were provided in the Hungarian Department of the British Council for Aid to Refugees and in hostels which had been established for the refugees. In the same way, when British subjects were expelled from Egypt by President Nasser, they were first accommodated in nine hostels in most of which CAB services were provided. The workers concerned were responsible for dealing with the personal problems of individual residents.

A domestic occurrence of a rather different nature was the failure in 1963 of a cooperative bank in Whalley, Lancashire. The response to this was channelled through the Community Council of Lancashire, with the help of experienced bureau workers from Liverpool.

The tragedy at Aberfan in 1967, when the local school was engulfed in a landslide of mud, with a heavy loss of life among the children, and there was widespread damage to other properties, took the Area Advisory Officer to the scene. She remembers that

We offered our services to Merthyr Council and they said that they had already appointed somebody to be responsible for passing information to the bereaved families. It was very much at that time that people were sending toys etc. We felt that we did not have much of a role to play in that, but the next thing that happened was that the government sent assessors in to assess the value of the losses. We then sent in a retired District Valuer from Swansea CAB to advise the people whether they were getting a fair deal. He and the government assessors worked out some sort of formula and afterwards we arranged for CAB back-up support for him. That lasted about 6 to 8 weeks. People from all over South Wales went up to Aberfan on a rota basis. Once there was no further role for us we withdrew. The emotional problems arising were shelved at the time; the Council did make an appointment but that was not for six months. CAB had by then carried out the task which it felt it was qualified to undertake.

The flooding which occurred in Kent in 1968 was much more localised than the earlier East Coast floods. Two bureaux which were affected were Tonbridge, which was completely flooded and lost its papers and equipment, and Sevenoaks, which set up an emergency service in Edenbridge. The Tonbridge bureau workers

> were prevented by the Police from going near the Bureau for three days and when we arrived the scene was one of total devastation. Everything up to 3½ feet from the floor was ruined. We tried to dry the Day Books with a fan heater but not very successfully; the write-ups were nearly all unreadable. The drying of the office was carried out by the Army but the smell of drying river was almost unbearable.

There were problems in parts of London, too.

> 64 roads in the London Borough of Lewisham turned overnight into swiftly flowing rivers, and Local Authority Services and other agencies, including the CAB, visited the affected areas giving advice and help where it was needed. The Borough Council set up a control room from which the Bureau was supplied with appropriate information and advice to give the public. This became a two-way service, the CAB explaining the needs of the public through its direct contacts with them and the relief services expanding their services to meet those needs.

Experience of previous disasters led the Council to conclude that

> the real problems would only emerge some time after the floods and the information department was supplying bureaux in the affected areas with special material about such questions as insurance.

In Belfast, August 1969 saw riots, as a result of which the main CAB at Bryson House received 7,500 enquiries and struggled to help those who had had their homes burnt down or were having to move because of intimidation. This was the beginning of a long history of stress and difficulty.

The next major emergency action in England was different in duration, scale and scope from those which had occurred since the 1953 floods. This was the expulsion of the Ugandan Asians by President Amin in the autumn of 1972. Those who were deported arrived at various airports but the greatest number were brought to Stansted, the final total being something like 12,000 people.

The emergency began with a briefing meeting held in the newly opened reception building at Stansted Airport at which voluntary organisations were asked for their cooperation in running the reception teams. CAB was asked to provide teams for documentation and the Area Advisory Officer was seconded for the purpose of organising the teams.

A brief account of this extended emergency runs as follows;

> The first flight, which arrived on September 17th, comprised people who had been subjected to harassment, maltreatment and theft on the way to Entebbe. They were in a state of shock when they landed and it did not

help that the volunteers receiving them were not yet clear about what was needed, nor that there were about 250 press and television people milling about in the small reception block. Immediately after the flight had been cleared a post-mortem was held and changes were made in the arrangements. Without the media teams to impede them, the volunteer groups soon worked out efficient and effective means of dealing with the processing of the arrivals.

During the first days about 60% of the expellees arrived with the intention of proceeding to private destinations and the CAB teams were greatly stretched as, with the help of interpreters, they struggled to find out whether families could be collected, if they had enough money for fares and enough English to enable them to travel independently. Most of the planes arrived in the early hours of the morning and after a time it became clear that working in the night hours was imposing a severe strain on the teams and the CAB workers, some of whom were elderly, could not continue to carry the burden unaided. At the same time there was a sharp drop in the number of refugees proceeding to private destinations.

One of the elements which made for fatigue and strain was the sheer unpredictability of arrivals. On one occasion the WRVS, Red Cross, medical team and volunteer marshalls, etc., had gone home when, at 04.10 hrs the message came through that a plane would be landing at 05.25 hrs – which meant a frantic call to everyone within easy reach to bring them in to man the building! Another day an SOS was sent to a local High School and the co-operation of the Headmistress and Sixth Form girls was a great help in dealing with a totally unexpected arrival.

Such alterations were due to many factors. The usual hazards of flying were complicated by the unpredictable happenings at the other end. For example, a plane had been loaded with passengers and luggage when the Ugandan authorities objected to something concerning the last family who should have joined the flight. All the passengers and luggage were taken off the plane and searched again with consequent delay. On another occasion the women and children were all put on one plane and the men were held and then put on a second plane, with the result that the women were completely hysterical with fear on their arrival.

Because of the difficulties it was decided to recruit teams of students who could sleep on camp beds in the building, be available for any arrivals during the night and deal with the documentation of those destined for the resettlement camps. They were backed by experienced CAB workers who dealt with the Asians going to private destinations. This system worked well for a brief period but then, without warning, night arrivals suddenly stopped and for a few days all arrivals slackened and became even more irregular.

After the lull, arrivals built up again towards the final deadline, with planes coming thick and fast and large numbers of the sick and the elderly being moved by ambulance, by coach and by train to the reception camps. At the end of the three month period the building was shut down again and the volunteers, from the IVS, the CSV, WRVS, the Red Cross & St John Ambulance, and the CAB, went home and hoped to rest after their labours.

One of those who took part in the documentation process remembers it:

> The planes usually seemed to arrive during the night. 1 a.m. – the phone ringing, the Advisory Officer's voice – 'There's a plane due in about an hour.' Driving through the deserted Essex countryside, arriving at the airport and meeting members of the reception team from other bureaux in Essex. The hectic activity for a few hours as a plane came in and a crowd of frightened, bewildered people, old and young, complete families from grandparents to babes in arms, crowded into the reception area. The WRVS was there to provide hot food, clothes etc.; our task was to talk to each person or family group, often needing the help of interpreters, to find out and register all the necessary details about them. If they had relatives already in this country we telephoned them, we arranged for travel warrants, we gave what help and advice we could. These were people who had been frightened and intimidated, lost their homes and possessions, often their businesses and livelihood, many even told of being stripped of their personal jewellery. We tried to make the bureaucratic process as human and friendly as possible – just CAB on a large and concentrated scale.
>
> Gradually the queues disperse, our task is over for the moment – time for the flask of coffee and sandwiches we've brought with us. One day we might be asked to stay on for a few more hours as another plane is expected, another day it's home by mid-day and the chance for a few hours' rest before the family comes home from school and office.

The Annual Report of the Brentwood bureau also mentions their contribution:

> Eight advisers from Brentwood took part in this work and those who did will never forget the experience. The majority of planes landed during the night and those 'on call' were frequently roused from their slumbers at 3 or 4 a.m. to be told a plane was arriving in an hour's time. After the lonely drive through the Essex countryside, the airport was a scene of bustle and activity. The tired and bewildered refugees were interviewed with the aid of interpreters, 'phone calls made to relatives throughout the United Kingdom, or places found in reception centres for those with no one to turn to for hospitality, and a welcome, food and clothing provided by the WRVS and other voluntary agencies.

At the other end of the process, CAB workers were involved in the reception of the expellees at the camps. Tunbridge Wells CAB was one bureau which helped:

> We were asked if we could help with the documentation during the arrival of the Ugandan Asians at the reception centres at West Malling and at Maresfield and we were able to put on an immediate 24 hr coverage over the first few days and continued until the arrivals were complete. Included among our volunteers for this unusual task we had those who could speak the languages, which was a tremendous bonus. It was a difficult task to get the details required from an endless stream of expellees, all looking very lost, bewildered, yet dignified. Most had been obliged to leave all their personal possessions behind.

In London the main contribution was made by CAB workers who helped in the office established in the Bayswater Student Centre by the Coordinating Committee for the Welfare of Evacuees from Uganda. The office acted as a clearing house for the many offers of help which poured in, coordinating and collating and directing personnel to appropriate tasks. Offers of employment were passed to individuals, camps and the Uganda Resettlement Board. Three CAB workers helped to man the office during evenings and weekends; four others worked regularly, between them giving six days a week. In addition, CAB all over London handled enquiries from Ugandan Asians who called of their own accord or who were referred to the nearest CAB following a phone call to the Bayswater office. In a report made at the time the comment is made that:

> One of the heartwarming and exciting aspects of this work was that despite the Committee's inevitable problems of integrating the efforts of fifty or so voluntary organisations, and keeping in communication with the Uganda Resettlement Board, the office itself rapidly developed a closely-knit, enthusiastic and hard-working team of paid and voluntary workers. Therefore while attention has been drawn to the spontaneous and useful contribution of London's CAB workers it must be seen alongside the efforts made by many other individuals and organisations.

Others helped at Heathrow and for some weeks after the evacuation had been completed there were CAB workers in some of the reception camps. Volunteers were sent in from the neighbouring bureaux and found themselves involved in all kinds of 'first aid' work, some of it unlike normal CAB work. In the camps in Lincolnshire it was found that one of the first, most urgent, needs was for maps. These people had been snatched from their homes, transported across continents, bundled into coaches and trains, and they now wanted to know where they were! British Rail supplied a large number of maps and though these were strictly rail maps they made it possible for the workers to point out the relative positions of the camps and, for instance, London or Leicester, where relatives were living.

A rather more short-term and limited initiative concerned the tragic explosion at the Nypro Plant, Flixborough on 1 June 1974. This left everyone in the area sad and dazed and the grief suffered through loss of life and personal injury brought much distress; the tremendous amount of damage to property covering a vast area presented many problems. The Scunthorpe bureau was able to assist by making its premises available to the Chairman and Deputy Chairman of the British Insurance Association, and to a local insurance representative, to interview potential claimants. The bureau also held a supply of claim forms for both personal injury and damage to property which were issued in the days which followed.

In July 1975, it was reported in Council that the CAB service had been involved in advising and supporting the survivors of another disaster, namely the Dibbles Bridge bus crash.

It was in the seventies that a new phenomenon began to hit the bureaux – one which called for a different kind of response, a response which soon came to be widespread in the areas where the workforces were hit by large-scale redundancies. An anecdotal example of the unpredictable effect of redundancy on individuals is quoted by a worker from the the Sunderland bureau, who tells how in December 1978:

> On a day that fell between Christmas and New Year with only a skeleton staff of volunteers on duty a chap walked in and said 'I need to get this money, can you help? I've lived on tick all over Christmas.' From his back pocket he produced a crumpled and by now almost illegible cheque for £24,500. Having picked myself off the floor, I enquired why he hadn't paid it into a bank. It turned out he was illiterate, had no idea what the money was or how much it was, certainly had no bank account and obviously would not be able to cope. Luckily, we were able to arrange all these things for him but it was the first of the batch. After that, banks, building societies, insurance companies and the like camped outside shipyards etc. which were closing and gave free advice to all. By the time of the large-scale redundancies at British Steel, Consett, and Tyneside ship-builders everything was much better organised.

In the years that followed, as mass redundancies became common, bureaux in many parts of the country began mounting special initiatives to deal with the problems arising. These varied in size and character. One which exhibited special difficulties was the Birmetals dispute in 1981.

Birmetals Ltd, a Birmingham firm, had dismissed 700 of its hourly paid employees during a dispute at the beginning of June. Although the firm announced that it was to close down completely at the end of November, it refused to pay the employees redundancy pay. The sacked employees were refused Unemployment Benefit and were allowed Supplementary Benefit only for their dependants. During the five month 'crisis' the neighbouring Halesowen bureau set up a multi-agency weekly advice session for the 700 employees. The CAB workers discovered that widowers, single and divorced men were not receiving any money. Neither were husbands and wives where both had worked for the firm. Savings were being used up; mortgages were in arrears, as were payments for rent, rates, gas, electricity and hire purchase, and parents were unable to provide nourishing food for their children. Some workers were unable to get new jobs because the firm refused to give references. At the end of November the National Insurance Commissioners decided, on appeal, that the sacked workers were entitled to Unemployment Benefit and the immediate crisis was over.

It was not only the bureaux in traditional industrial districts which had to cope with mass redundancies. Two rural bureaux, typical of their fellows, which were involved are West Wiltshire and Norwich. The former gave help in the cases of the Avon Rubber Company at

Melksham, Avon Industrial Polymers at Bradford on Avon, GEC at Melksham, Bowyers (Meat Products) at Trowbridge and Hurn Fencing at Melksham. Norwich CAB provided a service for the employees of Eastern Coachworks over a period of three months – mid October 1986 to mid January 1987.

> Five workers shared the work, going three days a week, two at a time. There were some 450 employees involved. A large proportion of these had worked at Eastern Coachworks all their lives, and not a few had started within the past year or two. One thing they all had in common was a total lack of knowledge of the State Benefits System, never having had to use it. Redundancy payments meant that a lot of the older ones were outside the scope of benefits, except for Housing Benefit, which in those days had no capital limit.
>
> We found ourselves advising on the ways in which they could spend some of their money without running into 'Abandonment of Resources' trouble; how to get advice on setting up in business on their own; where to get advice on investing their money; tax matters; how to fill in the Unemployment Benefit form; what they would get and the meaning of signing on; national insurance credits; how to make the most of increases for spouses – if they were working part-time.
>
> Once a week we gave a 'Tutorial' on the whole Benefits system – at which both management and shop floor would attend – so that they got an idea of what the system was, and therefore what questions they might wish to ask us in private.
>
> Of course, in addition to benefits, all sorts of other personal problems came up. The chief thing which struck us was the amazingly good humour of all the staff we came across, and their very positive attitude to their situation. It was very sad to see the works running down. When we first started there were some 30 bus chassis parked awaiting their bodies and day by day the number dwindled, until there were none. The men had a tremendous pride in their work and were certain that the division of British Leyland in the Midlands which was supposed to take over what was to remain of the coachbody business would be totally unable to do the job as well as they did! Probably they were right, as they virtually did the whole thing by hand – no production line nonsense for them – which is perhaps why they were ditched.

The needs which came to light in the course of the miners' strike of 1984/85 presented a challenge and demanded a response which crossed the usual boundaries of support. A major factor which affected NACAB's response was the impossibility of predicting the length of the dispute. Despite this NACAB was able to provide some support for those bureaux most directly affected by the strike. Three mobile units were used by Walsall CAB, the Yorks./Humberside Area Office and the North East Area office to take help to the bureaux and the miners whom they were attempting to help. The need for CAB involvement varied with the extent to which the local NUM was able to give advice. In some localities the provision of advice was quite extensive; in others the NUM welcomed

CAB and worked closely with local bureaux. During the course of the strike a large amount of information, focussed around the issues which were thrown up for the striking miners, was produced both locally and nationally by NACAB. The arrival in bureaux in January 1985 of a long-planned debt information package was particularly timely since the burden of debt was one of the long-lasting effects of the strike.

The final emergencies to be listed are once again ones which come into the category of 'Acts of God'.

On 22 October 1987 the rivers Strule, Mourne, Finn Dennett and Owenkillew burst their banks, flooding hundreds of homes and the complete town-centre shopping area of Strabane. Following moves by the District Council and the MEP for the area, an all-party delegation to Westminster was organised and, through the local CAB, the Parliamentary Liaison Officer of NACAB was contacted. She agreed to facilitate the visit to Parliament and as a result the delegation managed to lobby both peers and MPs. The outcome of the visit was that considerable extra provision was gained for the disaster areas, to cover the cost of some housing repairs, extra coal and heating allowances, plus other help in specific areas. £45,000 was given to statutory and voluntary organisations to distribute to flood-damaged households. The CAB has continued to be involved with the administration of this money and with the follow-up work resulting from the floods.

October 1987 was also the month when the hurricane-force winds in the south of England created a huge number of enquiries for bureaux in those areas, many of which were referred to the consultancy service. The problems causing most concern were not those involving disputes with insurance companies (which, in the main, acted quite swiftly) but rather those involving neighbours and damage caused by fallen debris, particularly trees. The incidents had all the ingredients of the classic neighbour dispute – trespass, nuisance, negligence, questions of rights and responsibilities. The most useful advice that could be offered was for the neighbours to come to an agreement between themselves. Good use was made of the DTI's grant for emergency needs in these areas to put additional resources into 24 bureaux to enable them to cope with the flood of extra enquiries concerning insurance claims, housing repairs, urgent needs payments etc., and dealing with cowboy builders.

It has not been possible to cover all emergencies and examples of special needs where the CAB service has had a part to play. The Notting Hill and Toxteth riots are two such episodes which have not been included, but if this list does nothing else, it demonstrates the ability which the service has shown through the years to rise to the situation, to meet the need of the moment and to absorb and integrate within itself the lessons which special emergency operations often bring in their wake.

CHAPTER FIVE

People

There could have been no CAB service without the people – the volunteers, on whom the whole was built, and the Honorary Officers and paid members of staff who constructed the framework which enabled the service to open its doors on the outbreak of war and to keep those doors open for the following fifty years.

In the first formative years three people were instrumental in shaping the service and establishing it for the future. These were Sir Wyndham Deedes, Miss Dorothy Keeling and Miss Kay Oswald. Sir Wyndham chaired the consultation which produced the Statement of July 1939 and he continued to take an active interest in the CAB, becoming Chairman of the CAB Committee of the NCSS in 1941. He has been described by someone who knew both Sir Wyndham and Dorothy Keeling as 'a wonderful man – a stunner. He was a very remarkable person and he and Dorothy Keeling worked well together – they had a very good rapport.' Since much of the history of voluntary organisations is tied up with the personalities of those who pioneered them, the CAB service was lucky in having two outstanding people working in harmony in the years when the foundations were laid.

Dorothy Keeling took part in the initial discussions in 1938/39 and sat on the sub-committee which was set up to consider the development of family casework and of Citizens Advice Bureaux in time of war. She thus took a large part in planning the service. She was seconded by the Liverpool Personal Service Society to the NCSS in February 1940 for six months but she says in her autobiography that 'towards the end of this period I decided, in view of the great importance of the movement, to accept the headship of the CAB Department, the appointment to last until the end of the war. This was a very difficult decision to make, causing me many sleepless nights.' She resigned as CAB Secretary when peace was declared and returned to Liverpool. This was not the end of her association with the CAB service as she later became Chairman of the CAB Committee of the Lancashire Community Council and, when she had moved to Yorkshire, chaired the Yorkshire CAB Committee, serving as a member of the Central/National CAB Committee for a number of years.

Dorothy Keeling was the sister of Ernest Keeling, a Tory MP, though her own political outlook was very different, doubtless as a result of her experiences as a social worker in the most deprived areas of Liverpool during the Depression.

She was succeeded as CAB Secretary by Kay Oswald, who took over towards the end of 1945 and remained in post for nearly twenty years. Like Dorothy Keeling she came from a background of social work. After service with the Sheffield Council of Social Service, she joined the NCSS in 1928 and remained with it until shortly before the war. During the war years she served as a Regional Welfare Officer of the Ministry of Health. Her return to the NCSS as CAB Secretary was crucial. It was largely due to her belief in the continuing need in peacetime for advice and help for ordinary people that the service – which had been launched purely as a wartime measure – was retained after peace had been declared. She has been described as 'an absolute gem of a woman – highly respected in every field' and 'slim, pretty, thoughtful – a strong person', and the service as it developed was influenced by the qualities which she showed as its leader, through good times and bad. In the obituary published at the time of her death in 1964, the Director of the NCSS paid the tribute:

> She enshrined in herself the qualities of the best bureau worker. To be able to interpret the weak to the strong and the strong to the weak is a priceless quality for any social worker or administrator to possess. Kathleen Oswald had it and expressed it superbly in all she did.

It was also said of her that

> Everyone who met Kay Oswald felt her to be an outstanding person. In a remarkable way she created a personal link between herself and the individual workers and organisers in more than 400 bureaux up and down the country and at the same time built up a national service with a headquarters and field staff equipped to carry on her work when she laid it down.

These three are important in the history of the CAB service but they are by no means the only remarkable people who gave, and still give, their time and commitment to the CAB service. Many distinguished and able people have served in every capacity and given support to the bureaux. National, Regional and Area Chairmen and Honorary Officers, Council and Committee members, unofficial advisers and volunteer experts, Chairmen and members of Management Committees, Organisers and advice workers in bureaux – all have given their services on a voluntary basis over the years. The value of their devotion and dedication to the service and the benefit to the public is impossible to evaluate.

How they went about things varied over the years. In time of war divisions are largely forgotten – everyone is in it together – bombs fall and people are killed and injured whether they be rich or poor. It would be unrealistic to say that all constraints disappear but they are much less evident than in normal times. With the outbreak of war all manner of people felt the call to help their fellow citizens in any way they could, and for some involvement with the local Citizens Advice Bureau seemed an obvious way to do so. Many of these early helpers were also at work with the WVS, the Warden service, fire-watching or a multitude of other services.

In the years which followed, this feeling of oneness began to leak away and as bureaux became more and more isolated the tendency for bureau staff to become small, self-perpetuating groups with shared prejudices and attitudes becomes noticeable. Noticeable, too, is the weakness of many Management Committees at this time and, in many cases, their subservience to the ruling Organiser.

In an attempt to reach these isolated people after the disappearance from the scene of the Travelling Officers, and to influence them, the National Committee decided to publish a handbook which could be used as a training document for all new recruits to the CAB service and as advice for groups planning to open a new bureau. This handbook (subject to periodic up-dating and revision) remained in print for many years. The 'flavour' of this first, 1948, edition may seem a little quaint but it is possible to see within it a definition of working practices which today's workers can recognise and identify with. It is clearly what is now called 'client centred' – the principle to which the Association has returned in the late 1980s (*see Appendix 7*).

Staff in Bureaux: Change and Evolution

An article in *The Times Weekly Review* of 11 November 1954 refers to the staff of the bureaux in complimentary terms:

> It is indeed the quality of its workers that has won for the service the recognition it now enjoys. In background and experience they vary greatly from place to place. In the large towns they are mainly full-time professional social workers, but in smaller places they are often volunteers who give two or three days a week to the bureau, as well as a great deal of time outside it, keeping themselves up to date with the kind of information they need to be able to meet the many demands that are made upon them. Many have done this since the beginning of the war.

The use of volunteers has been central to the CAB service – with certain conspicuous exceptions – and it is sometimes believed that because the Organisers and some of the support staff in bureaux are now, in the main, being paid a proper salary for their work, the voluntary principle has been watered down and reduced. The evidence suggests otherwise. The present-day service estimates that its 13,500 volunteers represent about 90% of the workforce and it is therefore interesting to find that the Report of the CAB Service 1959/60 states that

A recent survey has shown that nearly seventy percent of bureaux workers are part-time volunteers ... These workers have made it their business to be fully conversant with social legislation and with local organisations and situations and in doing so have built up a close working relationship with officers of local and central government.

This is a large claim. What did being 'fully conversant with social legislation etc.' mean in reality?

From the beginning there had been consciousness of the need to have workers who were competent and knowledgeable. In the early years it was the responsibility of the NCSS Regional Officers and the CAB Travelling Officers to keep a close eye on what was happening in bureaux. The CAB Policy sub-Committee of May 1941, considered a proposal for 'improving the standard of efficiency of Bureau helpers, more particularly those who volunteer for post-blitz work'. An interesting slant is given to this by the comment that the training would be confined to those 'who were considered to be personally suitable for helping after raids' – the first indication of the need for selection.

In July 1944 the Committee contemplated the introduction of an intensive course for new workers after the war. The members 'considered that such a course, organised in close co-operation with the Universities in several different centres, would be useful and likely to interest the right type of recruit'. It was agreed at this time that a Certificate would only be given to those who passed an examination at the end of the course. This was yet another idea which remained submerged for many years.

Clearly, those who took part in these discussions knew what was needed, but the resources were not available and the progress of the process of recruitment, induction and training over the years, as reported and remembered by a number of long-serving bureau workers, shows just how big was the gap between the ideal and the reality.

I didn't even 'sit next to Nelly'. I was shown a large card index, CANS and HQ circulars and advised to read – which I did! (*Voluntary worker 1945*)

In 1945 a draft scheme for the training of workers was produced by the Midlands CAB Travelling Officer – a scheme which contains within it most of the elements which became the basis for such training as was done over the years. It consisted of lectures, a period of probation and visits of observation to other agencies and neighbouring bureaux (*see Appendix 8*).

The attitudes in the central organisation might be enlightened and far-sighted but there was a tendency for things to be different at the place of work. A good example of entrenched attitudes and, in particular, of the current view of the capabilities of women among some men, is demonstrated by an extract from a bureau Minute Book, dated 1948:

> [The Organiser, Mr Gibson] could not give the same amount of time to the CAB as in the past and he proposed to establish a panel of ladies to undertake duty spells and deal with the easy, straightforward cases; all other cases to be referred to him, or, if Mr Griffiths or Mr Drummond were present, to them. Special appointed times for personal interviews in the more difficult cases could be made.

Notice that there is no reference to any training to be undertaken by Mr Gibson's 'panel of ladies'!

More enlightened people were aware of the need to put the service's house in order, if only to prevent this kind of thing from happening. In 1949 the Standing Conference of Citizens Advice Bureaux passed a Resolution which underlined the importance of training for bureau workers and Organisers and asked the Central Committee to prepare a training syllabus. This was excellent stuff but nothing appears to have come out of it. Worker after worker reports the situation over the next few years; all of them report it in much the same terms.

> Training was not considered necessary. After being interviewed by the Organiser, the volunteer worker was just expected to get on with helping clients, with the aid of a few notices on the walls and a small number of files without index cards. (*Voluntary worker 1950*)

If the problem of training new workers had been difficult while the Travelling Officers were in post, it became almost impossible, save where there was some supporting agency such as a CSS on the scene, after the funding for these officers ran out. In January 1951 the Central Committee expressed anxieties about the recruitment of voluntary workers, particularly in the industrial districts of the Midlands. It was felt that because the work was 'increasing in complexity' recruitment was more difficult and the comment was made that the withdrawal of the travelling officers was beginning to have 'an adverse effect'. A couple of years later Kay Oswald drew the attention of the Central Committee to 'the difficulty of assessing standards of work in bureaux in the absence of field officers'. She judged it most difficult when it became necessary to criticise the work of a bureau, epecially where it was part of a Council of Social Service or other casework agency.

There was continued anxiety about maintaining standards and in July 1958 the Central Committee worried about the situation again. All the good intentions in the world were no help in the face of lack of resources. There was no sense in making attendance at training obligatory if the bureaux could not provide it and the recruits could not afford to attend when attendance involved travel costs. The Committee found itself helpless in the face of all the difficulties. It agreed that there was need for machinery for selection (and for rejection), and identified the desirability of compulsory training for Secretaries and Organisers, together with a commitment from these to the principles of the CAB service.

The Report of the CAB Service for 1962/64 touches on the subject and expresses high sentiments, but evidence received indicates that the sentiments were not possible to translate into positive action.

SELECTION AND TRAINING OF WORKERS

The last two years have shown that there is an ever-growing acceptance of the need for a careful selection procedure and preliminary training of the workers. Nowadays when new bureaux are being opened it is normal for local committees to require candidates to complete application forms and submit themselves to a selection committee. Before being appointed they must indicate their willingness to accept the discipline of training as a continuous process. Training organisation has progressed towards more modern methods and higher standards. There has been greater emphasis on group discussion and courses have alternated between weekly lectures and visits of observation.

It may be that this is what happened in some new bureaux; it is clear that it did not happen in all of them.

Picture an old primary school on a cold winter evening and in the hall an assortment of men and women of all ages, sizes and professions eager to learn the mysteries of National Insurance benefits, government legislation, local authority services etc. With a smattering of knowledge and even less confidence the thirty people who survived the training staffed the bureau which opened its doors in April 1966. (*Voluntary worker 1965*)

The large and very busy bureau in central Birmingham had its own induction and training system operating in 1969.

After trying different methods the most satisfactory approach has been found to give the workers about six months sitting in at the interviews with an experienced worker, with the opportunity after each interview of discussing the advice given and the method of arriving at it. After this experience, a short series of talks follows which deals with the methods used in the bureau, interviewing, and the welfare services. These talks can be fully discussed and are more valuable to the new workers after they have gained some experience than if they were given at an earlier stage. They are given by experienced workers who are used to being faced with difficult problems. It has been found that outside lecturers who are not in constant touch with the practical side of the work of the Citizens' Advice Bureau are far less helpful. It might be thought that having two people at an interview ... would inhibit the full usefulness of discussion ... the position of the observer is explained before the interview commences and permission for the trainee to stay is obtained. It is gratifying to know how seldom any objection is raised. (*THE STORY OF THE CITIZENS' ADVICE BUREAU IN BIRMINGHAM 1939/69 by Raymond V Wadsworth*)

New bureaux which opened during these years often took a long time to build up a clientele and this gave the workers time to familiarise themselves with such information as they had and to learn what to expect when the public eventually came in through their doors.

After twenty-five years the bureaux were still offering help.

Some premises were portable.

Originally we opened in the evenings because many of us were about our professions or vocations during the day. At the beginning we had few clients and I have gone as long as seven weeks without any. Business did pick up and we found that we were doing a considerable amount of casework. In short, we were dealing with clients' problems in depth and over a period of time. The majority of the bureau workers disagreed with this and had the opinion that we were, as they said, a referral agency. This I take to mean that when their button was pressed they replied 'GOTO'. Many of our workers were of the 'twin set' brigade; a few were of the professional world and some were in business. The general expectation was that our clients would be of the lower classes, expressing the greatest gratitude for the minimum of effort from the workers. The bureau's relations with local law firms was poor. (*Voluntary worker 1968*)

Newcomers sat in with more experienced workers to listen, and learned what they could from reading the Daybook entries. CANS was our bible. There were very few other reference books. For a number of years workers kept their own indexed notebooks, collecting items of information from national and local newspapers. We relied to a certain extent on making common sense sound authoritative! (*Voluntary worker 1970*)

The great breakthrough came with the introduction of categorised and referenced information so that bureaux were not dependent upon their own resources to such a degree but there was still little idea of formal recruitment and selection. Training continued to be subject-based, with lecture courses conducted by the local managers of departments, solicitors and others – all of whom tended to be looked upon respectfully as the 'experts' in their particular area of work.

On my first morning I joined about fifteen trainees. The lectures were all given by the experts working in their particular field – interesting, but not necessarily presenting the information needed from the point of view of working in the bureau. I remember being fascinated to hear the history and see the formal yardstick, etc., held by the Weights & Measures Department but did not find it relevant to the consumer queries that clients were bringing to us. (*Voluntary worker 1972*)

The course consisted of 8–10 lectures given by local members of the community, such as the Geriatric Health Visitor, social workers etc. They provided useful background information but were of little practical help to volunteers who were shortly to be faced with clients. The real training was given by the Organiser on an individual basis in the bureau and to a much more limited extent through workers' meetings. (*Voluntary worker 1973*)

There wasn't really any selection for training; everyone who thought CAB work sounded interesting went along to a series of evening classes, twenty in all I think. Needless to say, there was a fairly high fall-out of potential advisers; it was an endurance test, not training! (*Voluntary worker 1973/74*)

On moving to Goucestershire I rang the local bureau and an interview was arranged with the Organiser when the bureau was closed. This short interview was all that was needed in those days to let me in. My very first introduction to my fellow workers in the bureau was in my Organiser's drawing room at a monthly workers' meeting where we had coffee before we started our work. There was no Area Initial training but I did get first-class instruction from the start, working side-by-side with experienced workers in the only room we had and in which everything happened. Waiting clients had to sit in a draughty passage outside. Perhaps technically the help and advice we gave in those days was not as good but enthusiasm and care for others was certainly there. (*Voluntary worker 1974*)

Accounts of what work in a bureau was like at that time, compared with the same bureau today, all stress the much more leisurely pace.

After training sessions run as evening classes the bureau opened 'cold', not knowing what to expect, but gradually we built up a clientele and gained the public's confidence. This meant there was time for cases to be thrashed out among workers before and after the client left the bureau, time to read the case notes, information packs (then quite small), ask questions and check references. Our confidence and competence grew too. (*Voluntary worker 1973*)

A bureau worker arrived promptly at 9.15 a.m. – time to look out the notebook, check the Continuity book and read through the previous week's cases before opening at 9.30 a.m. There was time to read the monthly news bulletin and to be brought up to date with legislative changes by the Organiser. A coffee break allowed for chat with fellow workers. Clients were attended to – on one memorable occasion four members of staff found they had dealt with no fewer than seven cases – a very busy day indeed! Young people seldom came to the bureau for advice; middle-aged or senior citizens used us more. (*Voluntary worker 1974*)

It was still possible for some bureaux to operate in eccentric and idiosyncratic ways without any consciousness that they were not functioning as they should. Because the workforce (both Organisers and voluntary advice workers) were largely women, largely middle-aged and largely under-educated in that, though able and intelligent, they were drawn from a generation and a class which did not automatically think in terms of university education or of professional employment, such men as were about tended to be over-valued and to be treated with a deference that was not necessarily earned. Management Committees, in particular, tended to believe that the former Bank Manager who offered his services could not be expected to undertake any training. If he was good enough to be willing to help, so much the better! Deference to professional men was ingrained among many of the workers in bureaux.

Training was minimal. One of our workers, an ex-naval gentleman, refused to attend any lectures or to look anything up. He always knew 'A chap' and would dive out of the bureau to talk to a Solicitor, Insurance Broker or whoever it might be and returned well-informed. It was not possible to persuade him that if we all did it that way the bureau might become a bit unpopular in the town. Another worker always preferred to have a consensus of opinion and would never settle a problem on his own. I can visualise him, back to the fire, asking anyone at hand what they thought and then eventually going back to the client with the general opinion. (*Voluntary worker 1976*)

One of the first effects of the use of the Development Grant money was the establishment of much more adequate and satisfactory methods of recruitment and training.

When I stepped timorously into my original CAB office in 1976 I had no experience of current working conditions; what it meant to lose a job, to have to pay income tax, insurance, what was a P45, I wondered, and how did one 'sign on'? Having been to a certain extent cossetted I knew nothing of housing problems – at that time Rachmanism was at its height. It was all too easy to be ignorant of the sheer poverty with which many people struggle all their lives.

We did our original training at GLCABS. This too was an eye-opener – where the lecturers all seemed tenderly young and jeans and jargon were de rigeur. The training was a real challenge – making us concentrate on practical matters, on figures (not my forte), Supplementary Benefit, pensions and matrimonial problems. Having had some legal training, certain areas came more easily to me, but nonetheless I envied those who had graduated to CAB via careers and who knew how many beans made five. I was deeply impressed then, as now, by the breadth of the information available to us.

Training has continued throughout my years in CAB, courses have extended and updated my knowledge on a fantastic range of topics – redundancy, starting up a business, housing benefit, debt, domestic proceedings, employment, consumer, income tax – the courses have anticipated the needs of the clients and equipped workers to help. (*Voluntary worker 1976*)

I came into the CAB service in 1977 as a paid employee. Several fundamental changes were taking place around this time. There was still a feeling among many of the voluntary advisers that the service should remain totally voluntary. Many saw the service mainly as a referral agency. There was no mandatory training for Bureaux workers. the main training was finding out by doing the job or sitting in with other workers. There were some training courses for experienced workers, very much subject based. The volunteers were mainly over 45 years of age and many of them were elderly. They did one 2 hour session in the bureau. Bureau workers were recruited through the 'grape-vine'. There was a very stable staff and the Management Committee felt there was no need to advertise for volunteers. Any suggestion of selection for voluntary work was regarded as unacceptable. Case recording was in daybooks, these were indexed to try and link repeat enquiries but it was a very laborious system. (*Organiser/Council member 1977*)

Compared to today the few people who did come in during the first few months had fairly simple questions to ask, so we were able to look up

most of it. I well remember one heart-stopping moment when I was asked
if somebody would be breaking the Official Secrets Act if they gave some
information to the government of another country. This was only 6 days
after we opened! I often wonder if any of us would have stayed in the job if
we had known that the problems we are facing now were coming.
(*Organiser 1978*)

When I think back over our training and the types of problems we dealt
with I shudder at the cheek we had to call ourselves advice workers. Our
formal training was 2½ hours one evening a week for 6 weeks, after which
we opened our bureau and had to learn the rest as we went along. Some of
my volunteers did sit in at a bureau which was 5 or 6 miles away just for
one or two sessions to get the feel of things. I didn't get this chance as I
had to get the information files up to date. This was good practice for me
but it did nothing for the interview situation. To say we were apprehensive
is an understatement of massive proportions. (*Organiser 1978*)

By the beginning of the 1980s the picture had largely changed. Not
only was there a constantly developing training programme but the
people who were drawn into the work came into it from more varied
backgrounds and with very different assumptions. The young graduate
mothers who did not feel able to take a paid job while their children
were small and the newly retired largely replaced the older generation
of women, many of whom, even if they had not yet reached the official
retiring age, began to feel that the work was becoming too pressuring.
More men were recruited – in particular from those who had taken early
retirement or been made redundant – bright working-class women and
the unemployed were drawn in to work for the service, as were black
and Asian people. Gatherings of CAB workers began to look younger,
more varied and more interesting in their variety. Some recruits still
arrived with no previous work experience but there was now a well-
thought-out programme of selection, induction and training to prepare
them for the business of trying to help their fellow citizens through
difficulties and traumas.

Most, though not all, CAB workers come to the job after being employed in
full-time occupations where they may have acquired certain skills and a
knowledge of one aspect of modern life. Few of them realise how little they
know of what goes on in their town hall, shops, DHSS office, court,
consulting rooms or schools.

The training of a new adviser sets out to remedy this, initially by a
period of in-bureau training. By observation the trainee assimilates the
essentials of CAB work, of confidentiality, impartiality, patience and
sympathetic understanding of the clients' problems. By listening to
workers discussing cases, reading reports, looking through files and
examining government pamphlets the newcomer begins to appreciate
how much has to be learned. Visits to the local magistrates' court, to the
Job Centre, to the DHSS Office and to the Unemployment Office help one
to begin to understand what life is like for the less articulate, less

advantaged members of our society. A little self-examination is encouraged. Making an honest list of one's own prejudices is a salutary exercise.

Formal training is given at Area by tutors expert in those subjects CAB workers are most likely to meet. New workers are required to attend a Basic Training Course one day a week for nine weeks, in addition to their regular duty at the local bureau. The training is varied; it consists of lectures, practical exercises with case studies, group discussions and role play. Each course is attended by about 15 trainees. By the end they have learned to unravel official jargon, come to terms with the complexities of social legislation, struggled with financial computations, practised interviewing skills and, most important of all, begun to learn to use the CAB files.

Back in the bureau things begin to make sense. The new worker has gained in confidence which is helped by the friendly advice from the Organiser and more experienced workers. In-bureau sessions on specific subjects are held monthly, giving an opportunity to revise or update one's understanding.

A further Call-Back course is arranged after about six months' work in the bureau. This involves more detailed study of subjects encountered on the Basic Course. After a year in the bureau workers find themselves on the Intermediate Course, another 4 days spread over 4 weeks. This provides further opportunity to revise, reinforce and improve upon the skills already acquired. Advisers meet friends made at earlier training sessions, are able to exchange experiences, to see who has given up and who is battling on – hooked by the infinite variety the work has to offer!
(*Voluntary worker 1980s*)

All those who have served for more than a short length of time agree about the weight of demands upon advice workers in bureaux today. For those who take up advice work as a full-time job there is a phenomenon known as 'burn out' – which is the effect of spending all your time trying to solve the insoluble, absorb the misery of the helpless and accept the fact that there is no redress from circumstances in all too many cases. The stress involved in dealing with an unending stream of trouble, difficulties and dismay can become too great, forcing the worker to leave the job and do something else – if only for a time. Even for the voluntary worker, who has other commitments and who is present for a relatively limited amount of time, the stresses can reach the stage when he or she feels that enough is enough and resignation is the only sensible course to take. In these circumstances, many of the older workers are more resilient than the young.

One thing I notice in the workers in the bureau today is there are so many men, and young people coming forward, which is a good thing. Many are without a paid job and find bureau work very stimulating, challenging and excellent training for any future vocation. The pressure of work in bureaux today is phenomenal and demands much more extensive knowledge in greater depth than 23 years ago but we approached our job just as conscientiously and devotedly as workers nowadays. The devotion and enthusiasm of workers today is encouraging to see and, as our Manager said in one annual report, 'The atmosphere of the place is unique in my working experience. It seems like an oasis of affection, tolerance and humour.' No wonder I have stayed for 23 years and going on! (*Voluntary worker 1988*)

Now, as before, the voluntary workers support each other and there is in many bureaux a great sense of shared enterprise on behalf of the community. If there is sometimes a sense of sorrow that the more leisurely practices of the past are no more, there is still a feeling that the work itself is justification enough for the amount of effort required.

From opening time every day it is all 'go', reading is done at home, case notes left unread, chat (personal and otherwise) is limited. The service has gone 'professional' – reflected in the superb information supplied at great cost by NACAB – but on a voluntary, though trained, basis. Training is client oriented and relies heavily on the information files. (*Voluntary workers*)

Legislation is persistently on-going and so is updating the files and the jargon – just as Weights & Measures became Trading Standards, so Supplementary Benefit has become Income Support. Although my Organiser has now become my Manager, the tremendous support and friendly teamwork at CAB remains unchanged from when I started in 1972. (*Voluntary worker*)

Since I started in 1982 the work has become much more demanding and a good many workers do find the pressures too great and are only able to devote 2 to 3 years to the task. Having had four children and a busy business life, I am used to keeping several balls in the air at the same time but have noticed that the more academic the worker the less able they are to switch from problem to varied problem. Life has become much more complex during my years with the bureau and thus the problems with which we must cope have also become more difficult. Our workload has increased tremendously. Debt, and the difficulty it brings, is the problem which I find most stressful. Having taken a Debt Counselling course, that has been my main workload for the past two years and, although not easily daunted, I have had to ask for a break from the work. Two other colleagues have had to do likewise. I love the work at the bureau and find it very rewarding. I would not like to see too great an increase in paid staff, since that would bring a whole lot of other problems and CAB would become another type of social services department. The dedicated able voluntary worker has value beyond money. (*Voluntary worker*)

The one thing which never changes in the life of bureaux is its unpredictable nature. Mixed in with all the questions about the client's entitlement to welfare benefits are others of an obscure, startling or bizarre nature. Bureaux workers have to learn how to deal with the unexpected – with the little old lady who knows that THEY listen in to everything which happens in her house, with the unpredictable behaviour of the mental patient released to 'community care', with the indecent exposer and masturbator, with all the problems of the inarticulate and the illiterate. These, and many more, find their way to bureaux throughout the network and the staff manage to cope in one way or another.

I can confirm that as far as my own experience is concerned, since 1981, the type of enquiry has changed considerably. One is continually surprised even now, with the enormous variety of subjects on which advice is required. I can think of no other organisation which covers so wide a field. Training has also become much more intensive than it was even five years ago in order to cope with continually changing legislation. Advice is ever more frequently requested on legal matters as the fees charged by solicitors often put their services beyond the reach of people with only modest incomes, especially when the matter is one which cannot be supported by legal aid. Because of ever more complicated matters being brought for advice, the standard demanded by bureaux is much greater than even a few years ago. (*Voluntary worker*)

Life seemed simpler for the bureau workers 24 years ago, in that they were not required to pick their way through a maze of overlapping welfare benefits or tackle the complex task of assessing eligibility for housing benfit. Yet one senses the same concern and care for the individual and willingness to tackle any problem which we hope clients find in the bureau today. (*Voluntary worker*)

One important factor in 1965 was that we had time to LISTEN and lend a shoulder to our clients on which to cry (not that it isn't done today) but then life seemed so much more leisurely and possibly personal and of course much less complicated. We had no voluntary specialist services by professionals such as Legal Aid and Money Advice but we did have a friendly solicitor whom we could ring for 'off the cuff' advice. (*Voluntary worker*)

The contrast between the service when I joined in 1973 and now is immense. I shudder to think how we interviewed (in tandem!) with comparatively little information on file. A vast amount of common sense prevailed, combined with referral. (*Voluntary worker*)

Since 1965 the increasing demands from our clients on every imaginable topic and the lack of anywhere else to turn to for confidential help has made the need for a different approach to training essential for all bureaux staff. We have come to recognise more fully the needs of our clients to express their feelings and to be shown that they are accepted, before facts and figures, or options and their implications, can even be considered. Interviewing skills have at last been recognised to be of prime importance for the adequate delivery of the service and to achieve its aims. This recognition has been, I believe, a real revolution which will need to continue to develop if the quality of the service is to improve and be maintained. So many of our clients find themselves in lonely circumstances, unable to cope with ever-increasingly complex situations which affect their lives. They long to be shown they are of value, as well as finding that the law says something relevant to their situation. (*Voluntary worker*)

Increasingly, bureaux began to appoint Organisers to whom they paid a salary – often at a low level – but still a salary. There was much resistance on the part of some Management Committees to the whole idea of such payments. This group felt that to pay someone to do what his or her predecessor had done for nothing, or for a token 'honorarium', somehow made the CAB service déclassé, no longer demonstrating its superiority over the world of commercial considerations. Those who took this position were particularly unsympathetic towards bureaux, such as those in central London, which relied on the work of paid staff and did not use volunteers at all.

> The change of emphasis and attitude I have seen since 1977 is from amateur to professional. In 1977 the CAB service saw itself as a voluntary group giving a committed but limited service to the local community. I have seen a change in emphasis, still with a strong commitment to the voluntary principle but a realisation that the standard of service that the bureaux give can be professional. The other important change is the acceptance that having key paid staff does actually enable the bureaux to give this service. The biggest change in emphasis is in the enquiries themselves – Social Security and Debt now certainly take up the largest share of time in the bureaux. No one sees the CAB as simply a sign-posting organisation but one actually able to answer many complex enquiries fully. (*Organiser/Council member*)

> Management Committees in the old days (1962) considered that bureau work was 'voluntary work' and I clearly recall that the minute honorarium awarded to the organiser (£250 p.a I believe) was not considered necessary. This attitude took a long time to rectify, hence the lack of sympathy towards re-grading of paid staff and the proper funding of the CAB structure as it is today. (Sadly, this attitude still persists in some quarters.) When I consider the work taken on by volunteers today, compared with 25 years ago I am amazed at the dedication and loyalty expressed but we love it and seem to thrive on the challenge it offers. (*Voluntary worker*)

For some bureaux, particularly those in the areas of mass unemployment, the problem nowadays is to sustain the motivation to continue in spite of the conditions with which they are surrounded. One Annual Report pinpoints the feeling of disenchantment – and the optimism which persists in spite of everything.

> In the late 70s and 80s when the money has run out, industry is declining and all public spending has been cut, we have a shortage of council houses, poorer standards of education, not enough Home Helps, Old People's Homes or meals on wheels, disgracefully dirty and dangerous pavements and unrepaired roads, NHS charges rising beyond what many people can afford to pay, a lowering of standards in hospitals and – worst of all – long-term unemployment. From this comes the greatest proportion of our troubles today. Too much money; too little money; it makes no difference, the problems still increase. We try still to be a friendly local

bureau with time to talk but this grows more difficult as the pressure grows. One thing never changes – the quality of our voluntary workers. The job has grown more responsible and needs more commitment from everyone.

An Organiser currently in post sums up the pattern of development over the last twenty years or so, ending on a note of modified optimism.

In 1966 we had 12 workers, 10 women, of whom I was the only one with a child of under school age, with two male pensioners. Now we have five men, two younger and three rather older – and ten women, whose ages I shall not reveal. They are, if anything, keener and more conscientious than any of the earlier volunteers. Above all, the work has changed – from a leisure pastime to a demanding dominating commitment; from 129 queries in the first year to nearly 4,000 now [1987]. And yet it hasn't changed. The most distressing cases will always be family and personal problems; the ones where you listen helplessly, knowing that you can do nothing to help, then finding that all that is needed is someone to listen. Neighbours will always fall out and then have to go on living together. However tight the money is, most people will work out ways of managing, and although I've sometimes doubted it recently, the CAB will always have that edge over the rest. Our service is free, impartial and confidential, now as in 1939. We do the job for love, not money and that will not change.

There are, however, some who are not so happy, who feel that the CAB service has been politicised in a way which makes them uncomfortable. They find change difficult and the need to have formal policies, publicly displayed, to be distasteful compared with the previously understated stance of general goodwill and even-handedness. These attitudes are likely to show up in their starkest forms in those areas of the country where there has been relatively little change in either social attitudes or the racial mix over the last ten or twenty years. In trying to meet the needs of people throughout the country the Association has to go at the pace at which all the bureaux can travel. This inevitably means that it will be too slow for some and too fast for others. One volunteer writes:

I fully appreciate that it would be totally impossible and inappropriate for bureaux to be run now on the basis which existed during my early years with CAB. The service is now better informed, better organised, very much larger and of course much more widely accessible than twenty five years ago and consequently reaches a vastly increased number of clients offering them specialist advice in wide-ranging fields.

I know that without the increased paid staff at all levels it would not be possible to provide the service to our clients with their growing and changing needs that we would wish. However there is the danger that in our increased preoccupation with committees, special interest groups, working parties and management structures, the most vital part of the work becomes less valued. The whole point of the service is to help clients and I believe that it is still largely the volunteers who answer the telephones and receive and interview our clients in most bureaux. Volunteers are now recruited from a much wider spectrum of society than when I started and therefore have a wider range of talents and experience to bring to the work which is invaluable for our clients. As the paid staff grow in number within a bureau they tend to be the people who set the atmosphere and take the decisions and the volunteers may begin to feel powerless and unimportant within the new framework.

When I started in CAB there were virtually only volunteers and thus their importance was obvious. Their place in the service has widened and changed but there is the danger that their importance and consequently the importance of the clients gets less valued within the management structure. I hope we will be able to remedy this trend and restore volunteers to a more central position in the bureaux.

An Organiser from a rural bureau comments more positively on the formulation of policies.

I feel that possibly the service has got rather more enmeshed in 'politics', perhaps because of the economic problems of the last ten years and the number of unemployed. We have inevitably sided with the 'under-privileged' in money/benefit terms, which doesn't make us best loved by conservatives (with a large or small 'c').

Another feature has been the increased emphasis on an equal opportunities policy for ethnic minorities and (controversially in some quarters) lesbians/gays. I think we should give a lead here, although it can cause controversy within the service as well as outside. We should try harder to reflect the community, although I think the image of middle-class ladies with leisure 'doing good' has been replaced by a greater public respect for our professional approach.

A final perspective from a member of Council with ten years' experience as a bureau Organiser in central London is useful to put things into context:

The bureau is situated in an area where wealth sits side by side with a huge Council estate, vast rented mansions housing pensioners existing on retirement pension and relics of a much richer past supplemented by (now) Income Support, and bedsit land (and, of course, hotels). Ten years ago clients were as varied in background as were the questions posed – well-heeled, educated people sat with the poor on supplementary benefit, overseas students and commuting workers, and the range of enquiries was wide and comprehensive. We mainly solved the 'presenting' problems and if there were others people could return as they didn't have to wait very long to be seen. Problems could on the whole be dealt with on the day we saw the client and the DHSS or Department of Employment were reached by 'phone within minutes.

Now our opening hours have shrunk from 6 hours to 2–3 hours a day to deal with the 'follow-up' consequent on the problems – which have got more complex and complicated as they have reduced in variety. The categories are now welfare benefits, housing and homelessness, employment, matrimonial; the presenting problem inevitably brings 5 or 6 other queries in its wake which take weeks or months to solve (when a solution is possible). One spends months getting the DHSS to sort out a problem. Only the most desperate can afford to wait the 1–3 hours to be seen in our bureau. Some arrive to be furiously disappointed because the door is closed one hour early because the waiting room is bulging and there are only 2–3 interviewers available.

For three or four years we have been making time to do social policy work because it seems to us to be more constructive and time effective to try to solve the problem at source rather than only dealing with the problems on an individual basis. For instance, getting the Council to reconsider how their repair department works is better than fighting to get individual flats repaired in a reasonable time. However this does conflict with the 'Open Door' approach, with our limited resources, and it is very difficult convincing both the Council and workers used to the traditional approach (**and clients**) that social policy is as important as the individual work.

This same Organiser, speaking as a black woman, says:

I think the concept of equal opportunities has had the greatest impact on the service. From a cosy enthnocentric group of people, the service has opened to more (inevitably) uncomfortable multicultural forces with all the difficulties as well as potential rewards. I'm certainly conscious of the uneasy and tentative stances of colleagues during the transition but I'm also aware of the wholeheartedness with which many embrace the changes, however difficult.

Racial equality is real in practice and in principle for advisers and their clients.

CHAPTER SIX

The Support Services

The bureaux and the support services are the two arms of the Association – neither would be able to function without the other. It is not a simple relationship; the central servicing departments plan their work in ways which reflect both the life of the bureaux and the outside world. It is essential, for example, for both the information and the training staff to be in close touch with the progress of legislation in order to timetable their work for the benefit of bureaux. They must also respond to issues which arise from the day to day work of the bureaux and it is not always easy to keep the correct balance between the immediate and the long-term.

To look at some of the separate elements which constitute the support services is a slightly artificial undertaking but it is only by doing so that some idea can be conveyed of the way in which strengthening these has enabled the Association to progress and build up its strength. No department at the centre and no Area Office works in isolation: they are all part of NACAB and exist to provide as much and as varied support to the federation of bureaux as they can.

The Field Staff

The original structure of the CAB service was based on the combined elements of the Civil Defence Regions and the regional structure of the NCSS. The bureaux in various parts of the country were grouped in Regions and met together in the Regional Advisory Committees, serviced by the NCSS and the CAB Travelling Officers.

Changes took place over the years as the field staff shrank, although the committee structure survived. In the absence of CAB staff, many of the Regional Advisory Committees, with the later County Committees, were serviced by county bodies such as Rural Community Councils or the Councils of Social Service. The lines of communication became tenuous to the degree that, at the lowest ebb, one part-time Advisory Officer covered the whole of the north of England while, outside London, there were no advisory staff in the rest of the country. It was during these years that the handbook 'Advising the Citizen' became the key to the CAB service, since it was often the main guidance available on setting up and running a bureau. It is significant that the edition of 1966 has only one reference to the field staff, in connection with the promotion of new bureaux, about which it says 'The National Citizens Advice Bureau Committee makes available the services of its advisory officers to guide all stages of promotional work, the first of which is normally the organisation of a public meeting.' Once established, a bureau was very much on its own.

As funds became available over the years, the field staff expanded again until by 1972 there was an Advisory Officer in charge in the North East, Yorkshire, the North West, Wales, East Midlands, West Midlands, Eastern, Chilterns, the South East and Wessex Regions. (Two of these were only part-time posts.) Northern Ireland had one member of staff, while Scotland (which was at that time still under the Scottish Council of Social Service) had six, including three Advisory Officers. A staff of ten serviced the London bureaux under different arrangements.

When it is realised that the North West contained separate committees for Cheshire County, Greater Manchester, Greater Merseyside and Lancashire/Cumbria, and that the staff consisted of two (later three) people, it will be seen that the task of administering the Region was in itself almost impossible and the chance of promoting new bureaux or monitoring the performance of the existing ones was very limited. The workload facing an Advisory Officer was daunting to the extent of being quite impossible. He or she could only survive at all by being extremely selective about the work undertaken.

The Advisory Officer was employed by the NCSS to be the agent of the National CAB Council in promoting all aspects of the CAB service and, in particular, to maintain the link between the Council and the bureaux, principally by means of the Regional Advisory Committee. The Advisory Officer acted as Secretary to the Committee and, with the Chairman, was responsible for the agenda. He or she was expected to interpret the views of the central organisation to the bureaux of the Region and, conversely, to ensure that the views of the bureaux were communicated to the centre as effectively as possible. The direct link to the National CAB Council was provided by the Regional Representative on Council. The Council member was a representative, not a delegate, but the distinction was not always kept clearly in mind, with the result that some Council members felt that they were mandated to vote in a particular way no matter how the debate went in Council.

The acquisition of the Development Grant enabled NACAB to subdivide the Regions into more manageable Areas and this process continued until, in 1981, the large Regions had become a thing of the past. The Areas were still too large to be serviced adequately by the basic staff, which by then consisted of an Area Advisory Officer, an Administrative Assistant and a clerical worker, but the situation was not quite as impossible as it had been.

Scotland was separate but the rest of the country was divided into the North East, Yorkshire and Humberside, Lancashire and Cumbria, Greater Manchester, Merseyside, East Midlands, West Midlands, North Wales, South Wales, East Anglia, Essex, Chilterns, South East, Surrey and West Sussex, Southern, Wessex, Devon and Cornwall and Northern Ireland, plus four London Areas.

Even within these subdivisions great concentrations of bureaux existed. After a time the case was made for treating the West Midlands Area as a double Area and new ground was broken by the appointment of a second senior officer, so that there was both an Area Officer, with overall responsibility for the management of the Area, and an Advisory Officer who could work with the bureaux at the level previously solely the prerogative of the Area (Advisory) Officer. The West Midlands was the first, but as funds became available, more and more Areas gained the services of additional staff. Increasingly, the Area and Advisory Officers worked in close association with the bureaux in their Areas, taking part in the selection of all staff, whether voluntary or paid; attending meetings of Management Committees; advising on the preparation of applications for funding; helping management committees with personnel problems; discussing and interpreting new policies and introducing new practices into bureaux with the object of improving their effectiveness and efficiency; acting in support of Organisers, for whom one of the chief problems as workers had in the past been their isolation.

For some bureaux workers and Management Committees it was difficult to come to terms with this spate of activity. There was a certain amount of rebellion on the grounds that each bureau was supposed to be independent and yet it seemed that they were only independent as long as they toed the line and did exactly what they were told! Once again, the CAB service exhibited the classic conflicts between 'Us – here at the place where life is real!' and 'Them – up there, who have all these crazy, impractical ideas'. All dispersed organisations appear to suffer from this syndrome and the CAB service is no exception.

GLCABS had been the first to appoint a Training Officer and develop a coherent training strategy, but the start of the development of improved provision of training in the Areas in the rest of the country can be dated from a decision made in June 1974 that a Training Tutor should be appointed in every Area. This was not, in fact, implemented and part-time Course Organisers were the first training staff to be appointed in all Areas. South Wales appointed the second Training Officer in 1974, to develop training based on three of their bureaux in the Area, and Training Centres were opened in Manchester, Liverpool and Leeds to serve their respective Areas. By 1982 every Area which did not have a

Training Centre had at least the minimum establishment of a full-time Training Officer, together with the necessary support staff.

The closing of the Consumer Advice Centres in Birmingham opened the way for the appointment of the first specialist staff within Area Offices. The West Midlands established a Consumer Unit to work in support of its bureaux. This was the beginning of the development of specialist support to bureaux at the Area level, a trend which continues with the establishment of Tribunal Support Units, Money Advice and Debt Counselling – often by providing specialist services through support units servicing groups of bureaux rather than by placing individual specialists within a single bureau.

The Area staffs exist to give support to the bureaux within their Areas, to act as the interpreters, mediators, facilitators and negotiators. The Area and Advisory Officers are charged by Council with the tasks of applying the current membership scheme, monitoring the performance of the bureaux in the Area and promoting new bureaux and related services. Their place in the CAB service is central in every sense. For many bureaux, NACAB – by which they mean the people in the London office – is remote and unapproachable, while the Area staff are relatively near, more visible, known to be helpful and supportive in many ways and, apart from the occasional spat, trusted. The relationship between the bureaux and the Area Office is consequently crucial; if an Area can carry its member bureaux with it along the path which the Association has chosen to follow, the health of the whole is assured; when the bureaux become disaffected and feel excluded from decisions made on their behalf, the Association suffers. In their darker moments the field staff feel themselves to be 'Piggy in the Middle'; in more optimistic moods they realise that they function as the essential fulcrum which makes the system work.

The Information Service: Supplying the Tools

In order to enable the bureaux to instruct, inform and advise the civilian population on the conduct of their lives in the context of war, it was necessary for a steady flow of information to be distributed to them from the Central Office. Much of this comprised government leaflets and publications of all kinds. These were backed up by circulars which were compiled by the information staff of the NCSS. An indication of the type of subject covered by these is shown in the contents lists for two months in 1943.

17 March 1943

The following subjects are dealt with in this circular:

1 Clothes rationing
 (a) Towels: Special ration for certain priority users.
 (b) Services clothing coupons.

2 Shoe Exchange
3 Make Do and Mend Campaign
4 Simplified Army Pay
5 Employment of Women (Control of Engagement) Order 1943
6 Enquiries regarding missing relatives abroad
7 New address of Far East Section, BRCS
8 Rations of Relatives visiting service patients who are dangerously ill.

15th April 1943
The following subjects are dealt with in this circular:
 1 Work on the land.
 2 Restriction on Access to Coastal Towns.
 3 Utility Furniture.
 4 Civilian Internees in the Far East.
 5 Merchant Seamen: Rationed Food
 6 Application for Replacement of Lost clothing coupons.
 7 Air Letter Service to HM Forces.
 8 Sending Money to Troops Abroad.
 9 Domestic Food Production in Urban and Rural areas.
 10 Insurance cover for CABx: accidents on premises.
 11 Ministry of Information: extract from Letter regarding co-operation.

It was not until 1957 that the CAB service took over responsibility for the preparation and distribution of the Information Circular. CANS remained in the hands of the NCSS and continued to be an essential resource of bureaux for many years.

From 1951 the Information Service was freely available on subscription to any body which wished to have it. This did not last – in June 1966 the decision was taken to discontinue the supply on the grounds that the monthly Circular was now more specifically designed for bureaux and no longer appropriate for other bodies. There was a proposal for a precis to be produced and distributed to such bodies as Councils of Social Service.

It would seem that the decision was not acted on because the matter was raised again in Council in June 1969. Possibly as a result of this discussion, it is evident that action was taken because by October of the same year protests were being received about the discontinuance of the service. For the next few years the Information Service was no longer available to outside organisations but there was continued pressure from various bodies to be allowed to buy it. The issue of the sale of the Information Service became a perennial item on agendas of meetings held at all levels.

Many bureaux had misgivings about any possible sales. These were rooted, first, in doubts as to the use to which purchasers might put the information material and, in particular, whether it would be properly maintained and kept up to date; second, in the fear that if another body was given the resource a local authority might cut – or even withdraw – the funding of its local bureau.

Eventually, Council approved the sale of the Information Service to outside bodies under certain limitations and safeguards. The first sale under these circumstances is recorded as having been approved in October 1975. This was the beginning of a steadily increasing demand so that ten years later there were over 220 outside subscribers, listed as being 33% libraries, 33% generalist agencies, 9% specialist agencies, and 25% 'secondary advisers' such as colleges, students' unions, local authority departments and newspapers and magazines. In the Annual Report of 1975/76 the statement is made that

> Given ... the general increase in applications from outside groups, the CAB service is opening out the sale of the Information System. NACAB has allocated further resources with the aim of doubling subscriptions after first meeting the needs of new and existing CAB. Local bureaux and area offices will still be able to object to a particular sale if it affects the funding of a bureau.

This qualification was dropped in 1982 when Council agreed that all applicants should be accepted without reservation and sales continued on that basis until 1986 when the decision was reversed and conditions of sale were again imposed.

The paucity of information resources in post-war bureaux can be starkly illustrated by the 'List of essential information material and reference books which should be in a Citizens' Advice Bureau' as published in the 1966 edition of 'Advising the Citizen'. This contains the following:

> CANS (Citizens Advice Notes); Monthly Information Circulars; and supplementary memoranda; supplied as part of the central information and advisory service from CAB headquarters – minimum contribution £7 per annum.
> Public Social Services – 16s. 0d.
> Buying a House or Flat – Do's and Don'ts – 2s. 6d.
> Everyday Insurance – Some Questions Answered – 2s. 6d.
> Advising the Citizen – 5s. 0d.
> *All published by the National Council of Social Service*
> *Annual Charities Register & Digest – 18s 6d.
> *Family Welfare Association & Butterworth & Co Ltd*
> *Whitakers Almanack – 25s. 0d.
> *J Whitaker & Son*
> *Also recommended*
> Classified Telephone Directory; Street Directory and Map; Local Handbooks and timetables
> *Please order from booksellers*

Similarly, a list of 'Subject Files' is given. This is introduced with the note that 'The following list must not be regarded as exhaustive. It has been prepared only as a basis on which to start a filing system, and it will need to be expanded as more material is collected in a bureau.'

Financial Needs
– including National Assistance; sources of voluntary help in kind or money; specimen forms and stock of Form O.1; particulars of appeal procedures.

General Information
– to be sub-divided as and when desirable.

Health and Medical
Lists of doctors, dentists, clinics, convalescent homes etc; details of mental health services, home helps, hospital car service, equipment lending schemes ... (all to be collected locally).

Housing & House Purchase
– including information on Rent Act 1957, and other legislation, loan schemes, improvement grants, rating and valuation, property tax...

Legal Procedures
– Headquarters circulars on County Court, Legal Aid and Advice, Solicitors' Charges; Court of Protection pamphlet; lists of local solicitors, specimen forms ...

Local Information
Youth organisations; services for the elderly; (or have an Old People's Welfare file); places of interest ...

National Insurance
Specimen forms; particulars of appeal procedures ...

Prisoners and their families

Service matters
– including National Service, Service Pensions ...

Trading matters
– including information on dealing with hire purchase and credit buying problems; consumer protection ...

It can be seen from this list that no thought had gone into the construction of a suitable information system which would enable bureaux to handle and retrieve items in the most efficient way. Isolated individuals, often with backgrounds of librarianship, were conscious of the deficiencies and contrived comparatively sophisticated systems within their own bureaux but there was no means by which such systems could be introduced nationally, however good they were. Far too many bureaux lacked the requisite skills to set up and maintain good systems, and, as a result, only those who worked in a particular bureau could find the information they needed, because only they knew the peculiarities of the local set-up. A worker who moved from one part of the country to another and began to work in another bureau had to learn the second system before he or she could make use of it.

A new Chief Information Officer, Robin Forrest, a former bureau Organiser, discovered an equivalent state of affairs in the central information department. He decided that before anything else could be done the mass of information held at the centre must be re-classified. He therefore introduced a numerical system which contained within it the capacity for almost infinite expansion. An item classified, for instance, as 4.1.3.3 had as the first figure that of the major category, the second that of the first subdivision of that category, the third the subsection of the subdivision and the fourth the number of the item within that subsection. Followed through this gives:

4   ADMINISTRATION OF JUSTICE
4.1   Court Procedure
4.1.3   County Court
4.1.3.3 Using the County Court Office

Once the material held centrally had been re-classified it became possible to store and retrieve all items in the full confidence that the system could be understood and used by the most inexperienced worker in the shortest possible time.

The next step was to persuade bureaux to adopt the same system. All items would, in future, be issued with a classification number printed on them; therefore it was necessary that the bureaux should maintain their files under the same system. Only when this was done would it be possible for each piece of paper to be slotted into the system automatically on its arrival in the bureau. Mr Forrest embarked on a campaign to persuade bureaux that although it meant an initial upheaval and would involve the painful prospect of jettisoning cherished practices, the long-term gain would be immense. It took several years for the proposal to work through the committees of the Association but in February 1974 Council noted that 'it should be possible to introduce the National filing system on 1 April as planned'.

Many bureau workers have acknowledged that this was the key factor which enabled the CAB service to offer a well-grounded service to the public.

The organisation within Central Office at the time was such that the Senior Information Officer was responsible for writing almost all the information items which went out on a routine basis. The Information Officers spent a large proportion of their time answering questions from bureaux on the consultancy telephones and, when not so employed, might – if they were lucky – write one major item of information in a year. The information which went out on a monthly basis was designed to explain in clear language the provisions of all social legislation as it was enacted. The bureaux received a synopsis of the law, which made it possible to explain it to clients but was not much help in assessing how the law would apply to an individual in particular circumstances. The service prided itself on the succinct clarity of its explanations – it did not look at the usefulness or otherwise of each piece of information as perceived by the advice workers.

When a new Head of Information, Ms Mimi Sanderson – like Robin Forrest, a former Organiser of a bureau – took over the department the whole philosophy of the unit and the way it worked was re-examined. The first change made was to give each Information Officer a subject for which he or she was responsible. This worked for a time but was found to have limitations which inhibited further development. Ms Sanderson realised that the department needed to know more about the bureaux' requirements and an Information Officer conducted an enquiry to find out what they wanted and needed, at the same time culling their ideas about the future development of the Information Service.

The results of the survey were fed back to the information staff and it was decided that further changes in work practices should be introduced. The Information Officers were brought together into what became the Information Production Group, with the object of developing the work cooperatively. Instead of one person being responsible for a subject area, all subject areas were shared; decisions on work to be undertaken were made by members of the group; work was allocated to two or three people, working together, to complete.

As well as the slow but steady evolution of this method of working, a complementary change was the move away from information seen as a precis of legislation to that of information as a tool for the use of the interviewer in the bureau. The shift to the problem-solving aspects of information transformed the ability of bureau workers to venture into what many of them had previously seen as difficult or threatening areas of work. For example, the calculation of benefits and the assessment of entitlements became possible through the structured nature of the information as supplied to bureaux.

As part of the development of the Northumberland Advice & Information Project, an Information Officer had been engaged in December 1979 to design a condensed form of the Information Service. This was initially visualised as being for the use of contact persons in the rural areas. In order that he should have sufficient resources for his work, this Information Officer was placed in Central Office, not in Northumberland, and took his place within the existing information department staff. The nature of the project and the fact that he was doing something which had not been attempted before meant that he had to go back to first principles. He did this so successfully that it was not long before the work which he was doing began to affect the ideas which were held about the main Information Service. Unwittingly, in financing the 'Minipack' (as it came to be known) NACAB provided a way of influencing and improving the whole Information Service.

These three things had a combined effect on the information system which made it the powerful and effective tool it now is. A minor, but still important, element was the integration of the local information into the main system – previously the two had been held separately. Contrasting with the pitiful resources available to a bureau in 1966, a bureau twenty years later had in its files 18,000 pages of information, covering more than 900 topics, with an index of 1,200 main and 5,000 sub-headings. Additionally, all bureaux in 1986 had on their shelves a range of reference books, supplied as routine on an annual basis, which complemented the information held in their files.

The system is built on the assumption that the information held in bureaux is as up-to-date as it is physically possible for it to be. Every month the 'pack' as it is called, goes out to all bureaux and outside subscribers which are on the mailing list. Each pack contains information on new aspects of law or administration, together with up-dates on material already held. Although workers are not expected to remember the information contained in the pack each month, it is important that they should at least look through it, if only to note that some factor or other has changed. The better-funded bureaux took to buying second or 'reading' packs for this purpose. This avoided the danger of new information lying about the bureau office rather than being incorporated within the system at the earliest possible moment. It was a great advance when, in 1981, Council was able to give its approval to the supply of reading packs, free of charge, to all member bureaux so that each one, no matter how poor, could file the information as soon as it arrived without depriving the workers of the chance to look through it. Unhappily this concession was withdrawn in 1987 as part of the cost-cutting operation which NACAB was forced to undertake.

A major task which bureaux had always had to grapple with was the indexing of the information. The first improvement which was introduced was the issue of ready-printed index cards to obviate the necessity of bureaux having to compile their own. This, in itself, was an advance but the coming of computers enabled a still greater one to be made by means of the issue of a computerised index in the form of an A4-sized book. This made access to the information simpler than it had been before; it was also regularly amended from the centre.

An important aspect of the work of the information staff has always been the consultancy service. This is offered to bureaux which have failed to find the requisite information in the files they hold and which turn to Central Office, with its enormous bank of information, for help. The consultancy work is done either by telephone or by letter and may involve making enquiries of departments of state, professional bodies, specialist agencies or any number of other sources of authoritative information. In the early years the use of the telephone for consultancy work was almost entirely confined to bureaux in London and the South East, because of the cost of long-distance calls, but with the institution of the Freefone service in 1980 the consultancy became accessible to all bureaux, however remote their position. This resulted in an immediate increase of 50% in the number of calls received. The limitation today is that imposed by the amount of staff time which can be given to answering calls and taking the necessary action arising from them.

It has been said that to stand still is to go backwards and standing still is not an option open to the information staff of NACAB. The pressures on bureaux are reflected back to them and the activities of our legislators ensure that the task of keeping up with the provisions of the law becomes more, rather than less, arduous than it has been in the past. The staff are, in the main, recruited from those who have worked in bureaux and who understand the problems experienced when dealing with that awkward person, the individual who conforms to no statistical average. In their work they are conscious both of the problems of the interviewer who is faced with the client in crisis and of the client's need to come to terms with the world in which he has his being.

Information Retrieval: Evidence to Hand

The second Aim of the Association is

- to exercise a responsible influence on the development of social policies and services, both locally and nationally.

This is the final formulation of a statement first made in 1941, when it took the form

- to collect information on the kind of problems which are at any specific time causing difficulty or distress and to bring such problems to the notice of those who have power to prevent or solve them.

Once again, we have to refer back to Dorothy Keeling to see the origin of the idea that what could be deemed 'secondary action' should arise from the work of Citizens Advice Bureaux. In her autobiography she makes it clear that her commitment to this dated from 1922, when the Personal Service Society 'went so far as to appoint a Statistical Sub-Committee ... "to consider the desirability of collecting and making appropriate use of information on specific points gained through casework"'. As so often happens, good intentions were defeated by lack of resources and by the fact that the disciplines of what she called 'social investigations' lacked attraction for charitable donors. Shrewdly, Miss Keeling puts her finger on the other limiting factor:

the main reason was that 'research' makes little appeal to the average case-worker who is more anxious to get on with the all-absorbing job of setting a family on its feet than to stop and think and take a long view. Indeed a survey which does not lead to practical results is considered by many caseworkers to be a waste of time and money and merely a cause of irritation.

These comments were written in 1961 and remain true in many respects today.

The work of collecting evidence in a systematic way and presenting it to the authorities concerned was thus more honoured in the breach than the observance. That this was so was acknowledged as the reality when a Resolution was passed by the Standing Conference of April 1949. This drew the attention of bureau Organisers and their committees to the importance of using the information gathered in bureaux constructively, and called upon the Central Committee to work out a plan designed 'to develop to its fullest extent this aspect of CAB work'.

Like so many Resolutions which have been passed this one brought almost nothing in the way of results. It was to be many years before money was found for the development of 'this aspect of CAB work'.

This does not mean that the CAB service did not present evidence to many a Royal Commission, Parliamentary committee or other body investigating some issue or other. Reports appear regularly of the submission of evidence papers; what is not said is that the content of such papers was largely anecdotal and, while they often illuminated the subject, they could not contribute evidence which was based on statistical sampling or a scientific formula. There was a consequent tendency for the evidence to be welcomed by the body concerned but for it to be set on one side as incapable of proof.

A more systematic approach was not possible until, in 1977, the first Information Retrieval Officer was appointed to the staff of NACAB. Unfortunately, the initial appointment was tied to funding from the Office of Fair Trading, with the result that the subsequent exercises in information retrieval were almost entirely concerned with consumer matters, such as used cars etc. This was no help in persuading bureaux that IR was a serious subject to which a certain amount of time should be given. In the hustle of the bureau, and the care for clients, the view that IR was 'a waste of time and merely a cause for irritation' was only too widely held. Those who were trying to develop a workable system of IR were not helped by the fact that most bureaux recorded their cases in Daybooks – making the tracing of particular categories arduous, if not impossible – and that for many years such exercises had been conducted retrospectively. For example, bureaux had commonly been asked to specify how many cases of a particular kind they had had in the previous six months. Such a combination of circumstances made the reluctance of bureaux to pursue IR work only too understandable.

The small information retrieval section in Central Office worked hard to change attitudes to their work and, in parallel with the development of systematic information retrieval work, put effort into developing suitable systems of case recording so that the work of the bureaux could be monitored in such a way that emerging trends could be spotted, pressure points recognised early and evidence of particular problems gathered without difficulty. As more bureaux tried out various systems of recording, more became converted to the view that the time of the

Daybook was over. There are problems about the adoption of a national system of case recording but these should be capable of solution.

There is still some way to go before the work which results from the information retrieval section stands as high in public esteem as the other work undertaken by the Association, but already the social policy work which they do has a higher profile than was true in the past. In the words of the 1985/86 Annual Report of the Association

> Ministers, MPs, government departments and local authorities need and ask for this invaluable, independent insight into public opinion. How are people coping with the new benefit? Can people deal with their gas bills? Do people understand legal aid? CAB provides just this information, both in the form of centrally collated reports and by individual CABx talking with their DHSS Office, their MP and their fuel boards. Sometimes policy makers hear things from CAB they may not wish to know, but as an impartial service CAB does not tailor its evidence. CAB simply reports the reality. With improved methods of case recording and the increasing use of computers to store statistics, 'reporting back' will become easier and even more effective.

A Special Initiative: The Classification Research Project

It had been a long-cherished belief of Ms Sanderson that it ought to be possible to standardise the classification of information in such a way that the system was equally applicable to all users of information, whether they were to be found in libraries, professional bodies (such as the Law Society), Neighbourhood Advice Centres or elsewhere. Her position as Head of the Information Department gave her the opportunity to pursue this idea and she succeeded in interesting the British Library in a project to research the possibilities. The British Library agreed to put some money towards the research for three years, the balance of funding being found by NACAB, and a group of researchers was recruited and began work in 1981.

Research as such was a new departure for NACAB and the protocol for the project was an ambitious one:

> The functions of the new classification scheme will be to:
> – determine the order of information in documents and the order of those documents so as to facilitate the rapid retrieval of that information by the user;
> – provide an index to the classification, in which all the terms likely to be sought by users are present;
> – provide a system for keeping case records by the problem category, and also for the compilation of statistics.

It was recorded during the first year that

> The new scheme will be different from that in current use, in that it will be specifically organised to deal with the type of problems coming into CABx and other advice agencies. In order to achieve this the Project is carrying

out a large amount of fieldwork in bureaux and other agencies. The
fieldwork has taken the form of a case recording exercise in which
bureaux from all areas have participated and which is now being carried
out with other agencies. The main aim of the exercise is to collect actual
cases in order to see what problems and elements of problems occur
together; the second part of the exercise is designed to collect information
on the data needed to answer these problems.

Three years later, the research team was still far from completing the
task it had been given, though the fieldwork had been done and the data
processed, using a computer. No further funds were contributed by the
British Library, but NACAB agreed to continue the project for a further
period, in the hope that it could produce a result which would be of
value, given time. This was probably a mistaken decision; enough work
had been done for it to be clear that the project would be unable to
produce the results which Ms Sanderson had envisaged. To continue it
further was not likely to benefit the Association proportionately to the
amount of money it was costing. The death of hope is always difficult
but has to be faced from time to time; unfortunately, it was not until
1987 that the final decision was taken to close the project and cut the
Association's losses.

Training: Learning the Ropes

It is interesting first to look at some specimen questions, prepared for
the training of CAB workers in 1943, which indicate the expectations
which were placed upon those early workers.

Specimen queries prepared for training purposes:

*Lady, Boardinghouse proprietor. Boardinghouse destroyed by enemy
action. Two temporary residents killed; register destroyed; only known
particulars are place of residence (Weston-super-Mare); man local official;
second body female. All personal property destroyed, also property of
twelve boarders. House own property.*
'How can I inform relatives of casualties? Do I claim compensation on
behalf of boarders? Am I legally responsible?'

*Woman enquirer – My sister, an Austrian refugee, came here yesterday for
an interview for a post, I do not know with whom.*
'Could you tell me how I could trace whether she is alive or not? I do not
know where she stayed; her name was Katherine Muller, registration
number unknown.'

*Woman enquirer – My husband was killed in last night's raid; house also
slightly damaged, my brother and sister-in-law, living next door, were also
killed.*
'Can I get any help towards burial costs of husband, brother and sister-in-
law? What can I do about repairing my house? I am heir to my brother's
estate. Should I take any action about his destroyed house (his own
property and furniture) with regard to compensation?'

Male enquirer – I was staying at the 'Riviera Hotel' which was bombed last night. I have lost my note case (all my money except 3/6d in change), my identity card, my gas mask, my ration book, my clothing coupons and my petrol coupons (E coupons). I have only the clothes I stand up in and have only thin pyjamas underneath and am finding it chilly.
'What can I do about my lost property? Can I get a message to my wife in Swansea to reassure her?'

Woman enquirer – My house was badly damaged last night and I have nowhere to live. The Rest Centre is most unsympathetic. I have salvaged my cat, parrot and two dogs but she will not let me take them to the Rest Centre.
'What can I do about accommodation until my house is repaired? What can I do about my pets?'

Soldier – I am home on leave and I have found my house totally destroyed. There is no trace of my family on the Casualty List. I think they had an arrangement with the WVS to go somewhere else if the house was damaged.
'I have only got 48 hours and am going to find them even if I overstay. Can you help me?'

These examples illustrate why it was felt necessary for those who advised after raids to be specially selected and trained. Clearly, they needed resourcefulness and level-headedness as well as knowledge of all the regulations which might apply and the services available to the civilian population.

Such knowledge became redundant with the coming of peace but new things had to be learnt if the public was to be helped. Consequently, throughout the history of the CAB service, lip-service has always been paid to the concept of training for all workers but what this meant in practice, as has been shown, was often very different. An extract from a speech made by a bureau Chairman in 1960 illustrates a low estimate of what was needed which was typical of the time. After referring to the need for 'intensive' training she continues:

> The National Citizens Advice Bureau Committee is alive to this and helps the Bureau in many ways. It publishes the Citizens Advice Notes, with supplements and cancellations every three months. Every month it issues Circulars and, in the case of especially complicated Government regulations, a full explanation. Conferences are held regularly, with talks by members of the government department concerned. Every second year there is a two day national standing conference. As you see, we are kept up to date in new legislation.

Even allowing for the fact that the legislative programme of the 1950s was not as packed as it became later, this hardly seems to bring the process within the definition 'intensive' training. Indeed, the whole concept of training, as held at the time, was limited to instruction. Trainees were lectured to; the training day or the residential conference was organised on the assumption that if one person from each bureau attended the knowledge would somehow or other, by a process resembling osmosis, be passed to all the other workers in the bureau – in spite of the fact that the volunteers seldom met together as a group and, in far too many cases, had no programme of workers' meetings which they were expected to attend.

Even had the thinking been different, it is doubtful whether much could have been done to improve matters, given that resources were minimal. For example in 1964 the Board of Trade training grant comprised '£30 per region allocated for subsidies to residential or other training courses, with £10–£15 per region for travelling subsidies and a balance of £50–£75 held over for contingencies'.

Parallel with concern about training which began to develop from the early 1960s onwards was the question of a possible qualification in advice work, first put forward as a suggestion by the training group of the London Regional Advisory Committee. Once again, this could be seen as a divisive issue when related to the full-time professional worker as against the volunteer. Consequently Council took the view that while a formal qualification might be 'an encouragement to many bureau workers to achieve higher standards, any suggestion of its being imposed as a necessary condition of bureau work would endanger the voluntary principle of CAB'. Though the question of a formal qualification was dropped for the time being, plans went ahead for a special course for experienced CAB workers to begin in the autumn of 1969 at the North-Western Polytechnic of London. The course was to become a regular event for a number of years, at various venues, and proved both valuable and popular with those who attended it, both Organisers and advice workers.

The first post-graduate diploma course in Advice and Information Studies began at the North East London Polytechnic in October 1975. The course was attended by bureau staff and by people from outside the CAB service. It proved to be rigorous, demanding and 'completely worthwhile'. It gave the students time for study and thought about their own work and futures as well as gaining their diplomas. The problem which developed later was that it became difficult to persuade sufficient bureaux and other agencies to release staff to attend the courses, so that in the end they were discontinued through lack of support. Some people still believe that there should be a proper professional qualification for advice and information work but at the time of writing this has not yet become a practical possibility.

In the mainstream of the life of the Association a more general pattern of development was continuing. A national Training Committee was set up in 1973 and one of its first duties was that of advising on the appointment of the first national Training Officer. It was planned that, later, a consultative group would be assembled to advise the Committee and Council and to support and assist the Training Officer.

The Committee met for the first time on 3 October 1973 and established that it would have overall responsibility to Council for:

- the expenditure of available training funds
- the content of training
- the method of training
- the recruitment and remuneration of experienced CAB workers involved in training.

The Training Officer worked with the Committee and with the Training Officers from the centres in London, South Wales, Manchester, Liverpool and Leeds, to develop a strategy for the service as a whole.

The Development Grant made it possible from 1974 onwards to begin to construct a training network, the first step towards which was the selection and training of panels of tutors in every Area. This was followed in 1976 by the appointment of part-time Course Organisers, responsible for arranging and coordinating training courses in the Areas. The final step of appointing Training Officers in all the Areas was achieved in 1980, by which time there were, in some Areas, Assistant Training Officers as well.

In Central Office the training staff became more specialised, starting with the appointment in 1976 of a Learning Resources Officer, again someone with experience of bureau work, whose prime responsibility was the development of new training materials and methods. New ground was broken by a group comprising workers (Organisers, tutors and advice workers) from bureaux working with the LRO to draft, pilot and evaluate a number of Self-Instructor packs. These first packs covered the subjects of 'Helping your Client', 'Appropriate Action', 'Unfair Dismissal' and 'Using Reference Books'. Work was put into the development of a correspondence course covering the national Basic Training course and another on Money Problems. A different kind of innovation was the publication of a newsletter – 'CABLE' – designed to keep the tutors and trainers in touch with developments in training, training materials and issues of principle and practice.

The work of the training staff in the Areas and in Central Office, together with that of the Training Committee and the Learning Resources Working Group, involved the Association in the examination and review of all aspects of training. The work done in these groups was an expression of wide concern and constant debate. For instance, a small consultative group in GLCABS produced in 1976 a paper 'Towards a Training Policy' which restated belief in the importance of training and emphasised the crucial fact that training should be a continuing process for all bureau staff. Recommendations were made relating to the minimum commitment to training which should be required of staff, whether paid or voluntary, in the first and subsequent years of their career in the service.

Just as the examination of the work of the information staff had led to a re-think, so the discussion throughout the Association shifted the focus of training away from the transmission of facts and towards the development of skill training. More and more of the materials produced by the Training Department were concerned with active, rather than passive, learning. Such things as graded case studies, a film 'Take my Advice', to be used in interviewing training, training kits designed to equip workers to cope with particular areas of work, for example 'Changes in Housing Benefit', together with an ever-extended range of Self-Instructors and specialised Handbooks, changed the face of training. The amount of time and resources committed to the training and re-training of new entrants, experienced workers, Organisers and members of management committees expanded year by year.

An element in the training situation is that of timing. There had been many occasions over the years when new legislation had come into effect and new information items had been issued to bureaux in explanation of that legislation but the material for training the inter-viewing staff in bureaux on the application of the legislation to the client's situation had not been produced on the same timescale. Both the information staff and the training staff became much more sensitive to the need for coordination of effort, so that bureaux were fully armed in advance to deal with problems as they arose. It was partly the realisation of the importance of the integration of their programmes which led to the grouping together of Information and Training into one of the Divisions of NACAB which were set up as a result of the management review undertaken under the Chairmanship of Sir Douglas Lovelock.

The training programme of a typical bureau – Durham City CAB – serving the city and its rural area, dealing with 12,500 enquiries in 1987/88, as reported in its Annual Report, gives an idea of the amount of time volunteers are asked to set aside for this activity. The Bureau Manager writes:

We had a variety of speakers at our Workers' Meetings – from Housing Aid, from the Gas Consumers' Council, from the Business School and from CRUSE. Training Course days were also attended to cover

Aids	The new Insolvency Act
Money Advice	Debt and the County Court
Counselling	Racism Awareness
Managing change	Time Management

Visits were made to the DHSS, County and Magistrates' Courts.

However, the main thrust of our training was in the field of Social Security – refresher courses on the existing system and information courses on the April 11th changes. These have varied from 2 hour sessions to 2 day Courses. On average each worker has had over 25 hours training in this subject area, as well as reading materials and training packs that have been taken home to study. This time, along with that spent in the Bureau each week (at least 6 hours), was given on a voluntary basis.

The bureau has over thirty voluntary interviewers, supported by paid staff (some only part-time) comprising four clerical workers, a Tribunal Assistant and the Bureau Manager.

A comparatively light-hearted account by a trainee of what it is like to join the CAB service as a volunteer in the late 1980s gives an insight into the reality of induction and training in the average bureau.

MYTH AND REALITY – A TRAINEE'S VIEW OF THE CAB

When I applied to do voluntary work with the CAB, I knew very little about the organisation. I was unemployed and wanted to do something useful with my free time and something of benefit to my community. I had been to the CAB twice before with questions of my own and knew they gave information to help people sort out their problems. I am a qualified librarian and therefore I felt I had information skills to offer the CAB.

MYTH: That I could start the following week and deal with enquiries.

REALITY: Before I could start I had to go through a selection interview and provide references. Before I was able to interview clients on my own, I had to attend a training course, one day a week for 11 weeks and I had to attend the Bureau one day a week to observe interviews etc. In fact the professional approach of CAB to both selection and training altered my perception of work with them from the idea that it would fill in a few hours a week to the realisation that it was a qualified demanding job that just happened to be unpaid!

MYTH: That the CAB provides people with pamphlets or regurgitates precis of written information. Obviously such a service is needed.

REALITY: CAB workers also deal directly with clients' problems, e.g. write letters or make phone calls for them, represent them at tribunals and in departments etc. on their behalf, provide a sympathetic, neutral listener etc. In fact anything within reason that the clients need to solve their problems. However, in all these activities it is the client who directs and decides not the worker.

MYTH: That the CAB is staffed by middle-class, middle-aged women.

REALITY: CAB workers come from a wide range of backgrounds, experiences and age groups, and both sexes are represented.

The reality is that working for the CAB is demanding in skills, knowledge and time.

A wide range of skills is required from a CAB worker. Certainly my librarianship proved very useful in looking up information for clients. However, personal and communication skills were even more important. In dealing with a client we must first establish a rapport with them. Then finding out about their problems, without either sounding like an interrogator or missing important details. We must always be alert for any verbal or non-verbal clues from the client to help in the interview. Then the information needed by the client, often very complicated details, particularly about benefits and legal rights, must be interpreted and communicated. We have to try and ensure that the client goes away satisfied with the service and confident in handling the information provided. Communication skills are not only needed for talking with clients. Often clients want the CAB worker to negotiate on their behalf.

When we go to the next client in the queue we must be prepared to deal with anything, though most enquiries fall into social security, employment, consumer and financial categories. CAB is a generalist, not a specialist advice agency. The National Association of CAB's provides detailed information packs on all potential queries, classified and indexed for retrieval. Expertise in using this database is essential and my librarian skills are very useful in that respect. However, as the areas covered are so complex, particularly social security and employment, experience and practice are also necessary. It needs a few years' experience before a worker starts to feel on top of this material. But even experienced workers are wary of becoming over-confident as the information is continually updated in line with changes in laws, regulations etc.

CAB work is time consuming. When in the Bureau we have to deal with the client's enquiry no matter how long it takes. Often queues of people are waiting to be seen and some problems, particularly those involving social security or debt, require more than one interview to reach a satisfactory conclusion. All enquiries are recorded on case sheets so that another worker can help the client if they return and to provide evidence and statistics on the work of the CAB. Training is a continuous process requiring attendance at courses and workers' meetings and reading newsletters, information packs etc.

With all this reality you may wonder why I'm still a CAB trainee! I have found working for the CAB very interesting and rewarding. We are continually being required to learn new topics or gain new skills. Much of what we learn is not only of use to clients but also benefits us in our own lives eg finding out about rights we didn't know we had or pitfalls we should beware of. The other CAB workers are supportive, committed and very interesting to talk to. We are providing a very necessary service and working for an organisation with a huge degree of professionalism and integrity.

The distance which has been travelled from the day when 'the volunteer worker was just expected to get on with helping clients, with the aid of a few notices on the walls and a small number of files without index cards' to the carefully structured and monitored progress of a new trainee entering the CAB service today is immense but nothing stands still and the training staff of NACAB and the bureaux do not relax from the task of constantly reviewing and renewing training materials and practices.

Specialists and Special Units

The story of the association of specialist advisers with the CAB service is extremely detailed and complicated. Leaving aside the relationship between the bureaux and the legal profession, there has been a continuing dialogue with all manner of professional advisers and working arrangements have been set up under all kinds of local agreements, official and unofficial, at different times. To present a coherent account of these arrangements would take up a lot of space and it will therefore not be attempted.

Specialists have been defined in different ways at different times. The retired Tax Inspector on the staff of a bureau was often the 'specialist' Tax adviser for that bureau, while a practising Surveyor attending under a Surveyors' Voluntary Aid Scheme was similarly the 'specialist' – boundaries tend to become blurred and confusing.

The first specialist units which were opened under the aegis of the CAB service were the Consumer Advice Centres opened by Edinburgh and by Watford in 1974. Each was closely linked with the parent bureau but the effect which these and other such centres had on the service as a whole was limited.

A few consumer advisers were employed in bureaux but the expansion of services to the public as a result of these developments in consumer work was strictly limited. Because of the contribution which it has made to the development of the CAB service as a whole, the Wolverhampton Tribunal Representation Unit occupies a position which is different in kind from any other. The decision to go ahead with the establishment of this Unit was to have radical long-term effects on the development of the service the bureaux could offer their clients.

Most new initiatives in the CAB service arise directly from the experience of bureaux, which identify gaps, uncover new needs or decide upon a new approach to old ones. The TRU project began rather differently.

In the early 1970s there had been some consideration of the possibility of providing a lay advocacy service at Social Security Tribunals through the use of bureau workers. During 1975 the Lord Chancellor's office discussed the possibility with NACAB and suggested that an application could be put forward for funding under the EEC's 'Anti-Poverty Programme'. This was a modest two-year programme of both action projects and research studies. The action projects were to be 'pilot' projects, so the NACAB proposal of a project which would break new ground in its approach to Supplementary Benefit Appeal Tribunals and National Insurance Local Tribunals, fulfilled the criteria laid down by the European Commission.

Once a decision had been made to go ahead with an application, a further decision had to be made as to the nature of the project. It was decided that this should take the form of a Support Unit, acting as a second-tier agency working with a group of CABx to foster the ability of the bureaux staff to develop skills of advocacy. With the support of the government, an application was made to the EEC and funding was granted for the project.

It was decided to place the Project in the West Midlands Area and a group of bureaux was selected for it to work with. These bureaux were representative of a variety of catchment areas, from the intensely urban, through the suburban and the new town to the purely rural. The bureaux varied in size and competence, and from the old-established to the relatively new. The concept of the work of the Unit was that it would work directly with them to produce a generation of bureau workers capable of undertaking advocacy work for their clients.

The Project began work in 1976 and almost at once began to uncover a situation which had previously been hidden. This was the fact that although bureaux were registering a national percentage enquiry rate for Social Security problems of 7.5%, this was a false perspective, in that many bureau workers were failing to identify problems and to follow them through. An example taken from the Report of the Project illustrates what this could mean:

> Mr A was a middle-aged man who came into a bureau for advice. One of the unit workers was 'sitting in' on the interview he had with the volunteer worker. Mr A told the worker that he was having difficulty managing his money. He had not worked for some time because of various illnesses, especially bronchitis. His immediate problem was clothing for his wife and children. Having established that Mr A was on Supplementary Benefit, the volunteer suggested that he approach the Women's Royal Voluntary Service who ran a second-hand clothes depot, and her organiser agreed to arrange an appointment for him to go. It was also suggested that the bureau could contact Social Services to see if a social worker would visit to help the family budget on their scarce resources.
>
> *In practice, this could not be classified as 'wrong' advice as such. It was more inappropriate and shallow advice based on a failure to conduct an extensive enough interview and a general lack of knowledge of how Supplementary Benefit worked as a 'safety net' provision.*
>
> On further interview the unit worker found that the family were budgeting remarkably well on the limited resources available. The problem was that they were existing considerably below the poverty level because of Mr A's failure to claim benefit that he was entitled to but unaware of. The family lived in a difficult-to-heat, damp, terraced house which aggravated Mr A's bronchitis. He had been unaware that he could claim a weekly exceptional circumstances addition to his Supplementary Benefit because of this. It also emerged that his wife was diabetic and he had also been unaware that a similar weekly addition could be claimed to help with the cost of the special diet necessary. Although he had been on Supplementary Benefit for three years, he had never claimed an exceptional needs payment for clothing even though his stocks were very low.
>
> *When the Department of Health and Social Security were advised of the situation, a visiting officer ordered a payment for clothing and the local office awarded the additions for heating and diet, together with a back payment.*

The Report further comments: 'The concern with the quality of advice therefore, was not so much that there was a great deal of wrong advice as such being given, it was rather that much of it was possibly ineffectual or inappropriate advice that did not necessarily improve the financial situation of the claimant.'

The harsh facts to be faced were that many bureau workers were insufficiently aware (i) of the need to follow through all aspects of an interview and (ii) of the application of the provisions of the Social Security system in all its aspects. The Project team realised that it would have to take one step back and begin, not with advocacy as had been planned, but with an exercise in heightening the awareness of the interviewing staff. Quite apart from anything else, it was unlikely that workers would identify the possibility of an appeal to a Tribunal unless they understood the basis of a decision which had been made within the rules. A further discovery to be faced was that, despite the Association's Principle of Impartiality, it was hard to wean some workers from the unadmitted view that those on Supplementary Benefit were the 'undeserving' poor.

In the light of what was discovered the Project's goals were revised, so that the primary goals were identified as:

- to equip the generalist workers within the bureaux with the skills necessary to identify benefit problems
- to equip those same workers with the ability to inform, advise and effectively intervene on behalf of their clients to maximise their income as far as possible
- to enable all the bureaux to have the capacity to represent those appellants and potential appellants to Social Security Tribunals who sought its representation services, and
- to encourage poor people with Social Security problems to use the services of the CAB.

The Unit began to construct new training initiatives which reflected their goals and as these developed they became increasingly important nationally, so that by the end of 1979 training courses had been held in all the NACAB Areas. 'The idea behind these courses was to plant the seed for others to develop further initiatives and, following on from the courses, tribunal units were planned in Greater Manchester and Devon & Cornwall. Not only did this training programme enable the Unit workers to contribute to developments elsewhere, it also enabled them to gain a broader picture of the CAB and its level of development.'

Also thrown up by the activities of the Project workers was the discovery that the information being provided to bureaux on Social Security matters was inadequate. It was not fair to criticise workers for their lack of expertise in this area of work if the training which they had received was minimal and the information which they were using was insufficiently comprehensive and not well enough organised for workers to be able to use it with confidence. Difficulties within NACAB's Information Department led to the Project taking responsibility for producing a series of guides and a quarterly bulletin which was made available to outside agencies as well as to bureaux. The effects of the training programme, the improved information produced by the Project and the sharpened awareness of the plight of some Social Security claimants was to change the climate of opinion very widely through the CAB service.

By March 1980 Social Security enquiries had risen nationally from the 6.2% of 1976 to 8.5%; by 1984 the figure was 15.3% and by 1988 24.4%. This last figure demonstrates not only the level of hardship being experienced by many people but also the ability of the bureaux to deal with the consequences of that hardship. Without the pioneering work of the TRU, the bureaux would probably have taken a great deal longer to come to grips with the problems of income maintenance. Without that work it is quite certain that the Tribunal Representation work at present being undertaken by individual workers in bureaux and in Tribunal Representation Units would never have been tackled and countless citizens would be much worse off as a result. The TRU proved its value in examining the strengths and weaknesses of the generalist service of CABx when confronted with the problems of poor people enmeshed in the Social Security system and, as a result of its work, the whole service moved forward and became more active and competent in handling enquiries which came into this category.

One result of the increased awareness of need was that the appointment of Welfare Rights Officers in bureaux became steadily more widespread, as did the involvement of bureaux in 'Take Up' Campaigns, designed to alert the public to the provisions under Social Security legislation to which they were entitled. Some of these initiatives were funded directly by the local authority; others were achieved by means of various government schemes, such as Urban Aid or the Community Programme. The great disadvantage of short-term funding of this nature is that the employment of a specialist in a bureau tends to raise the expectations of the clientele; once funding is withdrawn the bureau is left with the problem of continuing a service which has become expected of it.

Perhaps the most significant specialist development which next occurred was that of Money Advice and Debt Counselling. Unlike the conception of the Wolverhampton Project, which was imposed from above, the initiatives in this field were taken by those who were faced with intractable difficulties and who felt the need to develop ways in which to address those difficulties. In the early 1980s the Birmingham Settlement opened a Money Advice Centre and it subsequently co-operated with the NACAB West Midlands Area to establish the West Midlands Money Advice Development Project. Similarly, the New Cross Money Advice Service was at work in London, and money advice specialists began to be appointed to work in bureaux in many parts of the country. By 1982 the Merseyside, North East and Yorks/Humberside Areas of NACAB had money advice units providing casework, consultancy and training support. These new units profited by the experience gained by the Wolverhampton Project and were able to avoid some of the difficulties experienced by it.

The number of specialist support units and the type of work which they undertake varies from year to year but the value which such units have as a back-up for the generalist service has been proved beyond all doubt. So, too, has the value of specialist workers placed in bureaux and available to help both the workers in that bureau and the clients who seek help.

The Chapeltown (Leeds) CAB is a bureau which has appointed specialists to its staff in order to meet the needs of its surrounding community. The Annual Report of 1987/88 lists a staff of 47 volunteers, supported by the paid staff of Organiser, two Deputy Organisers and the administrative staff, plus the following specialist workers:

- Asian Rights Worker
- Interpreter Welfare Rights Worker
- Consumer Worker
- Debt Worker
- Disability Worker
- Housing Worker
- Interviewer/Interpreter
- Tribunal Assistance Unit × 4

Chapeltown is not the only bureau which has so shaped its services to the local community; it is quoted as an exemplar of what can be done to develop beyond the purely generalist approach.

CHAPTER SEVEN

Other Aspects of Bureau Work

The Rural Scene

As early as 1942 anxieties about delivering a CAB service in rural areas were being expressed. Village contact people were established from time to time but there was general awareness that the country people were being neglected and deprived of access to any source of reliable information.

Twelve years later there were discussions with the Rural Community Councils about the possible use of mobile bureaux or the formalising of links with the traditional advisers in the villages. RCCs expressed interest in developing services and, in particular, in taking part in a process of identification of possible 'people of goodwill' on whom some sort of network might be based. It was suggested that the CAB department could make its experience available to the RCCs to assist them in this enterprise.

In practice nothing much happened and it is somewhat depressing to realise that early in 1982 it was estimated that there were still something like four million people in the rural areas who had no access to a Citizens Advice Bureau. The problem of the rural areas remained largely unresolved.

An early initiative was funded by the Carnegie Trust which in 1957 allocated £5,000 'over the next five years, for experimental rural advisory schemes'. Of this sum £750 was to be at the disposal of CAB headquarters for aiding small schemes and the remainder was already allocated to schemes approved by the Trustees. By the standards of the time, this was quite generous funding but it did not have noticeably lasting results.

The 1966/68 Report of the National Citizens Advice Bureaux Council outlines the position:

> The extension of the CAB Service to rural areas continues to be a subject of much concern to the Council, who hope that more efforts will be made at local level to put into practice some of the lessons already learned from

the experiments of some years ago. Further experiments are now being tried under the surveillance of headquarters and the results will be made available as soon as they can be assessed. The latest experiment is the launching of a mobile service based on the Braintree CAB. With the support of the Essex Community Council, which provided a capital sum for the purchase of a caravan, grants from six local authorities, and a contribution from the rural development fund of the CAB Council, the mobile bureau was officially set on its course by Sir John Wolfenden on 15th March 1968. Fully equipped with a complete set of information and reference material it is manned by trained workers from the Braintree CAB and makes regular visits to publicised points in six neighbouring small towns.

The three experiments which were announced in the last report, planned in conjunction with the GPO in Bedford, Ulverston and Wellington (Salop), were reviewed after fifteen months. These schemes were based on co-operation with sub-postmasters and postmen in surrounding villages through whom reply paid letters could be obtained to facilitate communication with the bureaux which, in suitable cases, would arrange home visits.

It was felt that the experiments had been useful and had helped to publicise the bureau service. They had however entailed a good deal more effort than had been anticipated on the part of the organisers – to all three of whom the thanks of the Council are due. Their efforts have underlined the four most important aspects of rural extension work; publicity, relationships with the leaders of village life, mobility of workers and sheer hard work on the part of the CAB people concerned.

The Braintree Mobile, which was a specially converted van, operated for nine years, during which it was used by 6,722 callers. The initial idea had been that it would visit a number of the large villages/small towns of Essex and establish the needs of each community. Places which were part of the programme included Witham, Halstead, Coggeshall, Dunmow, Thaxted, Sible Hedingham, Stansted and Saffron Walden. Of these, two, namely Witham and Saffron Walden, came to have their own bureaux, while Halstead (later an independent bureau) became an extension of Braintree.

Though not the first Mobile bureau – there had been a total of four operating during the war, and a 'Mobile CAB van' is reported as having been used as part of the Rural Scheme in North Staffordshire in 1962 – the Braintree Mobile seems to have been the first properly equipped, purpose-built Mobile to have been used. Running it proved to have inherent problems and the first Organiser of the service often had difficulties over manning it. At least two people were needed, one of whom must be a driver; if the driver was not a bureau interviewer he or she had to absent themself while the interviews took place. Even if the driver was a member of the interviewing staff there were still problems about space and confidentiality. For the interviewers the winter months were something of an endurance test. A small heater gave token warmth but to sit in the Mobile for several hours in cold weather was a chilling experience!

The first purpose-built mobile bureau, operating from Braintree, Essex.

*Work on the telephone is **unending**.*

The Braintree experiment proved that a Mobile was of some use in developing a service to small towns/large villages but it also proved to be an expensive way of delivering that service. It was A solution, not THE solution to the problem of extending services to rural communities.

The next innovation was the establishment in the autumn of 1975 of the East Devon peripatetic service. This was designed to bring an advice service to six towns and villages in East Devon through the medium of a mobile Organiser, who carried the information system in his car to locations in each place. A small group of volunteers was recruited in each location to work with the Organiser. The adminstrative work and correspondence was done at the Organiser's home. The Organiser also undertook a programme of home visits.

The experiment ran on these lines for a number of years but gradually evolved into something more like a standard bureau, in that it is now based on a full-time bureau in Honiton, with staff who move between it and four other centres. The Organiser still visits the outlets in the various places but the undertaking is not now so very different from any bureau with a number of extension outlets.

It was in 1977 that the National Consumer Council began to take an active interest in the promotion of rural services by establishing the Rural Advice Monitoring and Promotion Project in order to investigate the problems of providing advice and information to dispersed rural populations. NACAB was represented on the Steering Committee of the Project and worked closely with it, providing information out of its experience for inclusion in the final Report, 'The Right to Know'.

The present County of Northumberland had long been a wasteland as far as bureaux were concerned. Between Tyne & Wear and Scotland there was nothing. The Secretary of the Community Council lobbied NACAB about the situation for many years, but since the local authorities were both poor and unresponsive, action proved impossible until the decision was taken in 1975 to sacrifice one of the posts attached to the North East Area Office of NACAB and transfer it to Northumberland for development purposes. The Northumberland CC and NACAB then set up the Northumberland Advice & Information Project on the basis that NACAB would provide the member of staff and the NCC the accommodation and administrative support. A full-time Organiser was appointed to take charge of the Project. Her tasks were, first, to investigate the situation and, second, to establish a Rural Citizens Advice Bureau for the county. As one of the stages in this process a part-time research worker was engaged to carry out an investigation into the information and advice needs of a remote community. Out of this piece of research came the valuable information that, as had always been believed by the CAB service, though not necessarily by others, the rural population had just as many problems – though some were of a different nature – as people in suburban or city areas. It also pointed up the fact that, given access to competent advice, many of these problems could be at least alleviated.

The initial Project had been for three years but the work it was doing was clearly of such value that its life was extended. The first Organiser recruited and trained a group of village contact people and compiled a dossier of information material for their use. To back up her work an Information Officer was appointed in 1979, charged with the task of taking her dossier as a starting point and then progressing to the development of a Basic Information Pack, capable of use by the village contact people. Later there was a further appointment of a part-time trainer working with them to produce a Basic Information Training Pack. This was first produced in 1983 and proved of great value to a number of disparate groups (such as workers recruited on short-term 'Take-Up Campaigns'), who needed to familiarise themselves with the Basic Information Pack. It was also used for the initial training of ordinary CAB workers in some areas until it was discontinued in 1987.

The original concept of the Rural Citizens Advice Bureau had contained the elements of a skilled and experienced Organiser giving advice by telephone at certain times of the day, supplemented by village contact people and by home visits made by the Organiser. The built-in problems of this set-up eventually led to the return to 'conventional' bureaux. One of the many valuable things which the Project achieved was convincing the local authorities of the need for a service, with the result that bureaux were later established at Alnwick, Blyth, Hexham, Morpeth and Ashington; these bureaux also run a further six extension outlets. The final outcome of the Project was thus somewhat different from what had been envisaged at the start. It did, however, make possible developments in the County of Northumberland which went some way at least to meet the criticisms which had been levelled at NACAB over the years and provided, for the first time, a service for many of the people of that sparsely populated county.

In 1982 a Conference on Rural Advice and Information was jointly sponsored by NACAB and the Rural Department of the NCVO. This drew together examples of information work (and information technology), many on a small scale, local basis, which was being done (or utilised) in various parts of the country. The Conference was well attended and out of its deliberations came the Rural Advice and Information Committee, serviced by the Rural Department of the NCVO, drawn from a variety of agencies, including NACAB. The Committee met over nearly two years and, as well as its final Report, it produced and distributed a 'Briefing Pack' designed for Parish Councillors,and developed liaison with MPs and others interested in the welfare of the rural population.

Other initiatives taken over the years included the South Molton Project (developed in co-operation with the Devon Library Service); the Norfolk Rural Advice & Information Project, the Cumbria Rural Bureau and the Freefone service in East Anglia. Starting from a limited base, this last was extended progressively to cover more of the East Anglian counties and proved of value in providing a means of access for people living in isolation.

Perhaps the most significant development, apart from the Basic Information Pack, was the microfiche system produced by Royston CAB. The Management Committee of Royston believed that it should be possible to put the entire information system on to microfiche so that, with a small portable reader, it could be taken to the villages of rural Hertfordshire which Royston was trying to serve. With financial backing from NACAB, Royston embarked upon some trials and, once the initial teething problems had been overcome, the idea proved valuable and popular. The technology was simple and unfrightening; workers could master its use in a short time and the total equipment was no bigger than a large briefcase. It proved to be flexible and appropriate to use in all kinds of situations, not only at sessions in the villages but also in Old People's Homes, libraries, hospitals, community centres and prisons – the possibilities are infinite.

A significant advance for the rural areas was the designation of the Rural Development Areas, which opened the door to some additional funding in a way similar to what had resulted from the Urban Aid Programme in the cities. Both the local authorities and the Development Commission were able to take a more positive attitude as a result and in 1986 the Development Commission and NACAB each put £50,000 into jointly funded initiatives which attracted local authority funding in Cornwall, Lincolnshire, County Durham, Norfolk, Suffolk, West Cheshire, South Humberside and the Forest of Dean. Another Development Commission contribution was the funding of the Cornwall Money Advice and Welfare Information Project.

The difficulties of supplying a personal service to people living in small communities are not easily overcome but the CAB service has, over the years, made concerted efforts to tackle them. A variety of approaches have been tried – none of them ideal. Some prove, like the mobile services, to be excessively expensive, others, like village contact schemes, to be ineffective. It may be that eventually new technology will contain the answer; for the time being experiment will continue and every effort possible will be made to serve the country people as adequately as those in the towns.

The CAB Service and the Legal Profession

Some of the first CABx had access to legal services. Cambridge House in Camberwell has been cited and there were others which either employed a lawyer themselves or made use of volunteer lawyers attending at intervals to help the clients of the Settlement or the associated bureau. There are also many references in the early accounts to Poor

Bureaux now work cooperatively with other agencies.

The microfiche system in use.

Man's Lawyer services. It is impossible to know at this stage how effective these services were for those who needed them. The suspicion is that they were of limited use.

As for the legal profession itself, there is little doubt that the opinion among solicitors was that the bureaux had better be careful not to stray into giving any kind of legal advice. There was for many years a piece of paper which was supplied to all bureaux as they opened, warning against the danger of purporting to give legal advice or acting as a solicitor. This made many bureau workers nervous and contributed to the feeling that there was an almost mystical character in the law as a profession. Contrasting with this deferential attitude towards lawyers, there was – often in the same person and at the same time – a strong feeling that many lawyers were not really much use. The reasons for this second, gut reaction were rooted in two facts (i) the number of complaints made about the inefficiency or sluggardy of solicitors (some of which complaints were undoubtedly justified) and (ii) the lack of knowledge shown by many solicitors of the areas of law which impinged most painfully upon the clients coming into bureaux, for example housing law.

It became clear that there was need for a dialogue between the CAB service and the legal profession as a whole. The Law Society, like the CAB service, has both its local and its national bodies and it was necessary for them to talk to each other at the appropriate levels.

The concept of the Legal Services Group of NACAB was an interesting one, in that it provided not only a forum within which the CAB service could meet with the different arms of the law but also one in which those who represented them could talk to each other. The membership has varied over the years: for example, that of 1972 included five members drawn from CABx, two from the Legal Action Group, three from the Bar Council, two from the Law Society, one from the Child Poverty Action Group, one from the Citizens' Rights Office, two from the Lord Chancellor's Office, one each from the Societies of Labour and Conservative Lawyers, one from the Birmingham University Faculty of Law, two from GLCABS staff and four from NACAB staff. At various times there has been representation from the Law Society of Scotland; the Criminal Justice Department, Home Office; the Westminster Small Claims Court; the Law Centres Working Group; the Manchester Legal Services Committee; the National Consumer Council; and the Law Centres Federation, plus a number of solicitors in private practice and various academic lawyers. The great value of the group to the CAB service has been that of the duality of the legal expertise round the table and the experience of the CAB element. Thus a debate which tends to become somewhat divorced from practicalities is often brought back from academic theorising by the contribution of the bureaux representatives on the lines of 'but what actually happens is . . .'. The lawyers contribute to the understanding of the legal situation; the bureaux people make many of the lawyers aware of aspects of the legal system of which they have no personal experience.

In 1977, in order to prepare its evidence to the Royal Commission on Legal Services, NACAB carried out a Legal Services Survey which came up with a result which surprised many bureau workers into thinking again about the work they did. It showed that at least one-third of enquiries contained a legal element and that more than half of these were answered by bureau workers themselves without further referral.

A later summary of the situation was that

> More people with legal problems go to Citizens Advice Bureaux than to any other advice service. They go because a legal question can be cleared up at once in a bureau if it is simple and straightforward, and if it is not, the bureau will know where expert help can be obtained. Lay advisers in CABx are trained to spot legal problems, to know how far they can go in explaining the law and legal procedures and at what point the lawyer's expertise must be brought in. The adviser knows what sort of legal help is available in the vicinity of the bureau and in still a very few, but a slowly increasing number of bureaux, there is either a full-time solicitor colleague who can be consulted on the spot, or there is a law centre linked with the CAB.
>
> There is a long tradition of lawyers involving themselves in the provision of legal services for the poor. Many of today's eminent lawyers have contributed to voluntary legal advice sessions in CAB and have themselves learned at first hand something about the problems of poor people and the way in which the law and the legal system can help them.

A crucial stage in the development of relations with the legal profession was the establishment of Rota Schemes. The withdrawal of the Voluntary Legal Aid Scheme had left the bureaux with a need to establish a source of legal help for their clients. It was hoped that it would be possible to persuade the Law Society to introduce a national scheme which would enable a general waiver of the practice rules to be issued. Once a waiver had been granted all solicitors would then be free to undertake voluntary sessions within bureaux and take any resulting cases back to their offices. This proved impossible to arrange and led to the Area Officers being given the task of negotiating with their local Law Societies to set up schemes; each of these then had to obtain a waiver from the national Law Society.

Rota Schemes were introduced on the basis that all solicitors in a local Law Society were invited to put their names on a list of those attending in turn at a bureau to give voluntary legal advice to clients referred by the bureau workers. The particular value of the solicitor attending in the bureau is that it overcomes the fall-out factor which had been found to be heavy among clients recommended to visit a solicitor, for whom an appointment was made and who then failed to attend.

There were several reasons for this, one being an inherent fear of the law, another being the dread of perhaps becoming liable for higher charges than the client could pay. The idea that costs started clocking up from the moment you walked into a solicitor's office was widely held. Rota Schemes held in bureaux meant that a client could be seen on premises which were already familiar and unthreatening and where he or she had already received help without charge. At about the same time as the Rota Scheme discussions with the Law Society were taking place, others were also going on about the possibility of a replacement for the defunct Voluntary Legal Advice Scheme and, once again, it was the Area Officers who, in 1976, were given the job of trying to negotiate with their local Law Societies a 'fixed fee' scheme which would enable the public to get half an hour of preliminary advice in a solicitor's office for a predictable cost.

While the efforts of the Area Officers enabled an ever-increasing number of bureaux to offer the facility of a Rota Scheme to their clients, progress was slower on the 'fixed fee' front and by the end of 1977 it was reported that only 200 bureaux out of a total of 710 were able to refer enquirers to solicitors for such an interview. The trouble was that, in the absence of a national scheme, these were all at different levels of cost. One scheme might be £2, another £3 or £5. There was no consistency to be found. Fortunately the Law Society acted and the 1978 edition of the Legal Aid Solicitors List introduced a national fixed fee interview scheme, with a standard fee of £5, which meant an end to the previous 'horrible patchwork'.

Setting up Rota Schemes was only the first step towards delivering a satisfactory form of service in the bureaux. There had been a long tradition that the CAB service in no way discriminated between different firms of solicitors. All local firms were included in the lists handed over, or shown, to clients for whom a consultation with a solicitor was being recommended. It behoved the bureau workers to show no preference and make no recommendation. In practice, there were various devices by which bureaux got round the difficulty of being unable to recommend those firms which they knew to be sympathetic and good, such as printing the names and addresses of these at the top of the list, on the premiss that the client would look down the list and choose the first firm which was near their home or in some other way convenient for them and look no further. Sometimes the discrimination was conducted negatively, as for instance

> For all new volunteers there was the problem of learning about the work done by solicitors in the area and how to ensure that the names of those experienced in a particular matter were given to the enquirer. It was seen as wrong to have a list marked 'good' and 'bad' but we felt it essential to have some guide as often a volunteer would have no-one to refer to. We therefore had a coded list – the names to avoid were those marked 'NWB' which, being interpreted, meant 'not with a barge pole! (*Voluntary worker 1960s*)

The problem about recommending or not recommending a particular solicitor or firm of solicitors was very real and one about which both the CAB service and the individual CAB had to think very carefully. Part of the difficulty lay in the fact that, like the CAB service, the solicitor held himself out to be a generalist, able to tackle whatever came through the door. That this was unrealistic the bureaux knew from experience of what their clients reported back to them. Some firms were virtually convey-ancing and will factors – but should it therefore be taken that they would not perform well if a matrimonial problem was referred to them? Perhaps they were simply in the position of not doing matrimonial work because it did not come to them; they could not advertise and attract such work, yet given the chance, might be very good at it. The problem of discrimination was a thorny one from all points of view. The bureaux were trapped between their desire to ensure the best for their clients and the need to take proper cognisance of the rules of the Law Society.

The setting up of Rota Schemes led in some places to there being initially a hundred or more solicitors on the list. There was no way in which a satisfactory relationship could be built up with a solicitor who attended once a year and yet there was a feeling at this time that the work must be fairly shared out so that all firms had a chance of picking up some of the work which arose from the Rota sessions. There were difficulties about firms who thought it sufficient to send one of their Legal Executives along; there were problems about who was to manage the Rota Scheme – the Law Society or the bureau; there were polite battles about the control of the scheme – who was in charge? All these were relationship problems which had to be worked through and in the end the logic of circumstances placed the running of the schemes in the hands of the bureaux. Over time the difficulties were ironed out, including the vexed problem of the integration of records. In the early days of Rota Schemes many lawyers held that bureau workers could not see the casenotes which they compiled during a session, on the grounds of legal confidentiality, but it became increasingly clear that this was a bar to a proper service to clients and one which caused them some puzzlement. If a client had first seen a bureau worker, then a lawyer (also in the bureau), his perception was that he was dealing with the bureau in all aspects of his troubles and if on his return the bureau worker knew nothing of what had transpired between the client and the lawyer it was a cause of frustration and misunderstanding. Equal access to case records was the only solution.

As the years went by the trend was to establish smaller rotas of solicitors who were prepared to work closely with bureaux and who became more familiar with the work of the bureaux and how the services which they gave could be integrated with it.

The publication of the Law Society's Legal Aid Referral List in 1977 was the first step towards the identification of those areas of work covered by firms of solicitors. The 1978 List, introducing the fixed fee scheme, while it gave some information, did not contain the names of individual members of the firm nor did it give any indication of the firm's expertise; it merely gave a list of the categories of work which it would accept. A few years later the new Solicitors Directory came much nearer to meeting the needs of bureaux. It contained most of the information for which the Association had been pressing over the years and the underlying attitude which led to its compilation was very different from that held by the Law Society earlier in its history.

An illustration of the progress made in this respect comes from the 1987/88 Annual Report of the Sevenoaks CAB. Sevenoaks dealt with 7,254 enquiries during that year.

> We added up the figures and found that in a year we had referred 300 clients to solicitors. We wondered how helpful we had been in making these referrals and whether we knew enough about the individual specialisms of the firms. We therefore asked each participant to complete a questionnaire and invited all respondents to a review meeting. At the meeting we exchanged experiences with a view to making more appropriate referrals. We now have a much clearer idea of who deals with what. We have produced a leaflet to help our clients maximise the benefit of an appointment with a solicitor. We are grateful to the solicitors for their help in this.

The Association's dialogue with the Law Society was not the only way in which it related to the legal profession, nor did the profession itself stand still. From the early 1970s onwards the Law Centres movement gathered momentum. The North Paddington Law Centre, which was set up in 1973, was the first Law Centre which was linked to a bureau. There was optimism at the time that Law Centres could be developed throughout the country but this proved a false hope and in the long term the financial vulnerability of Law Centres was unfortunately proved to be extreme.

The anxiety of bureaux to provide as complete a service as possible for their clients led to some bureaux employing their own resource lawyers. Some of these were funded under Urban Aid Programmes, which meant that at the end of the Programme, unless the local authority was prepared to pick up the costs, it was impossible to continue to employ them. There could be difficulties other than funding difficulties. For instance 'It took 2 years for one CAB resource solicitor, financed by a 4 year Urban Aid Grant, to obtain his waiver to enable him lawfully to assist individual clients to the full extent that may be needed; indeed this has been a common and frustrating experience of full-time resource solicitors.'

Even at the peak, there were never many lawyers employed directly by bureaux but those that were had an important role to play and influenced the CAB service quite significantly through their work.

An indicator of the changed position of the CAB service in relation to the legal profession is the degree to which lawyers have proved themselves willing to listen to and take note of what the service is saying. One milestone was when a CAB Organiser was appointed as one of the two lay members of the Law Society's Legal Aid Committee. The first Legal Services Committee outside London was set up in Manchester and the Area Officer was appointed a member. An even more significant development occurred in 1984 when

> a network of 40 Regional Duty Solicitor Committees was set up to supervise the statutory duty solicitors schemes for magistrates courts introduced under the Legal Aid Bill 1982. Following representations by NACAB and others these committees are required to include lay members. The lay members have now been appointed and almost every committee includes a CAB representative.

Those who were appointed to these committees found that they had to establish their right to be there and win individual respect for their contribution to the discussions. It was tough on the pioneers but the battle was won in the end.

A long-standing problem in bureaux was that of handling complaints against solicitors. For years the workers had battled to deal with clients' complaints and the Association continually pressed the Law Society to take the appropriate action to put their house in order. The climax was reached when at the Annual General Meeting of the Association in 1982, a Motion was put 'That this Association, noting the recommendations of the Royal Commission on Legal Services concerning complaints about solicitors, urges the Law Society to introduce without further delay a means of settling minor complaints, and that this should include lay involvement'. Before putting the Motion to the Meeting, the President asked all those who had had a complaint about a solicitor in their bureau during the previous year to put up their hands. The resulting forest of hands was widely reported in the national press and, whatever else could be deduced from it, proved that there was definitely a problem to be addressed. Eventually, along came the Solicitors' Complaints Bureau, to the establishment of which the Association had certainly contributed its weight.

Alongside the improved ability of the bureaux to help clients with legal problems through the medium of trained lawyers, there was the other development of increased ability on the part of CAB workers to undertake work to help clients to appeal to tribunals of various kinds and to make use of the County Courts, together with things like 'Do it Yourself' divorce procedures. The spin-off from the work of the Tribunal Assistance Units working in different parts of the country was a sharpening up of many of the workers' abilities when dealing with the law.

When the statutory right for most suspects to have free legal advice was included in the provisions of the Police & Criminal Evidence Act the government invited tenders from interested parties to provide the necessary service to ensure this. NACAB decided that this new provision warranted more than the efficient transmission of messages from client to solicitor and decided to put in a tender. This incorporated an advanced communications and information system, plus a great deal more. In the event the contract went elsewhere but the exercise proved a worthwile one in terms of the planning which went into it.

Perhaps the last word can lie with a Report which appeared in the 1986/87 Annual Report of the Association, which illustrates just how far the Association has travelled in the last twenty years.

> Welfare Rights is an area of the law traditionally under-served by solicitors. A unique initiative by the Tyne and Wear Project Group aims to encourage solicitors to fill the gap. After contact with the Newcastle Law Society the CAB Welfare Rights Officer designed a welfare rights course for the local solicitors. The Law Society advertised the course in its mail-out to members and the response has been enthusiastic.

The CAB service is no longer merely a handmaiden of the law; it now comes nearer to being a respected collaborator.

Selling the Service: (i) The Media, Press and Publicity

The Owl of Minerva was the first symbol of the Citizens Advice Bureaux. It was produced in 1941 and was made available to all bureaux approved by the Central Committee. It was used over the years on paper and publications used by bureaux and attracted a good deal of sentimental attachment from many of the volunteers. They did not like it when the Owl was up-dated and deprived of its laurel wreath; they liked it even less when its use was discontinued.

This occurred after the firm of Wolff Olins had been employed to produce a suitable 'corporate image' for the National Association. They were the people who designed the colour scheme, typeface and roundel which were eventually adopted. They also suggested that the word 'bureau' should be dropped from the title, on the grounds first that it was not a word commonly used in English and second that for many people it signified either an office or a piece of furniture. The issue was heavily canvassed and opinion was fairly evenly divided. The Director of the day, Jeremy Leighton, felt that 'Citizens Advice' was all that was needed but he failed to carry Council with him and the vote went for the retention of the full title. Once the decision had been made, the corporate image was launched and became known and recognised countrywide as it came into general use from 1976 onwards.

The attitude to publicity in bureaux was fairly ambivalent. On the one hand many bureaux felt that their work was insufficiently well known and understood; on the other there was nervousness that if the service was publicised they would be unable to cope with the resulting rise in enquiries. Annual General Meetings, if held, were often attended only by members of the Management Committee and the staff. There was in some bureaux a slightly neurotic fear of the danger of inadvertently disclosing details of a case, even in a fictionalised form, which might lead to the identification of the original client concerned. One result was that the activities of such bureaux were as blanketed in secrecy as any Masonic Lodge meeting. For these bureaux the idea of a 'Question and Answer' type column in the local paper was out of the question.

Others, however, took a more progressive view and believed that the CAB service as a whole should develop its own publicity materials, with Central Office making itself responsible for providing these. The limiting factor, as always, was the lack of resources, and although the first formal request to Council that there should be a 'public relations officer' is recorded in 1969, it was not until the acquisition of the Development Grant that it became possible to make an appointment of a Press & Publicity Officer to the staff of NACAB.

This appointment was the only beginning. As time went by a small but active Press and Publicity section was built up, with responsibility both for the production of internal material such as posters and leaflets and for external press relations, including the issue of press releases and the publicising of the activities of the Association in general. A great deal of work was done in support of bureaux, helping them to raise their standards in respect of their Annual Reports, their relations with the local press, radio and television and their use of publicity in relation to their funding authorities and Members of Parliament.

It was important to develop more positive links with radio and television nationally and this began in 1975 with the provision of back-up services to the television series 'The 60-70-80 Show'. An experienced Organiser was seconded to deal with the letters which came in to the BBC as a result of the programmes.

Over the years the Association began to be more sophisticated about the use which could be made of television; one example of this was the collaborative effort in 1981 with Yorkshire Television, producing a series of programmes called 'That's the Way' which showed viewers how to cope with bureaucracy. Involvement with radio programmes such as 'You and Yours' on Radio 4 and the 'Jimmy Young Show' on Radio 2 established the CAB service as a resource for the use of broadcasters and their audiences, until the climate was such that it became automatic for the programme makers to look to the CAB service, in one or other of its manifestations, to provide evidence, instances and comment on all kinds of social issues.

1983 saw the employment of a Broadcasting Adviser, Ms Sally

Hawkins, who developed the exposure of the CAB service to television both through linkages with various programmes and by appearing as a presenter herself. In addition, the BBC appointed a Bureau Organiser to their Central Advisory Committee.

All of this activity meant that the CAB service had become a commonly accepted part of the social comment scene, through the local and national newspapers, through local and national radio and through local and national television.

Another use of the media has been the development, under the aegis of the Training Department of NACAB, of the production of videos designed for training or educational purposes in the CAB service and for sale to interested groups outside. The titles of those listed in the Annual Report of 1987/88 include

TAKE MY ADVICE
Two simulated interviews provide a basis for discussing interviewing skills.

PERCEPTIONS
A film to encourage social awareness as integral to interviewing skills.

TALK ABOUT TROUBLE
A film to introduce basic interviewing skills.

FACE TO FACE
A series of 'trigger' scenes portraying clients talking directly to camera in situations which many people find uncomfortable or threatening.

HOW CAN WE HELP?
A film for those new to CAB giving basic information about the service.

ADVICE FOR ALL
A short programme which answers questions about the kind of problems that come to CABx, what advice means, who becomes an advice worker etc.

COUNSELLING AT WORK
The programme explores the principles and applications of effective basic counselling skills.

AVOIDING DANGER
Explores the ways in which the dangers of attack at work can be minimised.

A POSITIVE APPROACH
For professionals and volunteers who offer help and support to those who are HIV positive or who have AIDS.
The last three of these were produced in collaboration with the Employee Advisory Resource (Control Data Ltd), The Suzy Lamplugh Trust and The Terrence Higgins Trust and others.

Many well-known actors and presenters kindly helped with the making of these videos, giving their services either voluntarily or at a merely token charge.

Selling the Service: (ii) The Funders

Once NACAB had left the NCVO and become independent it relied almost entirely on its government grant for its maintenance. Should the grant be withdrawn, the whole structure would collapse. It therefore became important that the Association's knowledge of the working of Parliament should be improved and, even more vitally, that the support of ordinary backbench MPs should be fostered.

As part of the strategy of building up fruitful contacts, a Parliamentary Liaison Officer was appointed and began work as an oiler of wheels, learning the ways in which the case for the bureaux could be brought to the notice of the Members. She arranged for presentations, for displays and for receptions in the House of Commons, at party and local government conferences, both national and local; liaison was established with groupings of Chief Officers and other appropriate people who might influence the decision makers when it came to the granting of funds; a fund of information was built up and friends and supporters identified. The CAB service began to realise that it was closely tied to the political life of the country, both locally and nationally, and that it was necessary to understand the decision processes of both local and national governments if the service was to survive in a difficult political climate.

New Technology

The Association found it difficult to come to grips with new technology. There were those who heralded the advent of computers as the solution to all troubles, whereas others took a more sceptical view of the possibilities. NACAB was represented in early discussions on the uses of the Prestel system, and bureaux in Cardiff and Norwich took part in experimental projects relating to Prestel and computerised welfare benefits provision. Enthusiasts in various bureaux worked at designing welfare benefits or other computer programmes and sporadic initiatives flourished and died again. To try and cope with the situation, a New Technology Advisory Group was set up in 1981, in particular to consider the possibilities which might arise from the Department of Industry's declared intention of fostering the spread of computerisation during the Information Technology Year of 1982.

Despite the difficulties of finding matching funding, it was possible to obtain backing from the Department of Industry for a three year Microcomputer Project in 1983, designed to examine the use of microcomputers in bureaux. The appointment of the Project Team marked an advance in the Association's ability to deal with the possibilities of computers and their application to bureau work. Several programmes developed by bureaux or by other agencies became available, including

The computer solves some problems and is increasingly useful.

ones on Welfare Benefits, Housing Benefit and money advice. The Project Team was responsible for introducing computers into 150 bureaux during its life as well as advising many others on suitable equipment. All bureaux in GLCABS were supplied with computers paid for by a grant from the former GLC. It has become widespread for bureaux to make use of computers for word-processing, statistical work and the calculation of Social Security entitlements. As the workers become more proficient, no doubt the uses to which computers can be put will extend considerably.

An interesting example of this kind of extension is the legal information system LAWTEL which is available from British Telecom's Prestel service. This combines thousands of pages of legal data with an electronic mailbox. It is just one of the developments which may be built on.

New technology – in its various forms – will undoubtedly have a great deal to contribute to the development of the service for clients in the future but one thing is certain; it must remain the tool of the interviewer, not the master, and it must in no way come between the client and the helper in a way that diminishes the client's perception of the relationship.

Overseas

Many groups and individuals, ranging from formal delegations of Japanese civil servants to advice workers from Europe and America in Britain on holiday, make it their business to visit the Central Office and one or more bureaux during their stay. At various times over the years there have been CAB-type advice agencies operating in Australia, Hong Kong, India, Eire, Israel, New Zealand, Rhodesia, Canada, South Africa, the USA, Holland, the West Indies and others. Where these have proved to be lasting initiatives they have formed themselves into their own National Associations or their equivalents.

In addition, interest has been shown in Greece, Fiji, France, Canada, Cyprus, Sri-Lanka, Sweden, Japan, and Germany.

Sometimes it has been possible for reciprocal visits to be made; CAB workers on holiday have contacted their counterparts abroad and have enjoyed being introduced to systems which were different but, in many respects, familiar. Nowhere is there a system which is strictly comparable to the CAB service in the United Kingdom; in this respect the British CAB service remains not only the pioneer but also the model for the rest of the world.

CHAPTER EIGHT
A Personal Perspective

Sitting in the laundrette waiting for the dryer to finish, I heard two middle-aged Fen women discussing a complicated series of misfortunes and troubles over the council house occupied by one. I was leafing through my daily paper as I waited and not really listening until I heard the trigger words 'so I went up to the Citizens Advice'. My attention sharpened and I waited to hear the outcome. 'They sorted it', she said, 'they got on the phone and in an hour got someone to promise to come.' That, I said to myself, is the authentic voice of the satisfied client, and I went round to the bureau to tell them that they had a good publicity agent at work! This woman, and the millions like her, is what it is all about.

Conceived as an emergency measure fifty years ago, the CAB service is now an integral part of the life of the nation and, in these days when the pressures of poverty grow ever more difficult to manage, one which plays a crucial role in the lives of many of the most vulnerable people in the country. Those who volunteer to work in a bureau are brought face-to-face with harsh facts which may have passed them by in their relatively comfortable lives. The fascination which interviewers find in the work of the bureaux, a fascination that grips them, comes through in the comments of long-serving workers. The work may have been more varied in earlier days but it is still full of interest. Consequently, many of the voluntary interviewers stay for years – disenchanted at times, impatient over stupidities, bruised by conflict with officials, unsure of what they are trying to do, suspicious of the way the service seems to them to be going, wary about change – still they find enough satisfaction in doing the actual job to keep turning up week by week to undertake their duty. The old jeers about twinsets and pearls ring hollow today; those who still wear the rig are nobody's fools and have found their way through the heights and depths of human behaviour to reach the point when nothing surprises them. The one universal about bureau life is that you can't judge by appearances and 'twinset and pearls' can be as good an adviser as 'pink hair and jeans'. Long may it last that bureau advisers are drawn from a wide mix of ages and types, all of them capable of working together with and for their clients.

I have tried to chart the health or otherwise of the CAB service over the years and it strikes me that any candid friend would have to admit that it came close to dying on its feet for some years. It was only the injection of money into the centre which brought the patient back from the brink. The idea of a purely voluntary organisation is beguiling but even on a small scale there are limitations about a voluntary group which cannot be overcome. Once a body reaches a certain level of function it becomes impractical to rely on voluntary effort only. The hours required to manage even quite a small project effectively are such that to expect them to be contributed voluntarily is not reasonable. The deterioration of the CAB service following the withdrawal of funding in 1951 was marked. The service cannot but be grateful to the volunteers who kept it in being during the famine years and enabled it to survive in a rudimentary condition until the restoration of funding from 1960 onwards, but those ten years constituted an influence on the development of the CAB service which it took a long time to overcome. Whether keeping the bureaux ticking over with untrained workers, without reliable information except on a very limited scale, was a good thing or not is debatable. It left a legacy of dilettante attitudes which were not easy to root out. The inheritance was one of low aspirations, inertia and resistance to change, together with a hostility towards professionalism which it took years to eradicate. If the founders of the CAB service had not laid such a solid foundation it might have been healthier to close the whole down and await the opportunity to establish a new and more solid agency to provide for the information needs of the nation. As it was, there was sufficient strength in the foundations to enable the whole to be rebuilt when material help was available again.

The establishment of standards is a difficult thing to achieve. It has been a worry for the Association for years and Organisers have told me of their worries on this score. How effective are their interviewers? How many of them overlook vital factors, do not follow up all leads? How many clients are satisfied only because they do not know that another possible solution was available and yet not offered to them? How many clients are not satisfied at all but fail to tell us so because it is too much trouble? A complaints system will only pick up those sufficiently angered and/or motivated to return to the fray. I am sure that when I started with the CAB service in 1970 many clients merely shrugged their shoulders at the inadequate service they received from some bureaux and wrote the whole episode off as a waste of time. The excellence of the 'flagship' bureaux only made the contrasting standards of some of the others stand out more starkly.

And what was the dominating characteristic of these 'flagship' bureaux? Almost without exception, they had at the least a full-time paid Organiser in charge. Where the bureau was purely voluntary it was often the case that the Organiser had begun in the bureau as one of the interviewers and had been prevailed upon by the Management Committee to take on the job of Organiser when an earlier incumbent left. Usually there was no suggestion of selection – it was a question of finding someone willing to take it on out of loyalty to the bureau rather than choosing the person best qualified for the job. The result was that many of the Organisers of purely voluntary bureaux were frustrated interviewers who carried the responsibility for the bureau reluctantly. There is no question that they were devoted and committed people but in many cases they were people in the wrong job. The idea that management needed skills and techniques would have been foreign to them. Mostly they muddled along somehow, often running the bureau into the ground through shortsightedness. This type of Organiser tended to be so busy interviewing clients that she had no time to recruit or train new workers and the bureau staff suffered erosion and diminishment.

The study of the evolution of the central organisation has left me with the impression that it could hardly have been better designed to make life difficult and unworkable for those trying to get things done. The service was designed to deal with the emergencies of war and, like so many things at the time, was thrown together with enthusiasm and flair. It was never intended that it should continue as a peacetime service and it does not seem to have occurred to anyone to look at the way it was organised and to decide whether it needed to be changed to meet changed conditions. To set up a system which demanded that those theoretically in charge had no executive authority was not the best way to ensure that decisions were made on a realistic basis or that decisions made were capable of being carried through. The amazing thing is that it worked at all for so many years.

The long history of voluntary work in this country has to a large degree been bound up with the moneyed classes. Elizabeth Fry, Josephine Butler, Baroness Burdett-Coutts and countless other social reformers were supported by private incomes, either their own or their husbands'. From this tradition came the unspoken assumption that in order to work for a voluntary organisation the qualifications required were willingness to work for less than the market rate for the job and commitment to the organisation, coupled with the capacity to ignore the number of hours of work put in. Recruitment (both for bureaux and for the centre) was therefore from a limited pool of people – those who already had some sort of pension or a private income; those who, because they had no formal qualifications or work experience, were unable to enter the commercial employment market, and those who were sufficiently idealistic to make the necessary sacrifices. Sometimes excellent people could be recruited; sometimes the quality was simply not high enough. An organisation is only as good as the people who work for it.

It was not until the NACAB staff Union won its appeal to the Central Arbitration Committee that it became possible to offer salaries on a par with those of the civil service. From that time, NACAB found the recruitment of qualified and experienced staff easier, though civil service rates were still uncompetitive in the market, since the 'fringe benefits' available to permanent civil servants were not available to NACAB employees.

When selection can be based upon the qualities of the candidate rather than his or her ability or willingness to work for a pittance the possibility of recruiting able and experienced staff clearly becomes more likely. The impact of both the CAC award and the LAMSAC Report on the work of the Association has been profound. Whether or not this situation will continue depends on the future relation of civil service and local authority scales to other salaries being paid. If they fall too far behind, the Association may find itself facing the same difficulties over recruitment in the future as it faced in the past.

At the time of the abortive bid for independence from the NCSS in 1971 many bureaux expressed their fears about the erosion of independence which might result from a high level of government funding. These bureaux felt that their own independence was guaranteed by the voluntary nature of the local units. They were not dependent on more than a very basic level of support from their local council and believed that, if the worst came to the worst, they could stay in existence through their own fund-raising efforts. This is no longer a practical possibility; without proper funding bureaux could not remain open; cuts in funding mean the curtailment of services; withdrawal would mean closure; there is no way in which a voluntary service could be substituted for the present mixture of part voluntary/part paid. It has to be faced, therefore, that both NACAB and the bureaux are to a degree at the mercy of the whims of their political paymasters. What the bureaux in that meeting of 1971 feared has come about – independence has been compromised. For most of the time the Association is able to continue its work without interference but if the sudden attack by Dr Gerard Vaughan did nothing else it reminded the Association of its vulnerability in the face of a hostile Minister or administration.

This vulnerability has made many Management Committees nervous about their legal responsibilities as the Charity Trustees of their bureaux and there is an increasing tendency for large bureaux to become incorporated bodies. It is important that their position should be made secure if the aim of having Committees which are representative of their local communities is to be achieved. Strong and competent Management Committees are important in the life of bureaux. It is to be hoped that there will be changes in charity law in the future which will make their position more comfortable.

Having acquired more resources, both centrally and in bureaux, and developed its public presentation of itself, the CAB service no longer feels on the defensive. The days have long gone when a bureau felt that if a Housing or Consumer Advice Centre opened down the road it represented an attack and was a cause for defensive action. The service has grown more adult in its attitudes and now works cooperatively with other advice services, Law Centres (where they still exist) and special- ised bodies of all kinds in a confident and expansive way.

Looking back, I wonder whether it was right to cling so stubbornly to the idea of a purely generalist service. Had CABx grasped the opportuni- ties which arose from time to time to graft specialisms on to the body of the generalist service development might well have been more dynamic. The services offered to the public are constantly extended but, like the Red Queen, the Association has to keep running faster and faster in order to stay in the same place.

One reason why the analogy with the Red Queen is pertinent is that Parliament has of late years passed a great deal of complicated and poorly-thought-out legislation. The best law is relatively simple and its provisions are easily understood and applied. Bad law is invariably opaque and difficult to apply in practice; it also tends to have un- expected by-products. The same applies to tinkering with regulations without proper thought; a good example of this was the introduction of the Board & Lodgings rule for young people in receipt of Supplementary Benefit (as it was then). The changes in the Social Security system in 1988 illustrate the kind of thing which can happen. Every effort was made to prepare for these. There was a massive input of staff time at NACAB and in the bureaux, yet no one could have anticipated the huge volume of enquiries received by the bureaux when the deadline date was approaching. There was an increase of 39% (from the already high level) in Social Security enquiries in bureaux in the quarter running up to the introduction of the new provisions. It would have been impossible to plan for this increase; as a 'demand led' service, all the Association can do is to try and anticipate such demand and make arrangements which it believes will be adequate to cope with it. This can be extremely difficult and is more successful in some cases than others.

As the effects of the so-called enterprise culture bite harder on poor people and their situation becomes more desperate, the bureaux find themselves increasingly to be the only source of help to which the poor can turn with confidence. The possibility that society is turning its back on the idea of the safety net which was encapsulated in the Beveridge Report could mean a return to the situation described by a worker in the 1950s, when 'We spent many hours making out cases for financial assistance to the many local and national charities.' One long-serving bureau worker commented that every Cabinet Minister should be forced to spend a month interviewing in a bureau so that he or she experienced at first hand the difficulties with which many people have to contend and the courage with which many of them face appalling situations.

The danger signals over housing were visible years ago and the increasing volume of debt could be seen to be building up over a long period. Debt problems can originate in basic poverty – simply not enough money to meet the day to day needs of a family; in the effects of changed circumstances, such as unemployment, illness, redundancy, divorce or premature retirement; or in the insidious effects of the climate of 'buy today, pay later' on those who find it difficult to live on anything but a day to day basis. Debt itself is no simple matter to deal with; it brings with it a trail of effects, such as family discord and breakup, eviction, depression, nervous breakdown, alcoholism and attempted suicide. It is no wonder that dealing with debt problems is extremely time-consuming and puts great pressure on the workers concerned. It seems that things have come full circle, since the great problem in 1939/40 was also that of debt, as people tried to cope with the suddenly changed circumstances of their lives. The scale may be different; the pain is the same.

Volunteers remain an important element in the CAB service. The contribution of the volunteer is not just that of service given free. If the selection has been sound, the training adequate and the commitment to the client's interest is real, the volunteer has something a little different to offer, which is peculiar to him or her. If the volunteer is less conversant with all the minutiae of regulations and requirements this is balanced by a freshness of approach which does not fall into the danger of seeing situations in standard terms. In the foreseeable future the Association will continue to need them in ever-increasing numbers.

Will it be able to find them? Does it already ask too much of its volunteers? Does it give them enough say in the conduct of the Association as a whole?

The answer to the first question is probably 'yes' and to the other questions probably 'no'. Over the years the great majority of volunteers have responded positively to the additional expectations placed upon them. The CAB service is one of the limited number of voluntary organisations which ask them to use their intelligence, perspicacity and perseverance not their muscles. These characteristics lead them to respond to challenge and to cope with all kinds of situations. There seems every reason to suppose that this will remain true in the future.

Whether the place of the volunteer in the structure of the organisation as a whole can or should change is problematical. The Association faces an ever-increasing problem of size; for 700 or so separate units not only to feel themselves to be part of the whole but also to feel that there is the opportunity to make their views known and for those views to be listened to is an ideal which is hard to realise. As the number of bureaux grows ever larger the distance between them and their governing body – the Council – feels greater, though in fact the structure has remained constant, with bureaux sending representatives to their Area Committee and from the Area Committee to Council. It is not that the distance has increased; it is that the perception of that distance has changed.

The politics of voluntary organisations are as needle-sharp as academic politics, and debates are often savage and intense. This is partly because those concerned are committed and care greatly for the cause they are fighting for; it is also because, in many cases, the opportunity to take decisive action is severely limited. On the one hand there are all the processes of democratic consultation; on the other the tensions arising from the need for action. The cry 'We was robbed' is frequently raised and the most curious aspect of life among the committed is their readiness to ascribe motives to others which they would never entertain themselves! There have been many squabbles over the years; in most cases they are soon forgotten but sometimes people are damaged and the wounds remain. The fact that the Association has weathered many a storm gives me confidence that it will not founder in the future, provided always that it never loses sight of the fact that the client is the reason for the existence of the bureaux. If that is forgotten the CAB service might as well shut up shop and go home. The whole structure – the volunteers, the salaried bureau staff, the Management Committees, the Area Committees, the Council and the staff it employs – is constructed for the sake of the person in trouble, distress or indecision who opens the door and comes looking for help. For fifty years that help has been available to a greater or lesser degree; it is essential that it should continue, should be tailored to the needs of the people it seeks to serve and should never, as it develops, lose sight of the Principles on which it is founded, the Principles of Confidentiality, Impartiality and Objectivity, and of Independence.

Appendices

CITIZENS ADVICE BUREAUX
A Service of Advice and Help in Time of War

This statement has been prepared as a result of discussions which have taken place under the aegis of the Standing Conference of Voluntary Organisations, convened by the National Council of Social Service, to consider the services which voluntary service organisations should offer to the country in war time, and to co-operate in establishing them.

. . . .

The proposal for the establishment of Citizens' Advice Bureaux is one example of the co-operative action which might be taken by voluntary societies in assisting statutory authorities to meet social needs in a national emergency.

THE CITIZENS ADVICE BUREAU – A FOCAL POINT OF EFFORT

The purpose of this Statement is to suggest ways in which the peace-time activities of [Voluntary organisations, Charities and Councils of Social Service] can be extended to cover the needs which will arise in war, and to provide a co-ordination of effort between the voluntary societies through a focal point of consultation with statutory bodies.

It is proposed that ... Citizens' Advice Bureaux should be established throughout the country, particularly in the large cities and industrial areas where social disorganisation may be acute.

. . . .

Local Authorities, Government Departments and voluntary organisations will give explanations and instructions in the matters with which they deal. But there will arise many cases which cannot be dealt with by any one department... In addition there are bound to be personal problems which no existing organisation can meet, and it will be necessary for the Bureaux to consider how these cases can be assisted.

. . . .

It cannot be emphasised too strongly that the plans for a Bureau should be discussed from the beginning with the Local Authority and its approval and support secured for the proposal.

. . . .

The Bureau should be situated in a prominent position, providing easy access for all people in the neighbourhood.... The amount of accommodation required will depend upon the size of the area to be served and upon the range of service to be provided.... There should be as a minimum a large room for ... general enquiries, and several smaller rooms for more personal interviews and for the keeping of records.

. . . .

The effectiveness of the Bureau would depend upon the number, ability and experience of the staff. As a minimum there would have to be one full-time person ... in charge of the Bureau, assisted by part-time helpers ... whose zeal and ability will command the confidence of the public.

This Statement has been abridged in the cause of brevity.

May 1941 **APPENDIX 2**

PRINCIPLES OF THE CITIZENS' ADVICE BUREAU SERVICE

Introduction
In a movement so new and so varied as the Citizens' Advice Bureau Service, it is difficult to lay down very definite principles. It is, however, possible to state broadly the objects for which Citizens' Advice Bureaux are set up and a few guiding principles as to how these should be attained.

Objects
1 To provide for all citizens a centre of advice and information on all kinds of personal and domestic problems.
2 To explain legislation and to endeavour to see that no-one misses out through ignorance of the provisions made on his behalf.
3 To put people in touch with the best means of obtaining the help they need, whether it be legal, financial or any other kind.
4 To collect information on the kind of problems which are at any specific time causing difficulty or distress and to bring such problems to the notice of those who have power to prevent or solve them.
5 To provide friendship and sympathy to all who are in need of it.
6 To play its part, in common with other social organisations as opportunities arise in the course of its work, in bringing to the notice of enquirers the opportunities and responsibilities of civic service.

Guiding Principles
1 A Citizens' Advice Bureau should be organised by a community for a community. It therefore follows:
   (a) that a committee representative of local interests, statutory, voluntary, religious and political, should be responsible for its work;
   (b) that every effort should be made to secure premises which are not associated with one political party or religious sect.
2 A Citizens' Advice Bureau should set out to attract all kinds of citizens, rich and poor, employer and employee, worker and leisured, landlord and tenant. It therefore follows:

(a) that the premises should be central, accessible, cheerful and businesslike.
(b) that steps should be taken to secure the support of the Local Authority.
(b) that voluntary subscriptions should be solicited;
(c) that where essential expenses cannot fully be met the Regional Officer should be consulted.

3 It is of the utmost importance that the standard of advice given in the Bureau should be the highest which it is possible to attain. It therefore follows:
(a) that it should endeavour to call upon the services of as many experts of various kinds as are available;
(b) that it should endeavour to enlist the services of a Poor Man's Lawyer;
(c) that its workers should take every possible opportunity of enlarging their knowledge by study, by conference and by all other means within their reach.

4 The success of a Bureau depends very largely upon the extent to which it co-operates with other organisations, both public and voluntary, in its area. It therefore follows:
(a) that close contact should be maintained with the Local Authority and with local representatives of Central Government Departments;
(b) that every opportunity should be taken to understand what other voluntary organisations are doing;
(c) that a plan should be worked out to make clear the kind of cases which should be dealt with by the Bureau and the kind which should be referred to other bodies.

5 A Bureau should be sensitive to the needs and reactions of the people in its district, its workers learning from the enquiries which are causing difficulty, anxiety and distress. It therefore follows:
(a) that a careful record should be kept of the number and nature of enquiries being dealt with;
(b) that the summary of these enquiries should be sent regularly to head-quarters.
(c) that a Bureau should be prepared to promote, or co-operate with other bodies in promoting such special services as may appear necessary.

April, 1940   **APPENDIX 3**

CITIZENS ADVICE BUREAUX
SIGNS OF RECOGNITION

Since the outbreak of war, some nine hundred CABx have been set up in various parts of the country. For the most part they have been formed on a purely voluntary basis and as might have been expected in a service which has developed with such rapidity, the various bureaux differ considerably both in type and quality. In order to establish the Bureaux as a national service on a firm foundation, some recognised standard of organisation and efficiency is clearly needed, and the NCSS acting on behalf of the Personal Service Group of the Standing Conference of Voluntary Organisations in time of War, has decided that the time has come to issue a sign of recognition to all these Bureaux, whether large or small, in large cities or in small areas of population, which conform to a minimum standard. Careful consideration has been given to the conditions which such a standard would imply, and due regard has been paid to the differing circumstances under which the Bureaux have been established and are now working.

In order to qualify for a sign, the Bureau must satisfy the National Council of Social Service:

(I) that it has a representative committee responsible for the Bureau, on which the Statutory Authority and voluntary societies of the neighbourhood have been invited to appoint representatives;

(II) that its basis is non-party and non-sectarian and that it is available to all citizens;

(III) that it has been in existence for a minimum period of three months and that it is open at least once a week at regular stated hours:

(IV) that it has taken adequate steps to bring its services to the notice of the public;

(V) that it has an adequate staff of voluntary workers, serving under a responsible leader;

(VI) that it is keeping an accurate record of enquiries;

(VII) that it is housed in accessible premises with suitable facilities for privacy.

The sign will, of course, remain with the Bureau so long as it keeps up its standard of efficiency, but will remain the property of the National Council of Social Service, which reserves the right to ask for its return should the work of the Bureau fall below the minimum standard. The sign which it is proposed to issue, free of cost, is the picture of a yellow owl on a blue background, round which are the words "Citizens' Advice Bureau".

We very much hope that the Bureaux which have reached this standard will apply for signs. We believe that it will be a real strength to the movement to have an accredited sign, easily recognised by those who wish to make use of the Bureaux.

1947 **APPENDIX 4**

CONDITIONS OF REGISTRATION FOR A CITIZENS' ADVICE BUREAU

The Conditions of Registration as approved by the National Committee are as follows:

1 That the Bureau shall have been in existence at least three months.
2 That the Bureau is carrying out the functions of a Citizens Advice Bureau as set out in the current edition of the printed "Aims and Methods" of the CAB Service.
3 That the Bureau has a committee, so far as possible representative of the voluntary societies of the neighbourhood and of the appropriate statutory authorities; and that it meets at regular stated intervals.
4 That its basis is non-party and non-sectarian and that it is available to all citizens.
5 That it is open at times convenient to all sections of the community.
6 That it is housed in the most accessible premises available with facilities for privacy.
7 That it has taken adequate steps to bring its services to the notice of the public.

8 That it has an adequate staff of competent workers.
9 That it is keeping a record of enquiries, making such monthly returns as are required.
10 That the National Citizens' Advice Bureaux Committee is satisfied that the work of the Bureau is carried on in a satisfactory and efficient manner in relation to the needs of the district which it serves.

NOTES
(a) Registration shall normally be for a three-year period except where there is some material change in the staffing or organisation of the Bureau.
(b) The form of application shall be signed by the Secretary or Organiser and countersigned by an officer designated by the National Committee.
(c) Where registration is required for Sub or Branch Bureaux, a separate form shall be completed.
(d) A small number of enquiries and limited hours of opening will not necessarily be a bar to the granting of the Certificate of Registration where a Bureau is otherwise providing an efficient service for the local community.
(e) It should be noted that the National Committee requires that all new workers should receive adequate training and considers that all bureau workers should periodically attend courses of instruction provided through regional and country machinery.

1st January 1967   **APPENDIX 5**

CITIZENS' ADVICE BUREAU CONDITIONS OF REGISTRATION

1 The National Citizens' Advice Bureaux Council is the body which undertakes on behalf of individual citizens' advice bureaux responsibility for the general policy, administration and coverage of the CAB Service; the provision at national level of the means of consultation and co-operation between the service and other organisations both voluntary and statutory; and the maintenance of an overall standard of work which the bureaux themselves establish, and which the public has come to expect from CABx as an integral part of the social services. This standard is related to the demands made upon the service as a result of the new responsibilities which are laid upon it from time to time, e.g. by new legislation or changes in social conditions.

Maintenance of Standards
2 In assuming these responsibilities the National CAB Council undertakes to provide, inter alia:
   (a) a headquarters and field advisory service to promote and develop new bureaux, to give guidance and support on all aspects of the administration of existing bureaux and to provide a continuous training programme;
   (b) a central and comprehensive information service for registered citizens' advice bureaux to enable them to keep up-to-date with changing legislation and other social provisions.
3 For their part the bureaux undertake to maintain the established standard of organisation and work and in particular to accept that, for both established workers and new recruits, training on a continuous basis is essential and that this entails study and use of reference material.

Purpose of Registration

4 The purpose of registration is to demonstrate the mutual obligations between the individual bureaux and the National CAB Council and their joint responsibility in maintaining a reasonable standard of service to the public. The certificate of registration is given on the understanding that the bureau maintains the necessary standard of work by conforming to the conditions of registration as laid down by the National CAB Council from time to time, and that it is open to visits by an advisory officer of, or a person designated by, the National CAB Council.

If the conditions are not adhered to, the certificate of registration and the information service would be withdrawn, but such action would not be taken until every possible effort had been made by the National Council and the advisory officer to bring the bureau up to the required standard.

Conditions of registration

5 The conditions of registration as at present approved by the National CAB Council are as follows:

(a) the bureau shall have been in existence not less than three months

(b) (i) where a bureau is an independent organisation:

it is under the direction of an independent committee of management representative of the appropriate voluntary organisations and statutory authorities, and of the bureau workers; which meets at least four times a year and which is governed by a charitable constitution;

(ii) where a bureau is part of another organisation such as a CSS:

it is under the direction of a committee of the organisation representative as in (i) above with responsibility for the maintenance and management of the bureau; which meets at least four times a year and which is governed by a charitable constitution.

(c) it carries out the functions of a citizens' advice bureau by providing a confidential and impartial service of information and advice to all citizens on a non-party, non-racial and non-sectarian basis as described in the current edition of AIMS AND METHODS OF THE CAB SERVICE: in particular that

(i) it is open for at least five sessions on different days of the week in order to make itself sufficiently available and well known to the public;

(ii) it is housed in suitable premises clearly marked as CAB, which are readily accessible and which have facilities for confidential interviews;

(iii) it has taken adequate steps to bring its service to the notice of the public in the town in which the bureau is situated as well as in the surrounding areas;

(iv) it is keeping an adequate daily record of enquiries and making such monthly returns as are required, in order to provide information needed from time to time either locally or by the National CAB Council for research or other purposes;

(v) it is maintaining an efficient and up-to-date information index and filing system;

(d) it has an adequate staff of competent workers who have undertaken the basic training course in accordance with the national syllabus and accepted the need for such further training as is required by the National CAB Council from time to time; and who are willing to accept the obligation of regular weekly duty;

(e) it makes itself available (in addition to the routine visits referred to in paragraph 4) for a formal registration visit each year by an advisory officer of, or a person designated by, the National CAB Council for the purpose of satisfying the Council that its work is carried on in a satisfactory and efficient manner in relation to the needs of the district which it serves;

(f) it makes an annual contribution towards the information service and pays a registration fee which entitles it to use the name CITIZENS' ADVICE BUREAU.

NOTE: The form of application shall be signed by the Organiser and the Chairman, and a recommendation made by an advisory officer of, or a person designated by, the National CAB Council.

January 1974   **APPENDIX 6**

GUIDE TO REGISTRATION

1   INTRODUCTION

1.1 Over a million and a half people consult Citizens' Advice Bureaux each year. Some want simple information. Some want detailed guidance through the labyrinth of regulations and provisions of a complex society. Others may be in doubt, confusion or distress (for instance following bereavement, accident or divorce or illness or through loss of a job) and will require tactful sympathy and personal understanding as well as informed guidance.

1.2 The CAB service is a voluntary and charitable organisation. To maintain the standard and effectiveness of the service offered it is thus a major concern of the National Association of Citizens' Advice Bureaux to establish and maintain the highest possible standards of both training and organisation and to ensure the provision of adequate premises.

1.3 Membership of the National Association is confined to Bureaux who have been registered with the Council of the National Association of Citizens' Advice Bureaux. This membership involves both rights and obligations.

1.4 To qualify for such registration a Bureau is required to meet certain conditions, as set out in the guide below. However, details of registration for any particular bureau should be discussed with the Advisory Officer, who will be in attendance when the Council's Registration Committee considers the application.

1.5 Each member Bureau is an entity in its own right, not a subsidiary of the central office. It is responsible for running its own affairs within the agreed policy and standards of the National Association.

2   THE RIGHTS OF MEMBERSHIP include:

2.1 Use of the name Citizens' Advice Bureau

2.2　Voting participation nationally and regionally in the management of the service as a whole.

2.3　The complete services of NACAB advisory staff, giving close support in selection, recruitment and training of new staff in the Bureau, regional in-service training, Bureau organisation, filing of the information service, advice to the Bureau's management committee, and support in approaches to the local authority.

2.4　Receipt of the National Association's information service. This includes the structure and basic material for an information system; the monthly parcel of new and up-dated material; the consultancy service of its information staff; access to comprehensive information files held in the central office; and participation in the national network of Information Retrieval.

3　THE OBLIGATIONS OF MEMBERSHIP include:

3.1　Complying with the policy and procedures operated by or on behalf of the Association;

3.2　Maintaining standards of organisation and efficiency in accordance with the procedures of the Association;

4　BASIC REQUIREMENTS
　　The following are the essential requirements for a registered Bureau:

4.1　*Constitution*

4.1.1　The Bureau is governed by a constitution that is acceptable to the NACAB and where applicable registered with the Charity Commission;

4.1.2　If the Bureau is part of another organisation (such as a Council of Social Service) its management committee has the status of a standing committee, concerned exclusively with CAB matters.

4.2　*Management Committee*

4.2.1　The committee meets at least four times a year, including an annual meeting;

4.2.2　The Bureau appoints Honorary officers from among the members of the committee;

4.2.3　The Organiser, together with up to three elected representatives of the bureau staff, are members of the committee; except that they do not have a vote on any matter affecting payment or conditions of employment of staff in the Bureau;

4.2.4　The Area Advisory Officer is invited to attend all committee meetings;

4.2.5　The committee prepares an annual estimate of expenditure; presents an annual audited statement of accounts to the annual meeting; and has a written report on the work of the Bureau available for circulation.

4.3　*Organiser*

4.3.1　The management committee, with the Advisory Officer, appoints an Organiser with appropriate experience, and a deputy. Induction, including sessions in other Bureaux, is arranged with the Advisory Officer, and training is undertaken as provided by the NACAB.

4.4　*Bureau workers*

4.4.1　The management committee appoints a panel, which, with the Advisory Officer and Organiser, selects and appoints new workers;

4.4.2 Each worker helps staff the Bureau for sufficient time each week to ensure an adequate and growing experience of handling enquirers, subject to a minimum of one session per week;

4.4.3 All Bureau workers are expected to attend regular staff meetings, of which at least six are held annually.

4.5 *Training*

4.5.1 All members of the Bureau staff attend basic training approved by the NACAB and such further training as is provided;

4.5.2 The Organiser maintains a record of attendance at training.

4.6 *Premises*

4.6.1 The enquirer is not required to state the nature of his/her problem in the presence of others;

4.6.2 Interviews are held so that the confidential nature of the service is not jeopardised;

4.6.3 The Bureau has its own telephone line(s), receiver(s) and entry in the telephone directory, and all telephone callers immediately hear "Citizens' Advice Bureau" and offer of help. Workers' home telephone numbers are not given to the public.

4.7 *Records and filing*

4.7.1 A daily record, in an approved form, is kept of all enquiries received;

4.7.2 Statistical and retrieval returns are punctually made;

4.7.3 An information index and filing system, agreed with the Advisory officer, are maintained.

4.8 *Representation on CAB Area Advisory Committee*
The Organiser, or a member of the management committee, is appointed to and regularly attends the Area Advisory Committee; is responsible for representing the Bureau's views on the Area Committee, and for reporting back to both the management committee and Bureau staff.

4.9 *Extensions to the service and experimental ventures*
Proposed new ventures are discussed with the Advisory Officer and approved by the Registration Committee.

5   OTHER FACTORS
The following points are as essential to the satisfactory running of the Bureau as are those which have so far been enumerated, but they are either more dependent on local circumstances and needs, or desirable characteristics which cannot be defined precisely.
The NACAB Council's Registration Committee gives detailed consideration to every application where fulfilment of all the requirements does not make recommendation for registration automatic. The application is prepared with the Advisory Officer to show how in qualitative terms, the Bureau's characteristics and arrangements add up to a level of assured service to the public.

5.1 *Hours of opening*

5.1.1 Normally a Bureau will be accepted for registration if it opens for at least two hours each day on five days of the week. Departure from this rule may be approved in exceptional circumstances by the Registration Committee to meet local conditions;

5.1.2 It is most desirable that a Bureau should open at the same hour each day though possibly with additional sessions (say on Saturday, market day, the evening or in a lunch hour);

5.1.3 Where lengthy or repeated interviews are necessary, consideration should be given to offering appointments in the Bureau out of normal opening hours, and home visits to disabled enquirers should be encouraged;

5.1.4 All available means of publicity should be used to bring the services of the Bureau to the notice of the public.

5.2 *Premises*

5.2.1 Premises should be readily accessible and well sign-posted;

5.2.2 The Bureau should be immediately identifiable, especially when physically incorporated into general purpose buildings, e.g. town hall or library. (Where premises house co-ordinated information and advice services combining local authority and independent agencies, the CAB will not be seeking to assert its separateness, and this principle will be modified.)

5.2.3 The premises should be so arranged that all interviews are held in private, with adequate additional space for waiting and reception.

5.3 *Management Committee*

5.3.1 The committee should include representatives of appropriate voluntary organisations, professions, social services and local government departments.

5.4 *Records*
Wherever appropriate, names and addresses of enquirers should be recorded.

6 CONCLUSION
It is essential that every Bureau seeking registration and membership should work in the closest consultation with the Advisory Officer who, it is repeated, will be in attendance when the Registration Committee considers the application.

APPENDIX 7

ADVISING THE CITIZEN
A Handbook for Workers in Advice Services
Published by NCSS June 1948

Principles of the CAB Service – as set out by Dorothy Keeling in the Foreword to Part II
(1) A real belief in Brotherhood and in the equality of Man
(2) A reasoned and intelligent understanding of those for whom we work
(3) A passionate sense of justice
(4) A wider outlook beyond the palliative to the constructive
(5) A determination to do everything possible to fit us for the work which we have taken in hand.

Work in a CAB is a test of sympathy. The worker finds himself literally face to face with all kinds of people.... Capacity to help depends partially on willingness to do so. Prejudices relating to class, creed or colour have no place in bureau work.... a CAB offers opportunity to understand an endless variety of people.... A sense of humour assists the exercise of tolerance.... safeguards a sense of proportion most valuable in work of this kind, where sympathy, no less than prejudice, may blind the view.... The daily life of a CAB is a swiftly moving drama, the scene changing from tragedy to comedy without warning.... This constant and ready switching of attention from tragedy to comedy, from the fundamental things of life to trivialities, from the sublime to the ridiculous. is most demanding and yet most refreshing.   (page 75)

Records
The making and keeping of record cards is of the utmost importance. These cards are not merely intended as reminders to the worker.... a record card should convey all relevant information as concisely as possible ... e.g. Name: Address: Nature of Request: Record of further visits, letters, telephone messages.

Requests involving merely the handing out of a form or the giving of an address require no further record. In such cases it is not essential to take the caller's name and address.   (page 80)

Interviewing
Courtesy sets the tone of an interview. Much depends on the way a client is received, on the manner and discretion used in asking his name, address and perhaps the nature of his problem. Use of a client's name at an early stage shows a sense of value for his identity. Here is not just "A caller" but a person, not Mrs X but Mrs Smith.

To the actual conduct of the interview the worker must bring complete concentration. For the good interviewer nothing exists for the moment but the client and his problem.   (page 95)

APPENDIX 8

Midland Advisory Officer
February 1945

TRAINING COURSE FOR CAB WORKERS

1 The following course on a Regional basis, has been designed to provide a background for fresh recruits and also to serve as a refresher course for those already taking part in CAB work.
2 The training should be concluded, if possible, in 3 months and be regarded as a probationary period.
3 At least 3 visits to other Bureaux are recommended (5 if possible) to gain some insight into different methods of organisation.
4 The Bureau Committee are asked to accept responsibility for completing a record form for each student, and this form should state whether the trainee is accepted by the Bureau as an accredited worker at the end of the probationary period.
5 It is suggested that the lectures should be held during the three months' training period and invitations should be extended to all CAB workers, members of Government Departments, Local Authorities, voluntary organisations and any individuals who may be interested.
6 It is hoped that the greater part of the practical side of the training may be arranged by the Bureaux; the Regional office will assist in arranging the lectures and in any matters of adjustment or difficulty that may arise.
7 The whole scheme is intended to be adaptable so that minor adjustments may be made in order that the training may be arranged to suit the needs of any particular district or Bureau.

INDEX